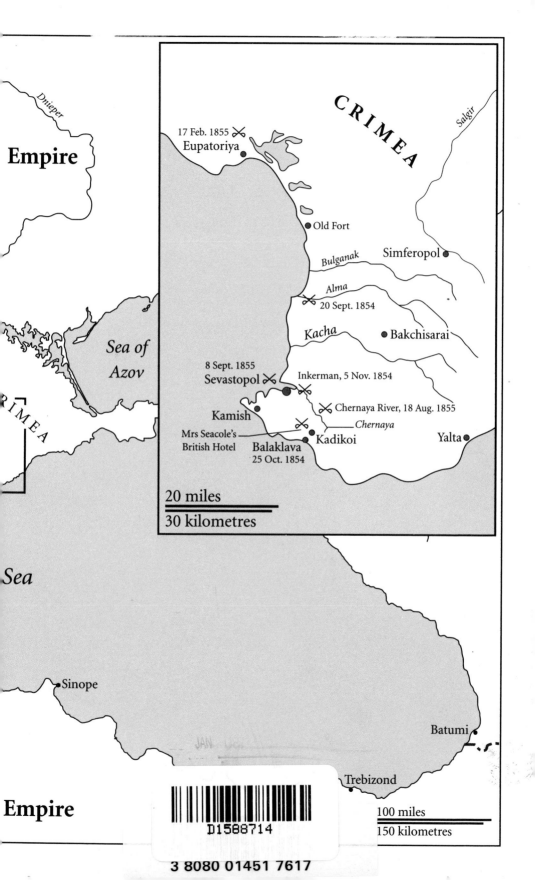

Empire

Dnieper

CRIMEA

Salgir

17 Feb. 1855 ✂
Eupatoriya

● Old Fort

Bulganak

Simferopol ●

Alma
✂ 20 Sept. 1854

Kacha

● Bakchisarai

Sea of
Azov

8 Sept. 1855
Sevastopol ✂   Inkerman, 5 Nov. 1854
●
✂
✂ Chernaya River, 18 Aug. 1855

CRIMEA

Kamish
Chernaya

Mrs Seacole's
British Hotel   ✂
● Kadikoi   Yalta ●
Balaklava
25 Oct. 1854

20 miles
30 kilometres

Sea

● Sinope

Batumi ●

Trebizond ●

Empire

100 miles
150 kilometres

D1588714

3 8080 01451 7617

NO PLACE FOR LADIES

No Place For Ladies

The Untold Story of Women in the Crimean War

...

HELEN RAPPAPORT

Aurum

First published in Great Britain
2007 by Aurum Press Ltd
25 Bedford Avenue, London WC1B 3AT
www.aurumpress.co.uk

Copyright © 2007 by Helen Rappaport

All rights reserved. No part of this book may be reproduced or utilized in
any form or by any means, electronic or mechanical, including photo-
copying, recording or by any information storage and retrieval system,
without permission in writing from Aurum Press Ltd.

A catalogue record for this book is available from the British Library.

ISBN-10: 1 84513 220 3
ISBN-13: 978 1 84513 220 0

10 9 8 7 6 5 4 3 2 1
2011 2010 2009 2008 2007

Design by Roger Hammond
Typeset in Goudy by SX Composing DTP, Rayleigh, Essex
Printed by Creative Print and Design, Wales

STOKE-ON-TRENT LIBRARIES	
38080014517617	
Bertrams	26.04.07
947.0737 HI	£18.99

WITHDRAWN AND SOLD BY STOKE-ON-TRENT LIBRARIES

For my mother
MARY MARGARET WARE

CONTENTS

ACKNOWLEDGEMENTS

The Crimean War first entered my imagination longer ago than I care to admit to – in the fourth form at Chatham Grammar School for Girls in the early 1960s, when it was my favourite topic for O-level history. From the outset there was something about the war, and its tragedy, that always fascinated me, even though later I got diverted into other areas of historical interest and other professional pursuits.

I do, however, know why it stayed with me and continued to lurk in my creative imagination long into my adult life, finally to be rekindled about five years ago by my discovery of the exploits in the Crimea of Mary Seacole. It stayed with me thanks to a wonderful history teacher – Miss Perkins. I'm ashamed to say I can't remember her full name, but I can remember her dark challenging eyes behind glinting spectacles, her long, dark plaited hair curled into a tight bun and her frightening, respect-inducing manner. I remember the compelling way in which she taught us history. She brought it alive for me and, I feel, lit a flame that still burns.

The research for this book was enormously facilitated by the collective expertise and generosity of the members of the Crimean War Research Society and its online discussion list. There are far too many people who offered suggestions, advice, titbits of information and encouragement for me to name them all here – but I am sure they know who they are and how grateful I am. I would wholeheartedly encourage anyone interested in studying the Crimean War in greater detail to join this wonderful society. For further information, see http://www.crimeanwar.org

There are however, a few Crimean specialists whom I must single out. First and foremost my good friend and colleague Douglas Austin, from the day we first exchanged our views about the many puzzles in Mary Seacole's life, has been a mine of information and expertise about the war. He has unstintingly given of his time in answering my endless questions, has shared source material and read this manuscript and provided valuable comments. My next debt of gratitude is to Keith Smith, who lent me many Crimean War books and the entire run of *The War Correspondent* back to the early Eighties, as well as generously providing maps of the Crimea. He also passed on to me the manuscript papers on nurses and army wives of the CWRS member the late Ken Horton. I must also thank Larry Crider, Glenn Fisher, Mike Hargreave-Mawson, Mike Hinton, Tony Margrave, and Major Colin Robins in particular for their helpful and insightful e-mails. Norman Gooding of the Orders and Medals Research Society helped me clarify information on awards to women; Mark Adkin offered some insightful comments on the Charge of the Light Brigade; Paul Benyon has been an invaluable source of information on nineteenth-century shipping; Steve Jones generously shared of his material on Nightingale nurses; Nick Mays at Times International provided me with insights on W. H. Russell and *The Times*; Teresa Watts and Alastair Massie at the National Army Museum helped with identifying Crimean images; Janie Hampton told me of her ancestors Felicia and Janie Skene; Megan Evans generously allowed me access to the letters of her ancestor Louisa Drake, and Elizabeth Balcombe to the letters of General Sir Richard C. H. Taylor; Roger Taylor answered questions on Roger Fenton and other Crimean photographers; Kay Priestley helped with researching documents in the National Archives, Kew; and Peter Skjol Horth in Denmark alerted me to the work of Dina Yafasova on Russian nurses. I could not end this list without finally thanking the long-suffering staff of the Bodleian Library's Upper and Lower Reserves for delivering endless piles of books to fuel the huge amount of speculative searching this project involved.

Several archives have granted permission for me to quote from documents in their collections. I am particularly grateful to Miss Pamela Clark and the staff of the Royal Archives at Windsor for their courtesy and assistance during my research there and reproduce material from that archive with the permission of Queen Elizabeth II. Caroline Roberts, curator of the Florence Nightingale Museum, allowed me access to the materials in its collection, notably the fascinating 'Register of Nurses Sent to the Hospitals in the East'. My thanks also for permission to quote from their archives goes to: Gloucestershire Archives for the diaries of Marianne Estcourt; the Trustees of the Army Medical Services Museum for the journals of William Menzies Calder and Sir John Hall; the University of British Columbia Library, Rare Books and Special Collections for the letters of Eliza Polidori from the Angeli-Dennis

Collection; Sir Edmund Verney and the Claydon House Trust for the Florence Nightingale Archive; Mr and Mrs I. McCurrach and the National Army Museum for the letters of Captain Charles Glazbrook, and the National Archives, Kew for War Office documents. I was also most kindly provided with photocopies from their archives of articles about Margaret Kerwin by the Green Howards Museum; Elizabeth Evans by the King's Own Royal Regiment Museum; Frances Driscoll by the Royal Scots Museum, and Christina Ross by the Argyll and Sutherland Highlanders Museum; Gillingham Public Library provided me with the full typescript of George Russell Dartnell's 'Notes of Queen Victoria's Visit to Fort Pitt and Chatham'.

My commissioning editor at Aurum Press, Karen Ings, offered her wholehearted support and enthusiasm for the project from the outset, as did my agent Heather Holden-Brown and her assistant James Pryor. Merlin Cox was a vigilant and highly efficient copyeditor. Several friends also offered encouragement in the writing of this book: my friend and fellow Russianist Orlando Figes got me thinking about the subject again back in 2003; Christine Kelly, herself an expert on Fanny Duberly, entered into lively exchanges with me on all things Crimean; Paul Kerr, with whom I had the pleasure of working on the Mary Seacole documentary for Channel 4 in 2005, offered valuable advice and passed on books and documents.

Finally, my thanks must go to my family for their love and support, and to my partner William Horwood, who tolerated my endless agonizing about the Crimean War and the writing of this book.

Oxford, November 2006

LIST OF ILLUSTRATIONS

Page One
Above: *The Farewell to the Scots Fusilier Guards at Buckingham Palace, 28 February 1854*, painting by George Housman Thomas. The Royal Collection © 2007, Her Majesty Queen Elizabeth II.
Below: Lady tourists to the Crimea on board HMS *Hecla*. Courtesy Mary Evans Picture Library.

Page Two
Top: *Coldstream Guards at Scutari, 1854*, photograph by James Robertson. Reproduced courtesy of the Keith Smith Collection.
Below: *Camp of the 4th Dragoon Guards, convivial party French and English*, photograph by Roger Fenton. Reproduced courtesy of the Council of the National Army Museum, London.

Page Three
Bottom left: *Fanny Duberly, Camp before Sebastopol*, photograph by Roger Fenton, 15 April 1855. The Royal Collection © 2007, Her Majesty Queen Elizabeth II.
Centre: *Lady Erroll at Devna Camp*, watercolour by Colonel (later Gen Sir) The Honourable George Cadogan, 1854. Reproduced courtesy of the Council of the National Army Museum, London.

Page Four
Top: Coloured lithograph of the exterior of the Barrack Hospital at Scutari, 1855. From a drawing by Lady Alicia Blackwood. Printed by Lavars, Bristol. Plate 13 from the second volume of Lady Blackwood's *Scutari. Bosphorus. Crimea* (1857). Reproduced courtesy of the Florence Nightingale Museum.
Centre: *The Mission of Mercy*, painting by Jerry Barrett, © National Portrait Gallery, London.
Bottom left: *Mary Seacole*, painting by Albert Charles Challen, 1869. Reproduced © courtesy Helen Rappaport/National Portrait Gallery.

Bottom right: Photograph of Florence Nightingale, seated on a couch in the Blue Room at Claydon House, 1891. By S. G. Payne & Son, Aylesbury. Reproduced courtesy of the Florence Nightingale Museum.

Page Five

Centre: 'A Reminiscence of the War in the Crimea – Sisters of Charity Succouring the Wounded on the Field of Battle (from a painting by Eugene Appert)', *Illustrated Times*, 5 July 1856.

Bottom: 'Costumes of the Imperial Guard', *Illustrated Family Paper*, 10 February 1855, by permission of the Syndics of Cambridge University Library.

Page Six

Above: *Privates Lockhurst and O'Brien*, photograph by Joseph Cundall and Robert Howlett, 1855. The Royal Collection © 2007, Her Majesty Queen Elizabeth II.

Below: Mrs Elizabeth Evans with Chelsea Pensioners of the King's Own Regiment, c.1912, photograph courtesy of King's Own Royal Regiment Museum, Lancaster.

Page Seven

Top: *Her Majesty and HRH the Prince Inspecting the Wounded Soldiers of the Grenadier Guards at Buckingham Palace, 20th February, 1855*, hand-coloured lithograph by and after George Housman Thomas, published by Dominic Colnaghi, 9 April 1855. Reproduced courtesy of the Council of the National Army Museum, London.

Below: *Reading the Queen's Letter, Scutari Hospital*, painting by Vincent Brooks, c.1855. The Royal Collection © 2007, Her Majesty Queen Elizabeth II.

Page Eight

Above: *The Roll Call*, painting by Elizabeth Thompson, 1874. The Royal Collection © 2007, Her Majesty Queen Elizabeth II.

Below: *The Field of Battle*, painting by Victoria, Princess Royal, 1855. The Royal Collection © 2007, Her Majesty Queen Elizabeth II.

'The Crimea is not the proper place for ladies.'

Edward Fisher-Rowe,
Extracts from the Letters of E. R. Fisher-Rowe, 26 September 1855

...

'You are quite right, this is no place for ladies.'

Lieut. Col. Anthony Sterling,
Letters from the Army in the Crimea, 15 June 1855

...

'This world is no place for women – at least for ladies.'

Fanny Duberly,
letter dated January 1855, in Compton, *Colonel's Lady and Camp Follower*

PROLOGUE

On the morning of Tuesday 28 February 1854, the whole of London took to the streets early, despite the bitter winter chill, to say a special farewell. Huge crowds had gathered to wave goodbye to the last battalion of bright-red-uniformed men of the Scots Fusilier Guards as they embarked for the 'War in the East' – or as we now know it, the Crimean War.

For one 34-year-old mother of eight in particular it was a poignant as well as an exciting moment, enamoured as she was of all things manly, military and Scottish. But this was no ordinary mother and certainly no ordinary woman. Uniquely of all the women alive that day she would give her name to a golden age of industry, of reform and of British military might. Over the course of the next two years she would unite the nation in war as it had never been united before.

That woman was Queen Victoria and like many other women that winter morning she had wanted to show her solidarity with one of the most legendary and admired of British regiments, famous for its heroism at the Battle of Waterloo. The sight of these fine fighting men marching off to war again after so many years of peace was, she would later record in her journal, 'a *touching and beautiful* sight',[1] and as the measured tramp of their boots pounded the streets and the bands played, the crowds thronging around the Guards watched in a state of high anticipation.

It didn't matter that they had no idea where their men were going – 'Somewhere in the Turkish territory' was all they had been told – or when their men would return. It didn't matter that they knew nothing of the Russian people or why Britain was going to war with them, except for what the papers had told them. Their men were heroes; 38 years on from Waterloo the British army was still invincible and it was going to give the nasty 'Rooshians' a jolly good beating.

Very soon, however, despite their initial ignorance of the Turkish and Russian territories in the East where the Crimean War would be conducted, every wife, mother, sister and daughter of a serving man in Britain would know exactly where the Crimea was located and how far away – a very long 3,000 miles. And for the women – including Queen Victoria –

who stood and waved the regiments of soldiers off during those heady February days, it would all too soon become painfully clear that war is never glorious but dreadful and that for many of their sex, 'this great and bloody war', as the queen herself would later describe it, would be endured in suffering and poverty and end in widowhood and destitution.[2]

This was an extraordinary war which had an extraordinary impact on the British psyche and on the way future wars would be fought. It was a war that would change for ever the public perception of what war really meant, brought home as it was to the front parlours of every Victorian household by the newspaper reports from the front. In so doing, it became a war that for the first time actively engaged the reader with the grim realities of military conflict. For it was a war that established the power of the press and the newspaper reporter and which saw the average daily circulation of The Times leap by a third, from 42,500 when war broke out in 1854, to 58,500 within the year.[3] It was a war which refused to brush culpability for administrative inefficiencies and military ineptitude under the carpet, and which led ultimately to major military, medical and public health reforms. It was a war in which women, so long confined to the domestic sphere, finally found an active and indispensable role as nurses, and one that would ultimately make nursing an acceptable profession for their sex. It was also the last war in which British army wives were allowed to accompany their husbands on campaign, and thus bear witness to and share in the terrible catalogue of suffering, death and disease that war brings in its wake.

ONE

The Girl
I Left Behind
Me

Reviled as an unnecessary drain on national resources, the British Army endured many years in the doldrums until, in February 1854, the romantic sight of a man in uniform made hearts beat a little faster and the British breast swell once more with patriotic pride. But now there was no Duke of Wellington to lead and inspire the rank and file; many of the older generation of senior commanders were professional diehards who looked upon war as a kind of recreational sport for aristocratic gentlemen, and they had now been joined by a much younger generation of fresh-faced boys – newly commissioned officers straight from public school who had never seen a war and probably hardly ever fired a musket. But although there had undoubtedly been a decline in the quality and quantity of rank-and-file recruits since the Napoleonic Wars, the army still had a core of disciplined, hardened soldiers of the old school – seasoned campaigners with a talent for fighting 'in the old dare-devil fashion',[1] who had served long years abroad in British colonies such as Canada and India. For, despite a reputation for drunkenness, the British soldier still remained 'stolid, shrewd and long-suffering'.[2]

But how many of this force had any real comprehension of the war they were going off to fight and the reasons why they had been ordered east?

Their old adversary 'Boney' had been only a short sail across the Channel, on familiar European terrain. But 'the East' was a nebulous location of which few ordinary soldiers had any geographical concept. Indeed, many of the illiterate army wives when they later sailed 'on the strength' – officially accompanying the army – were fearful that they were going to the very edge of the world itself.

The political crisis that became the Crimean War started as one of those 'quarrels in a far-away country', a phrase coined by Neville Chamberlain in 1938 when he alluded to the invasion of the Sudetenland by Hitler as being a war 'between people of whom we know nothing'.[3] So it was with the 'Eastern Question', which had been dragging on ever since Russia had first annexed the Crimea in 1783 and which was at the heart of the present hostilities between Russia and Turkey.

The British public had been aware of an escalating crisis for the previous year, but of the complex arguments involved they had little comprehension: these had largely been confined to the Byzantine memoranda of Victorian politicians and diplomats and the dense typeface of *The Times* – a newspaper many of the enlisted men now going off to war were unable to read (one-fifth of the army were totally illiterate). On the face of it, the two nations had been arguing over Russia's claim to defend the rights of Balkan Christians living under Turkish suzerainty within the crumbling Ottoman Empire, including their right of access to holy Christian shrines, notably those in Jerusalem, which lay in Ottoman-controlled Palestine. In July 1853 the Russians had turned threats into action by occupying the Turkish Danubian Principalities of Moldavia and Wallachia along Russia's south-western border with Bulgaria. The Russian tsar, Nicholas I, had shared the arrogant belief of his ministers that their incursion would go unchallenged; instead, in October, the Turks had declared war against the Russian 'infidel' and embarked on a campaign against them with all the zealotry of a jihad.

Britain was extremely reluctant at first to be drawn into the quarrel, having enjoyed such a long period of peace since the end of the Napoleonic Wars and having, as a result, wound down its military preparedness in order to concentrate on building an empire in India, Africa and the Far Eastern colonies, so much so that when war finally broke out in 1854, the greater part of the British army was based abroad. But whilst the British lion had been slumbering complacently through forty years of peace, the Russian eagle had been watching and waiting and fixing its eye ever further beyond its borders. Genuine anxieties had been growing in parliament about Russia's expansionist ambitions in the Middle East with its important land and sea routes to British dominions in India. Awakening finally to the Russian threat, 'England was aroused with the suddenness and the start of a man who from a peaceful slumber awakes to find his room on fire, or his bed surrounded by banditti', as one contemporary historian had it.[4] Once roused, there was no turning back the tide of British public enthusiasm for a war. During the winter of 1853–4, anti-Russian feeling in Britain ran high, particularly after the Turks lost some 3,000 men and 11 ships in a devastating Russian naval attack on the Turkish fleet at Sinope in November.

Frustrated by her prime minister, Lord Aberdeen, with his 'repugnance' of war and his desire to conciliate, an enraged Queen Victoria now turned on her erstwhile friend Nicholas I, a man with whom she had been on good terms during his state visit to Britain in 1844. If there was to be war, then it was, in the queen's view, the tsar's fault for failing to respond to the conciliatory messages she had sent to him; the conflict was a direct result of his ruthless ambition. With an inexorable tide of Russophobia now mounting in Britain, the queen judged that the time was ripe to challenge tsarist aggression; this despite the strength of pacifist feeling in radical circles that had prompted a Quaker mission to the tsar in the winter of 1853–4, attempting to broker conciliation. A war now, Queen Victoria asserted – and she did so with utter conviction – would be 'popular beyond belief'.[5] Such unbridled self-confidence was soon reflected in the popular press, which assured its readers that the British position was excellent: 'Never before was England so perfectly prepared for the necessity thrust upon her by the demented ambition of a disturber of mankind.'[6] The national mood, as Elizabeth Longford has defined it, was 'a kind of bellicose fatalism' that soon 'took wing on a jet of euphoria'.[7]

A British expeditionary force of about 27,000 men was now hastily assembled, later to be placed under the command of Lord Raglan, the ageing veteran of Waterloo. Day after day, from the middle of February 1854, at ports and railway stations all over Britain, regiments massed, marched and embarked by rail, steamship and sailing boat. Kingstown, Dublin, Leith, Liverpool, Manchester, Plymouth, Portsmouth and Southampton all said their fond farewells to sons and husbands and fathers en route to a war that had not yet even been officially declared.

On the morning of 14 February the citizens of London had been roused from sleep by the tread of heavy columns through the streets. The 1st Battalion of the much-loved Coldstream Guards had set off from nearby St George's Barracks to board South-Western Railway trains at Waterloo Station. Trafalgar Square had rapidly become crammed with people, both on the ground and at every available window and balcony, shouting and waving handkerchiefs. A day later, when further detachments of Guardsmen were piped by bands on their way to Waterloo, with crowds of women hanging on their steps as they marched, 'so great was the excitement to which the event gave rise that for some time the thoroughfare was entirely suspended. At Waterloo-bridge the toll keepers were completely overwhelmed by the torrent of people accompanying the troops, who were not to be stopped in their farewell greetings by any number of turnstiles.'[8]

On the morning of 28 February the Scots Fusilier Guards had been ordered to muster at 3 a.m. in heavy service marching order. Despite the dark, many people had begun patiently gathering and shivering in the early hours outside the Wellington Barracks on Birdcage Walk to watch them assemble – a good number of them the wives, sisters and mothers of those about to leave. By the time the regiment had marched its way, in slow time, to the esplanade in front of Buckingham Palace, with the regimental band playing 'O Where, and O Where is My Highland Laddie Gone?', the crowds, who had been waiting with exemplary patience in the cold, were ecstatic, waving their hats, walking sticks and handkerchiefs and frequently breaking into their own impromptu responses by singing 'God Save the Queen' or 'Rule Britannia'. But wedged in among them were many anxious women, some weeping, some shouting, some blessing the colours as they were carried past, standing on tiptoe and anxiously scanning the ranks of marching men in desperate hopes of catching sight of their own loved ones.

Queen Victoria, Prince Albert and the four oldest of their eight children – the Princess Royal, the Prince of Wales, Prince Alfred and Princess Helena – had had a front-row view of 'our beautiful Guards', a regiment for which the royal family had particular affection.[9] They had all got out of bed an hour early in order to gather on the balcony of Buckingham Palace for the march past at 7 a.m., the army having made special arrangements to delay the departure of the Scots Fusiliers in order to accommodate the queen's express wish of 'having the gratification of seeing the battalion pass in full marching order before them'.[10] Historically there was good reason too for her to so openly favour the Guards as an elite force, for in terms of blue blood they were the cream of the Army. During the Peninsular War they had been nicknamed 'the Gentlemen's Sons', with a third of their officers coming from the aristocracy.[11]

As the royal family appeared on the palace balcony – the first time they had done so since the death of the Duke of Wellington in 1852 – the sun was rising over the majestic towers of Westminster Abbey nearby. They could see huge crowds massing in the early-morning chill outside the palace gates below, crowds that stretched back down the Mall and spilled into nearby St James's and Regent's Parks. All stood waiting in eager anticipation of that rarest of spectacles – a force of British fighting men resplendent in their scarlet swallow-tailed coatees with white epaulettes and facings, their white cross belts and gleaming black bearskins, knapsacks on their backs and long muskets with fixed bayonets at their sides. It was a sight not witnessed since the euphoric days of victory after Napoleon's defeat in 1815.

The march past for the Queen would be a moment of high emotion – of patriotic pride and British bullishness accompanied by deafening cheers from the crowds. She had always been proud to call herself a soldier's daughter (her father the Duke of Kent having been Commander-in-Chief of the British forces in Canada) and would often express the wish that of her own four young sons, two would serve in the army and two in the navy. Throughout the war she would remain supremely conscious of the mystical bond between the army and its monarch and exploit it to the full. For her, these men were, quite simply, the epitome of manly beauty and courage, and it was in the triple role of wife, mother and sovereign that Victoria greeted them, bowing and waving from her balcony. 'They formed line, presented arms, and then cheered us *very heartily* and went off cheering,' she later wrote to her uncle King Leopold of Belgium, though she could not fail to register the solemnity of the moment: 'many sorrowing friends were there, and one saw the shake of many a hand'.[12]

As the ranks of the Scots Fusilier Guards wheeled and marched out through the palace gates, down the great thoroughfare of Pall Mall, along Cockspur Street, to Charing Cross and the Strand, their way was rendered virtually impassable by the crowds of ordinary public, by costermongers and cabbies and street children fighting for sight of them, pelting them with flowers and gifts of fruit and trying to grasp them by the hands as they crossed over Waterloo Bridge to the station. From Waterloo they would entrain for the troop frigate the *Simoom*, awaiting them in Portsmouth harbour.

As the soldiers marched, their bands of fifes and drums rang out the old familiar marching tunes of the day. The streets of central London echoed that morning to 'The British Grenadiers', 'We Are Going Far Away', 'Cheer Boys, Cheer', 'Auld Lang Syne' and, perhaps most poignantly of all, that favourite army song of leave-taking, 'The Girl I Left Behind Me', based on an Irish melody published in Dublin in 1791:

> Oh, ne'er shall I forget the night
> The stars were bright above me
> And gently lent their silv'ry light
> When first she vow'd to love me.
> But now I'm bound to Brighton Camp,
> Kind Heaven, then, pray guide me
> And send me safely back again
> To the girl I've left behind me.[13]

In stark contrast to the men in their bright scarlet jackets, a group of forty or so downtrodden women could also be discerned walking behind the Guards. Poorly dressed and wrapped in shawls, they were 'laden like packhorses, with large bundles, under which they appeared to walk with some difficulty'.[14] These, along with other contingents of army wives, such as the 32 women who had trailed off after the Coldstreams on 14 February, were supposedly the lucky ones. They were the women who had won the ballot and been chosen to go 'on the strength' as one of the six married women per 100 men allowed to accompany the army on campaign. But as the troop train pulled out of Waterloo with these women crammed on board clasping their few paltry belongings, another disconsolate group of careworn women, some of them with children hanging on their skirts, stood lingering on the empty platform. Suffering agonies of grief, they wept bitterly as the crowds around them dispersed. For these were the 'girls' who were to be left behind, in many cases abandoned to poverty and destitution for the duration of the war – few of them destined ever to see their husbands again.

In March this long sequence of farewells across Britain culminated in a final send-off on a remarkably fine day at Portsmouth, with the same 'immense concourse of spectators' crowded along the shoreline and waving from every available yacht and pleasure boat. But again, amidst the bands and the cheering and waving there was that same undercurrent of sadness and distress epitomized by the many 'sorrowful women, whose downcast looks and tearful eyes betokened that it was no high holiday for them'.[15]

Nervous that the Russian fleet massing in the Baltic might venture into the North Sea and threaten Britain, the British government had gathered together its own fleet under the command of Vice Admiral Sir Charles Napier. The departure of the British Baltic fleet's first division of fifteen ships of the line from Portsmouth on 11 March was witnessed by a huge influx of visitors to the town, who had for days beforehand taken advantage of special excursion trains from London and Brighton, or hired, at extortionate rates, any commercial sailing vessels available from Southampton, Hyde, Cowes and other ports along the south coast and on the Isle of Wight. The town was now filled to bursting point with noisy, excited crowds. Every bed in every inn, hotel and lodging house was taken; prices doubled, and those unfortunate enough not to secure rooms could be seen on the pavements in front of the hotels 'keeping disconsolate watch over carpet-bags and portmanteaux'.[16]

The sense of occasion and excitement was palpable, conveyed in a long-forgotten account by a woman subsequently identified only as 'Miss

Bird', whose prose, despite her winsome name and reticent nature (for she published anonymously), demonstrates a power of description to rival that of any male newspaper reporter of the day. From the morning of the 7th till the day of departure, the 11th, there had been scenes of turmoil at the dockyard gates where 'hundreds of women, some clean and sorrowful-looking, others noisy and slatternly' had been trying to beg a ride in a tug or rowing boat to get a closer sight of the ships. Added to the constant weeping of these and other groups of women dispersed around the town were the regular thunderous cannonades from the fleet at anchor, the carousing of drunken sailors, the incessant traffic of cabs and every kind of conveyance, and the constant and indecorous poking of elbows and umbrellas in the push and shove of crowds making their way to the shoreline – none of which, observed Miss Bird in sombre tones, could fail to remind people 'that we are on the eve of a war of which no human foresight can predict the close'.[17]

At the Sailors' Home in Queen Street she observed at first hand something of the misery that war engenders: young naval cadets – boys of only ten or twelve – in their gold-banded caps taking leave of their parents, and newly married officers bidding a painful farewell to their wives. It all brought home the stark reality of war – as opposed to 'the fictitious glitter' with which she had invested it till then – as she remarked on the gloomy mood of many officers who felt that they were setting off for a 'war of extermination particularly fatal to themselves'.[18]

By 8 a.m. on the 11th, with the moment of departure due at 1.45 p.m., enterprising 'cockney excursionists' from London, as Miss Bird dubbed them, had parked themselves in the best vantage points armed with picnic hampers full of 'eatables and porter'; elsewhere, 'woebegone ladies with sand in their eyes and their bonnets blown off' succumbed and fainted in the crush; those relatives of sailors in the fleet lucky enough to procure the hire of a vessel sailed or rowed out to the ships at anchor, armed with final packages and messages for their loved ones.[19]

Finally, Queen Victoria, in a fetching silk dress with sable muff and fur tippet and a blue veil, and carrying a redundant parasol whilst struggling to prevent her cloak being blown over her head, sailed out of the harbour mouth on board the royal yacht, the *Fairy*, in a brisk west wind. In the sheltered waters at Spithead, a location long favoured for naval reviews, the *Fairy* took its position at the head of the fleet, its name most fitting for it was dwarfed by the vast new troop transports and leviathan mail steamers encircling it.

'The fated hour was come,' intoned Miss Bird,

> friends, parents and children, husbands and wives, brothers and sisters, embraced for the last time, ere they were hurried over the ship's sides – the rigging of each vessel swarmed with men – huge anchors were seen ascending from the water – white sails were fluttering on every mast – and amid the loud accents of command, the shrill tones of the boatswain's whistle, and the deafening cheers of thousands, the beautiful *Tribune* turned round like a swan and fairly under-weigh, spread her cloud of swelling canvass to the wind and went forth to bear England's thunders to the Baltic.[20]

The experience had also been memorable for the queen – 'a never-to-be-forgotten' one, as she confided to her journal that evening. For her, the sight of the flagship, the *Duke of Wellington*, at the head of the fleet had been 'a harbinger of glory . . . an inspiriting and solemn sight . . . which we would not have missed for worlds'.[21] But it is Miss Bird whose observations convey the real dimension and drama of the occasion: 'On, on they went, their sails swelling with the breeze, their sides bristling with cannon, their poops with bayonets, their rigging swarming with seamen.' 'Through their open ports' she was thrilled to catch 'glimpses of marines in scarlet, and cadets and midshipmen in gold banded caps – joyous looking beings with flaxen hair, intoxicated with the excitement of the hour and dreams of Glory and the Gazette' – dreams that, as she sadly observed, would perhaps all too soon be realized 'in a shotted [sewn up] hammock on the floor of the dark Baltic'.

With the *Duke of Wellington*, a giant sail and screw battleship crewed by 1,100 seamen, now positioned at its head, the fleet moved off. As Her Majesty waved her handkerchief at the good British tars swarming like bees on every rope and spar and clinging precariously to the very topmost mast of the *Duke of Wellington*, her heart swelled with patriotic pride. She and the nation had fulfilled its collective duty by turning out to see them off. In the months that followed, the British Army would fulfil its duty too, in the bloody battles of Alma, Inkerman and Balaklava. But following this terrifying carnage the 'protective mantle' of 'perpetual peace, ever-growing prosperity and continual progress' that had given comfort to the self-satisfied citizens of mid-Victorian Britain would be gone for ever.[22]

As too would the traditional British Army: for it was no longer battle-hardened, its senior officers in the main long lacking in active military command. The army was also in fact being sent out on campaign fatally ill-equipped (many of its tents and guns and some of its ammunition dating back to the Napoleonic Wars) and poorly supplied for what would prove a difficult and protracted war for which the planners had not taken sufficient account of the exigencies of a Russian winter. And as the excitement of the first days turned to grim reality with the British Declaration of War on 28 March, the British public too seemed to wear a more 'earnest and thoughtful expression of countenance, and seemed fully alive to the importance of the coming struggle'.[23]

Throughout the war, Queen Victoria perpetually regretted that she was but a 'poor woman' and not a man, filled as she was 'with atavistic longings to don shining armour' and fight alongside her troops.[24] Her voluminous official correspondence with her ministers, combined with equally detailed contributions from the indefatigable Prince Albert, confirms her astute grasp of all the political and military aspects of the conflict. If she couldn't be out there watching it happen, then at least the queen could live out vicariously the hopes and anxieties of the women who had watched their men march off to war and must now sit and wait for news. She would share in their grief and their agony as, for month after endless month, the casualty lists relentlessly tolled out the names of the dead. She spent long hours writing letters of condolence to the wives and mothers of officers killed, soliciting detailed reports on the wounds and the recovery of those men transported home to the military hospitals at Chatham and privately paying for prosthetic limbs and dentures for those who needed them. She organized and paid for food parcels and consignments of books for the wounded at Scutari. Together with her daughters she knitted and sewed through the long winter evenings, her daughters repeatedly wishing that they could go to the Crimea as volunteer nurses to join Florence Nightingale's team at Scutari Hospital. She cajoled and begged and demanded news of the war from everyone and anyone returning from the front. In every way possible, Queen Victoria sought to *experience* the war, to be a witness.

Few women, in fact, would have that momentous privilege. In Jamaica, the Creole doctor and nurse Mary Seacole, long a friend of the officers of the British Army and Navy who regularly lodged at her boarding house in Kingston, also yearned to bear witness. 'I used to stand for hours in silent thought before an old map of the world, in a little corner of which someone had chalked a red cross, to enable me to distinguish where the Crimea was,' she would later recall, 'and as I traced the route thither, all difficulties would vanish.'[25] Through sheer grit and determination and a characteristically dogged refusal ever to accept 'no' for an answer from anyone, she would make her own way to the Crimea to be one of the campaign's most idiosyncratic female chroniclers.

It was the army's original intention that the women allowed to accompany the expeditionary force would be left at a depot in the rear – in this case Malta, Varna in Bulgaria, or Scutari, near Constantinople – but there were in fact a considerable number of women who did manage to become witnesses to the conflict on the Crimean peninsula itself: who saw the whole campaign through from the optimistic departures from the south coast, through the often stormy sea crossings to the Dardanelles, through the ravages of cholera epidemics at Varna, and on ultimately to the landings at Kalamita Bay and the front lines of the siege of Sevastopol. No official statistics survive for the exact number of army wives who went on the strength and the accounts of only a handful have come down to us, but they bear powerful witness to the sights they saw. For here were women as bold and courageous as any man, demonstrating equal levels of fortitude and endurance in the face of terrible deprivation and suffering. Women such as army wives Ellen Butler of the 95th Foot, Elizabeth Evans and Rebecca Box of the 4th King's Own, Margaret Kerwin of the 19th Foot, Marianne Young of the 28th, and Fanny Duberly of the 8th Hussars were forced to watch the British Army – which had marched off with such high optimism in those February days – rapidly melt away into needless death and suffering as the campaign unravelled.

But this was also a war that saw women travel to the Crimea for a wide range of other reasons: from the privileged officers' wives who watched the battles from a relatively safe distance and then retired to the safety of their yachts in Balaklava harbour; to the heroic British, French and Russian nurses – Catholic, Orthodox and Protestant – who served with great devotion on both sides of the battle; to the coquettish *cantinières* in their snappy uniforms, ever ready in the French front lines with their *bidons* of wine and water for the wounded; to the romantically inclined British lady tourists who looked upon war as an exciting form of entertainment and even managed to find romance in the Crimea. But back home too there was an army of dedicated women, from the queen herself to the humblest of servant girls, for whom war might have seemed 'a noise far away'[26] but who nevertheless knitted and sewed and fund-raised tirelessly to supply creature comforts to the troops in the Crimea.

All these women had their own sense of purpose. But for the hundreds of destitute women and children left stranded in the barrack towns of England, Scotland and Ireland as their men marched off to war, it would be a long and bitter time. The strains of 'The Girl I Left Behind Me', borne faintly away into the distance the day the soldiers marched from town, were left 'reverberating in thousands, nay, millions of English hearts, from the rocky fastnesses of the Scottish highlands . . . to the Cornish head-lands', and could be heard 'in the Queen's palace and the Grenadier's barrack-room; the labourer's cottage, and the ghillie's sheeling and the bogtrotter's shebeen'.[27]

It was a melody that had been the parting tune of the British Army on campaign for 60 years or more, to which the long slow agony of waiting and watching over the next two years would be played out, while death inexorably 'sang the bass to the fife's shrill treble'.

TWO

Nothing But My Needle to Depend On

Charles Dickens wrote in *Household Words* that the women left behind when their men went off to war could do nothing but resign themselves to their lot and 'weep and pray and hope'.[1] And in the first heady days of the troop embarkations they were indeed left to do so, with no thought being given to how they would survive. But the clamorous public reception given the troops did not for long disguise the entrenched and appalling official indifference not just to the welfare of the army itself but also the wives and children of its serving men. Many of the rank and file had themselves frequently expressed concern that their paltry wages were barely enough for them to survive on, let alone support families, a fact which in itself had long been used as a means of discouraging marriage in the army. To leave their dependants now without provision for their welfare caused a great deal of uneasiness. To make matters worse, even though many soldiers would have readily volunteered a portion of their pay to keep their wives and children from starvation during their absence, when war was eventually declared the army still had made no provisions for such money to be distributed to them. Army regulations forbade soldiers from arranging for 'half-pay notes' for their wives until three to six months *after* they had embarked for war.

The *Illustrated London News* was quick to take up the cause and to remind its readers that, at a time when other British regiments were being sent abroad, to India and, worse still, to that dreaded outpost of empire Van Diemen's Land (the penal colony in Tasmania), 'misery, bereavement and want have again and again been endured by women and children in precisely similar phases since the formation of our army'.[2] Public opinion slowly but surely was awakening to the suffering of soldiers' wives – 'this long-neglected class of our fellow creatures' – despite traditional hostility towards them.[3] The time had come for government to take responsibility for their support in time of war, instead of the traditional and complacent reliance on private donation and philanthropy.

The plight of the wives left behind became apparent the very same morning that the Scots Fusilier Guards marched out of London. One distraught wife, trailing two small children, four months pregnant with a third and faced with the bitter reality of her penniless state, went into premature labour. The following morning her baby was born dead. Fellow lodgers in the cheap boarding house in Carrington Street in London where she was staying took pity on her and raised a few shillings for her benefit, but the hapless Mrs Hawkins was nevertheless forced to throw herself on the mercy of the local Board of Guardians at Mount Street, who deemed her state of destitution worthy of one shilling and a loaf of bread and then sent her on her way. A subsequent letter from an officer in Private Hawkins's regiment revealed the true problem. He had concealed the fact that he was married from his commanding officers. As his wife had not been officially sanctioned as an army wife, the army technically refused all responsibility for her.

Mrs Hawkins's husband had, according to *The Times*, himself said before leaving that he 'should have been happier could he have followed them all [his family] to the grave ere he quitted the shores of England',[4] and there were many other soldiers who were distraught at being forced to abandon their families in this way. It was, *The Times* warned, detrimental to morale for soldiers to depart from home to 'face the fire and steel of the enemy in the open field'[5] knowing that their families would suffer hardship in their absence. One such man was Colour Sergeant John Wager, a loyal soldier of 15 years' service, who the night before sailing with the Rifle

Brigade cut his throat at the thought of leaving his wife and child destitute. It was a tale that would be told over and over again across the country, as more and more destitute wives appealing for help discovered either that their husbands had married them without army approval, or, as it turned out in many cases, had simply deserted them, enlisting in the army under false names. And under a clause that was added in 1837 to the annual renewal of the Mutiny Act, any man deserting his family to enlist was specifically exempted from any responsibility to support them.

Within days of Mrs Hawkins's story being published in The Times, a Mrs Walker wrote to the paper from the Edgware Road saying she had been left destitute, with one child and another unborn, and without money or the 'necessaries for her imminent confinement'. She had, she said, 'nothing but my needle to depend on' to keep herself and her children from the workhouse. Her letter prompted a speedy response and the offer of a bed at a charitable foundation, Queen Charlotte's Lying-in Hospital. But the committee of the hospital, despite their willingness to offer similar help to other soldiers' wives, was forced to admit that it was 'crippled from want of means' to do so; the hospital was in a desperate state of dilapidation and 'languishing for want of funds'.[6]

Similar appeals were made on the pages of The Times for Anne Godwin, denied relief after her husband William deserted her to enlist in the Royal Artillery, having taken a solemn oath that he was unmarried. When he was later killed in action, she was denied assistance as a war widow. Similarly, Mary Ann Tysoe was left pregnant and destitute with three children after her husband entrained with the 7th Fusiliers at Manchester for the war. She managed to obtain £1 8s. in handouts, only to discover, when she was hauled up in court on a charge of fraud, that her husband had never gone off to war at all. Despite twelve years of army service, Private Tysoe had deserted at Reading en route to his troopship at Portsmouth; he was picked up at Brampton, when it was discovered he had enlisted under the false name of Brown and had made no mention of his wife and children.

There were few romantic stories to leaven the relentless loop of penniless wives and starving children, but one such did make the pages of The Times in February. A recently married young wife of a Rifleman would stop at nothing in her desire to follow her husband on campaign, he having already sailed on the *Himalaya* troopship a few days earlier. Having lost out in the ballot to go 'on the strength', she cut off her long hair, donned her husband's regimental uniform which he had left at home, rehearsed sufficiently to get through the evening roll call and pass muster, and spent the night at her husband's barracks. The following morning she marched off through the dockyard gates at Portsmouth, musket at her side, and onto his troopship the *Vulcan*. When she was finally discovered, shortly before the ship set sail, she begged and pleaded to be allowed to travel on and join her husband. The incident was witnessed by several influential women, including the Duchess of Sutherland and the Marchioness of Stafford, who had come to see the ship depart, and who, together with Lady Erroll, wife of the Rifle Brigade's commander, prevailed on him to allow the woman to sail.[7]

Restrictions on numbers did not, of course, apply to officers' wives travelling with their husbands. Although some accompanied their husbands on the sea journey – and all the way to the camp at Varna in the case of Lady Erroll – many army as well as navy wives turned back at Malta or went no further than Constantinople. A few disappointed wives of NCOs managed to gain a passage thanks to a loophole in the rules by offering themselves as maidservants to officers' wives – women such as Mrs Williams, wife of a sergeant major in the 8th Hussars, who persuaded Fanny Duberly, wife of the regiment's paymaster travelling out on campaign, to take her on. Others tried applying to be sent out as Nightingale nurses in order to obtain a passage to Scutari and be nearer their men; one such woman was quickly dismissed for having shown no intention of nursing at all but of 'joining her soldier husband at the public expense'.[8]

For the hardened army wives who had already seen long years of service in Canada, India and elsewhere in the British colonies and had suffered the indignities and the shortages that such postings brought with them, life was always tough, often dehumanizing and for most, prematurely ageing. When the Crimean veteran Elizabeth Evans told her story in 1898, she did so with a justifiable air of superiority:

When I take my mind back to those distant years of suffering by young women in the Army, I marvel at the changes which time has wrought. Sometimes I listen to the wails of soldiers and their wives and sweethearts nowadays, and I smile almost pityingly, for, compared with the old order, they are ladies and gentlemen, and do not know what privation and iron discipline are.[9]

Life had always been harsh for the British foot soldier. From 1829 to 1847, enlisting in the army meant enlisting for life. The Limited Service Act of 1847 introduced a minimum term of 10 or 12 years, with the option to re-engage to complete 21 years of service, of which time a good part could be spent abroad. The low pay combined with a life spent constantly on the move, not to mention – until barracks were built – dossing down in billets, could not have been less conducive to marriage and family life. Back in the eighteenth century, wives had traditionally been looked upon as the ruination of a good soldier, many of whom married imprudently, or cohabited with a succession of women from posting to posting. Officers were urged to impress upon their men the importance of avoiding 'dishonourable connections' with women considered to be deviant or idle, while ensuring that their wives were modest, honest, sober and industrious, for a soldier's pay was certainly not enough for two to subsist on.

In fact everything about army life conspired against marriage, and officers actively discouraged it. 'I am fully and decidedly of opinion, that married men have no business whatever in the army,' wrote Major John Patterson in his 1840 study *Camp and Quarters*. Marriage was both a strain on and a distraction to the soldier when on active service, 'for constant uneasiness about the family he has left at home, when he himself is called abroad, and their anxiety for him, are painful things to think of; his happiness and peace of mind are marred, and all his best exertions paralized, by reflecting on his situation'.[10] Such diversions hindered a man's advancement in the service. Many of these opinions, of course, were expressed by commanding officers who had their own wives and families safely installed in nice homes in England, exposing the hypocrisy of a philosophy based on marriage as a social right – for officers and NCOs only.[11]

In the British army any soldier wishing to get married had to obtain the permission of his commanding officer, upon the receipt of which the wife would officially be deemed to be 'on the strength' and, if there was room, be allowed to live in barracks with her husband. But only between 4 and 6 per cent of soldiers were ever given formal permission to marry. Most married in secret and never told their commanders they had done so; their position as 'off the strength wives' meant that these women had to shift for themselves and find lodgings wherever they could near their husbands' barracks. Equally, many wives were unaware that by being 'illegal' in army terms they would not be eligible for such paltry benefits as the half-rations the army allowed to soldiers' families, or charitable donations if their husbands should die on active service. Other wives would find themselves and their children deserted when their soldier husband moved on to his next posting.

Before the construction of barracks in the late eighteenth century, soldiers had lived in tents in camp or been billeted out to taverns and alehouses. Barracks, when they were eventually constructed, were almost deliberately made to be as cheerless, comfortless and insalubrious as jails. Separate married quarters were not introduced until the late 1850s, and prior to that only a few regiments provided special rooms for married couples. Even by the end of the Crimean War only 20 out of 251 barracks in Britain had separate rooms catering for them. Even common criminals in jail had more cubic airspace than soldiers crammed into such over-crowded barracks (200–300 cubic feet per soldier; 600 for prisoners). Washing facilities were crude and unhygienic – wooden tubs for both washing and use as overnight urinals, with only a single towel and piece of soap provided, which had to be shared by many.

Barrack room life for the women who lived there was brutish, noisy, sweaty and undignified, obliged as they were to share the same living space not just with their husbands but with other men, crammed into folding iron beds, with barely standing room between them, where they slept on straw mattresses (the straw changed once a quarter) and with fresh sheets provided only once a month. Any thought of domestic or romantic seclusion as a couple was impossible: the best women could do to protect their modesty in such circumstances was to decamp to one end of the barrack and rig up a blanket or ragged sheet on string fastened with pegs to cordon off their own private area. Here, behind this thinnest of screens, babies were conceived and women sometimes died giving birth to them.

The rooms, lit by candles and penny dips, were often cold and damp, discouraging the opening of windows and not just trapping inside every fetid smell of cooking, unwashed bodies and bodily fluids, but also creating a breeding ground for infectious disease: in such crowded and insanitary conditions the death rate from tuberculosis among soldiers was five times higher than in civilian life. With so many single soldiers unable to marry and forced to resort to prostitutes, venereal disease was endemic – with as many as 40 per cent of the army needing treatment at one time or another.

It is not surprising that such an environment ground women down; poverty-stricken and downtrodden, army wives were looked upon as the dregs of society: drabs and slatterns whose only consolation was the gin bottle. Such was the poor public perception of them that it was generally assumed that all army wives were women of 'bad character', for barrack life had a rapidly corrupting influence even on the young and impressionable new wives thrown into this maelstrom. This, certainly, is what Mrs Marianne Young, surgeon's wife of the 28th Foot, had witnessed, writing on what she called the 'moral canker' of barrack life:

> Appalled at the position in which she finds herself placed, her ears assailed on every side by ribaldry and blasphemy, the woman perhaps sits down and weeps; while one who has passed through agony such as hers . . . draws near, jests at her condition, and recommends her to try the soothing influence of the dram-shop. The poison does its work; the poor creature's sensibilities are dulled; she now endures the horror of her position, and, day by day, becomes more indifferent to it.[12]

Young, who would go on to describe the terrible suffering of the army wives encamped at Varna in Bulgaria during the war, also vividly depicted the relentless, demoralizing misery of barrack life at the huge military camp at Aldershot. Elizabeth Evans admitted that she had been happiest when she had been the only woman in her barrack room at Ashton-under-Lyne after she married in 1852; once other women arrived to share the same space there was constant squabbling, recrimination and vying for position. Sometimes ten or more army wives per barrack, surrounded by hungry unwashed children and crying babies (and numerous army wives had as many as eight children), would find themselves fighting for use of the centre stove, 'the floor of the hut littered with bones and potato-peelings', their husbands lounging around and cursing as they awaited their meal, while the 'washing continued to drip from the lines overhead'. When they were not cooking and cleaning, the women spent their time struggling to do their laundry in a wash house ankle-deep in mud, 'productive of much cramp, rheumatism, and dangerous suffering . . . which a trellis-flooring of wood might at once have remedied'.[13]

Army food was grimly monotonous – each soldier was allowed one pound of bread and three-quarters of a pound of meat per day, plus an issue of potatoes, hard tack biscuits and coffee; any other food, particularly nutritionally important fruit and vegetables, would have to be bought out of what remained from his pay. This was a paltry 7 shillings a week (it rose by 7 pence in 1856 at war's end) for a private in the infantry, a greater part of which was deducted to pay for his food, laundry, kit, uniform, and haircuts. Stoppages were also made for medical treatment, lost equipment and any damage to his barracks, leaving the soldier on average less than three pence a week for the needs of his family; the only way in which a soldier could boost his pay was by acting as a servant to an officer or as a waiter in the officers' mess.

When the Crimean War broke out, the commander-in-chief, Lord Raglan, had made it absolutely clear that he did not favour women accompanying the army on campaign; many of his officers also questioned the logic and logistics of taking women to the East. Whilst women's lives in camp had been barely tolerable at the best of times, their presence in a war zone 'could not fail to be a misery to themselves, as well as a serious burden to the army's already seriously defective commissariat',[14] during the rigours of a campaign in an area where the army had no operations base or field depots. Nevertheless, the army also realized that to actively oppose marriage would discourage enlistment; it would also foster rather than put an end to prostitution and disease and encourage single soldiers to prey on women. Compromises had to be made. Anticipating a demand for a considerable number of 'on the strength' wives to be accommodated, the government ordered figures to be drawn up on precisely how many women might be eligible to travel with the army. Of the 31,394 NCOs and men ordered to the East during 1854, 3,266 had legal wives, of whom only a small percentage – under the regulations of six for every company of 100 men on colonial service – would be allowed to travel 'on the strength'. In order to reduce the numbers further, an official government circular was issued changing the old allowance to four women per company in time of war. The two additional women who might otherwise have gone received the consolation of half-rations for the duration. Children were excluded, so only those without offspring could take part in the ballot – drawing papers marked 'to go' or 'not to go', or one of six white pebbles in a hat full of black ones. This was held on the eve of departure in order to minimize the risk of desertion and deter attempts to smuggle wives on board ship. Those not selected to go were turned out of barracks immediately their men left for war and expected to find their own accommodation; the regimental schools for their children were also shut up and their children's education abandoned.

It was thus estimated that each infantry battalion would on average leave behind at least forty 'legally' married women and their children with no means of support. But this is not to include the 'illegal' wives, who technically did not exist in the army's eyes at all and who were eligible for no help whatsoever. The ramifications of this social problem were soon to be felt: with thousands of men going off to war leaving not just thousands of displaced wives and children, but aged and widowed parents who were dependent on them, the workhouse now loomed large for many. By the following January, 1855, the numbers of army and navy wives (both on and off the strength) receiving outdoor relief had risen from 598 to 2,217, not to mention their many dependent children.[15]

In Ireland the problem was particularly acute. A high proportion of Irish men had enlisted in the army to escape starvation during the devastating potato famines of the 1840s (7,000 of them would die during the Crimean War) and great numbers of their wives, as well as those Irishwomen English soldiers had married whilst serving in Ireland, were now abandoned. By late April these women were besieging the army paymaster's office in Dublin, begging for financial assistance in order to be able to return to their home parishes:

> Many were in rags, emaciated and care-worn, presenting most deplorable aspects. There were others more respectable in appearance, striving to maintain a decent exterior in the presence of spectators. Nearly all were accompanied by one or more children. Anxiety and sorrow were stamped on the features of these supplicants for the public bounty; but the generality shrunk from the exposure to which their pressing necessities urged them.[16]

Many of these desperate women expressed a desire to find honest employment in domestic service so that they could support their families, but they encountered a wall of prejudice when they attempted to do so, finding themselves shunned by polite Victorian society: 'The very fact of having lived in barracks militates against admission into private families,' wrote a correspondent of the *Illustrated London News*, 'and who would entrust needlework to one unpossessed of a fixed domicile, and regarding whose respectability it might be difficult to gain information?'[17] Such women found themselves in a double bind, for they could hardly expect a willing welcome from their own impoverished families if they turned up penniless on their doorstep trailing several children. Many were therefore forced to tramp hundreds of miles to apply for relief in their home parishes, as Catherine Wheeler did, walking 200 miles with two small children from Liverpool to her parish in Clerkenwell, London. In many cases these were parishes from which the women might long have been absent and into which they would arrive as friendless strangers.

As time went on the situation became more acute. Questions were raised in the House of Commons, with MP Augustus Stafford relating how he had seen letters from female relatives of soldiers stating that 'unless money was sent to them to purchase a mangle or set themselves up in some way of business, there was nothing left for them but the workhouse or prostitution'.[18] Any kind of employment was preferable to entering the workhouse, and the one thing they all dreaded – separation from their children.

With government slow to respond, clergymen all over Britain were being besieged by parishioners anxious to help; the British public was moved as it never had been before. It was also angry and conscience-stricken, as the pages of The Times increasingly revealed. But whilst there were many acts of benevolent sympathy and generous private donation, such as the £200 given for the relief of the wives of the 93rd Sutherland Highlanders by the Duke of Sutherland, it would not be until October 1854 that the Royal Patriotic Fund was established in direct response to public opinion. The Army and Navy Club in London, meanwhile, was spurred into philanthropic action by the example of the enterprising but anonymous wife of a captain in the Royal Engineers, who, after her husband's regiment left for the war, had set about finding employment for all the married women of his company who had been left behind; she had 'never relaxed her exertions until they were provided with situations'.[19]

Meanwhile, many Poor Law Guardians, unable to cope with the influx of destitute women, were questioning the additional strain on their limited funds, arguing that the War Office should take responsibility. In many cases they were refusing non-resident financial relief to women, insisting they enter the workhouse. The response of the government was stubborn and inhumane: every effort had been made to discourage the marriage of soldiers whose pay was sufficient only for maintaining themselves in 'health and military efficiency'; the soldier's wife must therefore 'depend on her own industry for her maintenance, whether her husband is in this country, in a colony, or at the seat of war'. Whilst the state would be willing to entertain cases deserving of compassionate consideration, to offer indiscriminate maintenance of any kind for wives of soldiers on active service would be an 'encouragement to marriage' without permission and deprive the woman of an 'incentive to industry'.[20]

In the meantime, a range of soldiers' and sailors' charitable organizations in the garrison towns, as well as some regimental funds, had swung into action, with the emphasis, as the war dead mounted, of assisting soldiers' widows and orphans, as well as aged dependants. In Portsmouth, where the local population had for weeks on end witnessed heartbreaking scenes as thousands of troops embarked for the East leaving desperate wives on the quayside, the problem was particularly severe. Many of the men of the 2nd Battalion of the Rifle Brigade who had been based there had brought back with them Canadian wives from their recent postings in the colony. These women, of whom there were around 200, had no home parish to go to and were forced to appeal for help to the good citizens of the city. A meeting had already been held in the Army and Navy Club in February to raise a subscription to assist them, the sum of £112 17s. 6d. being subscribed within an hour. The editorial column of the *Portsmouth Times and Naval Gazette* was proud to announce:

> The people of Portsmouth frequently apathetic in that which concerns their own immediate interest have during the past week evinced a zealous desire to be foremost in the good work of benefiting the destitute and unprotected. They have nobly taken up the case of the wives and families of those gallant men who have embarked . . . and have unanimously agreed to petition the government to make a permanent provision for those who by fortune of war
>
> 'Are cast abandoned to the world's wide stage
> And doomed in hopeless poverty to roam.'[21]

But, as ever, traditional British philanthropy made clear distinctions between the deserving and undeserving poor, and at all levels of fundraising such issues bedevilled decision-making. In March 1854 much of the charitable effort was coordinated under the Central Association in Aid of the Wives and Families of Soldiers Ordered to the East which had been set up in Pall Mall, London, under the patronage of Queen Victoria, Prince Albert and the eminent social reformer Lord Shaftesbury. Its primary objective was to provide relief to wives not selected in the ballot, until such time as they were able to find employment. But whilst assistance to the innocent children of soldiers would be unconditional, whether or not it was awarded to wives was entirely dependent on their good character and willingness to work. And soon the anomalous situation of wives whose husbands had concealed their marriages from the regiment or deserted them reared its head: under what pretext could the Central Association withhold charitable relief to a wronged or innocent wife? When cases emerged of such women being denied relief, the public response was emphatic: 'We wish that our donation be given to the widows and orphans of the noble fellows who have bravely fought our battles in the east,' wrote one correspondent to *The Times*, 'we want neither quibbles nor sophistry; we must have fair play, or we shall keep our money'.[22]

The repeated, hard-nosed objection to wide-ranging relief of impoverished army wives was always the same: to do so would encourage idleness and complacency in the women concerned and encourage even more soldiers to marry. Such blinkered attitudes did not allow for the dignity and pride of army wives such as Martha Brightwell, whose husband had sworn an oath that he was single on enlistment in the 19th Regiment and had given a false name. When her financial plight became known in the papers after the Central Association refused her assistance on this technicality, donations of money poured in. Mrs Brightwell was duly grateful but specifically stated that she would much rather be given the means of supporting herself by employment either as a needlewoman or laundress, or, failing this, that her small son be accommodated in an orphanage or suchlike so that she could take a job in service as a housemaid. An outcry on the pages of *The Times* was spearheaded by Major Henry Newland of the 60th Rifles, who declared that the Central Association had no right in imagining that 'matrimony and almsgiving – divine institutions both – are to be governed by regulations purely military';[23] his protest was joined by that of others who threatened to ask for their donations to the association to be returned if it failed to correct such discrimination and wrongheadedness. Eventually an allowance of five shillings a week for a period of six months was made to Mrs Brightwell, but she turned down the association's belated act of charity, having by then found work, and being 'unwilling to take the bread from those women who want it worse than she does'.[24]

Until the Crimean War raised once and for all the issue of whether women should accompany armies on campaign, soldiers' wives had traditionally performed an important function when they accompanied their regiments on active service, taking on the essential roles of cooks, laundresses, cleaners, needlewomen, and even providing basic nursing skills, whilst others became sutlers, trading in essential provisions of food and drink. Since the eighteenth century women had been an integral part of the workings of a regiment, but with the end of billeting of troops and the creation of specially built barracks for an increasingly professional army in the nineteenth century, many of the raggle-taggle of camp followers were now excluded. It was in fact as laundresses that many army wives earned much-needed additional income for their families – a halfpenny a day on average – and it was a valuable if not essential service that many would provide in the Crimea, some to considerable profit – but one which was never properly formalized by the army, which could and should have better exploited army wives for their skills. Why shouldn't otherwise destitute army wives be busily employed in the making of shirts and socks and mitts and cavalry flannels, asked one reader of The Times? Or could they not be given employment as domestic servants? The army failed to respond as well in formally employing army wives in the field as regimental nurses, a role they had performed in garrison hospitals on postings abroad since the eighteenth century. Women performing this task on the strength in British Columbia had earned sixpence a day and full rations, thus considerably enhancing the joint income of an army couple.[25]

As the war dragged on and letters from the front by soldiers expressed gratification for the presence of women in the field hospitals and at Scutari, it would become increasingly clear that the female role in the conflict was an important one. Women were to prove their worth in many ways throughout the war, both at home and in the Crimea, through many long-forgotten and unrecorded acts of charity and courage. And public perceptions of the army too began to shift: with thoughts of home, wife, mother, children dominating the letters of the rank and file, it was increasingly felt that the English private soldier was vastly 'improved in quality by the possession of a decent and an honourable domestic tie'.[26] It was finally recognized that much of the desertion and drunkenness as well as acts of insubordination by soldiers had been provoked by the existing system and the strains placed on married life for soldiers separated from their wives. By war's end, the steady iconization of the domestic and ministering virtues of British women – both in the Crimea and at home – as keepers of the flame with 'watchful eye, conciliating voice, helping hand, smiling face and consoling heart'[27] would raise them to unprecedented levels of respect and admiration and make marriage in the army far more acceptable.

In 1908, at the end of a long life as an army wife, having witnessed the Crimean War and the Indian Mutiny, Elizabeth Evans looked back on those 'stern and bitter days'. And it was not without affection. She might have spent her early married life sharing a barrack room with twenty-four men, but she had managed to maintain her dignity and make the most of her crude surroundings, later insisting that although the men of her Crimean days could not for the most part either read or write, they 'behaved to me like gentlemen' and were 'good and faithful friends' to her, as were the other army wives who shared her sufferings in the Crimea.[28] There was one great compensation for all the privations of army life in Elizabeth's view: 'I had my husband you see, and we were devoted to each other and that makes a lot of difference in your hard march through life, does it not?'

Devotion such as that of Elizabeth Evans would take her all the way to the Crimea on campaign. For two years she never slept in a bed and, along with the men of her regiment, endured indescribable privations, witnessing horrors which even in old age she still could not bear to talk about.

THREE

Tramp, Tramp, Tramp for Woman as Well as Man

N obody knows how many women travelled east with the British
expeditionary force in the spring of 1854. It may have been as many
as 1,200; it was certainly at least 750. It is likely that a good three-quarters
of the army wives never returned. By the end of the war, an additional 250
women had travelled out to Turkey and the Crimea as nurses. History,
until now, has had little to say about them; their fates are largely
unrecorded.

When the time came to leave Britain, an average of 30 army wives
travelled on campaign with each regiment. But despite the 'on the
strength' regulations, some regiments made up their own rules about how
many women they took, or looked the other way when those who lost out
in the ballot were smuggled on board. Other regiments took far fewer than
their complement; the Royal Artillery allowed seven wives per troop when
its first six transports sailed from Woolwich during the spring
embarkations but later appears to have rescinded the rules altogether, as
no women were allowed to embark with any of the artillery siege train

companies sent to Sevastopol in September 1854.

Only a small percentage of the women taken would make it all the way to the Crimea, and of these several, having been told they could go no further than Turkey, found their own way to the Crimea, so determined were they to get there. In the words of the popular song:

> Our wills are good, but lack-a-day,
> To catch the soldiers we will try for it;
> For where there's a will there's always a way,
> We'll walk a mile or two if we die for it.[1]

When they reached the Dardanelles the walking, and the dying, would begin.

Ellen Butler of the 95th Derbyshires was one of many women determined to go on campaign who had got married to their men shortly before they went off to war. Michael Butler was a natural charmer and fast talker; a Catholic from Tipperary, he had insisted on marrying Ellen Wateridge in the face of his padre's opposition, even prevailing on him for a loan of half a crown in order to publish the banns at Portsea, near his barracks in Portsmouth. Father Kelly, objecting to Ellen being an Anglican and a 'heretic', had asked what exactly they proposed to live on. 'On love, your reverence' had been their response.[2] That love would be put to the test when they sailed on the *Medway* on 7 April 1854.

Only fifteen women accompanied the 19th Foot (better known today as the Green Howards) the day they left the Tower of London for the war, among them Margaret Kerwin, wife of No. 1737, Private John Kerwin – one of the thousands of Irishmen who had enlisted in the British Army since the 1840s. They had married at Devonport in 1852 and would see out both the Crimean War and the Indian Mutiny together. Elizabeth Evans's regiment, the 4th Foot, were based at Leith in Edinburgh, when the orders came to mobilize. Over 900 men would embark for the Crimea, taking 30 wives and two 'ladies' (as officers' wives were always separately designated). Elizabeth and her husband William had the good fortune of travelling on a spanking new screw steamer, the *Golden Fleece*, a vessel commissioned for the new 'Golden Line' of Australian Mail Packets run by the General Screw Company. The 2,500-ton ship had been requisitioned by the government for use as a troop transport and had been made seaworthy at the East India Docks in a mad dash of only ten days, thanks to the efforts of its Captain Ford and the enlistment of 500 navvies and artisans. The sight of such a striking new vessel at Edinburgh's Granton Pier had brought out the crowds, many of whom ventured the two miles out from the pier in steam-tugs and small boats to take a closer look. The 4th sailed on 10 March, but its journey down to Plymouth to pick up coal, water and provisions was hampered by fog, rain and strong headwinds and it was not until 14 March that it finally left England for Malta.

Undoubtedly one of the most celebrated women of the campaign, alongside the Jamaican nurse Mary Seacole, would be Fanny Duberly. The daughter of a wealthy banker of Devizes in Devon, Frances Isabella Locke was the antithesis of her dull, acquiescent, phlegmatic husband Captain Henry Duberly, paymaster of the 8th Hussars. Bold, gregarious and opinionated, she was as fearless and uncompromising in what she said and did as she was in her riding. A superb horsewoman, she had an innate sensitivity to horses which made her agonize constantly over their well-being from the moment she saw her own three animals loaded on board ship for the East. Fanny's determination to see the campaign through to the end never left her and she remained in the Crimea till the fall of Sevastopol in September 1855. But her apprehensions had been great on 24 April as she left Exeter en route for the *Shooting Star* at Plymouth docks. That same day, when she began the journal she would keep of the Crimean War, she described how she left with a 'sad heart and eyes full of tears':

> The near approach of this long voyage, and the prospect of unknown
> trials and hardships to be endured for I know not how long, overwhelmed
> me at the last moment; and the remembrance of dear friends left behind,
> whom I never more might return to see, made me shrink most nervously
> from the new life on which I was to embark.[3]

In the journal Fanny would make little or no mention of the other officers' wives who embarked for the Crimea, and only on rare occasions would refer to the plight of the rank and file wives. With a probable view to posterity – and publication – she romanticizes herself as a lone woman in a hostile terrain, surrounded by her own coterie of officer admirers. She makes no mention of the 13 wives of the 8th Hussars who travelled out in the second instalment of troops in March and whom she must have been aware of in camp. For a brief while at least, she did have to share centre stage with the equally intrepid Mrs Adelaide Cresswell, wife of a captain in the 11th Hussars – another fearless horsewoman and a dead shot, who, like Fanny, announced her intention of riding throughout the campaign and 'being in the thick of it' with 'a complete suit of leather' and 'a brace of pistols', as one officer heard tell.[4] No doubt iron will and a dash of eccentricity was bred in the bone in Adelaide Cresswell's family – the Gordon-Cummings – for her brother Roualeyn was a celebrated 'lion-slayer' in Africa who would soon be thrilling audiences on London's Piccadilly with a nightly showing of a diorama illustrating his exploits.

Although the voyage to Gallipoli in Greece, from there to Constantinople, and finally to Varna on the Black Sea – where the allied troops assembled before the campaign moved to the Crimea – was a relatively short one, of two to three weeks, sea travel in the 1850s was still not without the hazards of fire, shipwreck and disease. Unlike their husbands, from whom they were segregated on board, the women did not enjoy the comfort of berths, or even the regulation 14-inch-wide hammocks unless they were very lucky. They had to bed down as best they could with their few possessions on blankets or pallets stuffed with cowhair in the orlop, the lowest deck of the sailings ships, amidst the vile smells emanating from the bilge below. (Those fortunate enough to travel on the modern screw steamers such as the *Himalaya* were accommodated in the rather more comfortable lower deck saloon, though even this huge vessel rolled uncomfortably in high seas.) But wherever you were on board the older, wooden sailing ships there was no escaping the smell of decades at sea, of stale food, human sweat and the taint of disease that pervaded everything. Their bilges were full of stagnating water; decomposing vegetable and animal matter stank no matter what time of year; and with the orlop deck located below the waterline, without ports or openings, there was no respite from the smell. It was dark, damp and airless and as time went on, if the voyage was a rough one, there was no escaping the pervading stench of vomit too. Nor was it possible to stand upright properly in such confined spaces.

For the more vulnerable, particularly women who were pregnant – and a surprising number followed their husbands on campaign in this condition – even a relatively brief sea journey exposed them to the dangers of shipboard fever and typhus, a disease spread by lice. They would all spend hours, in high seas, locked below being sick into buckets. Few were allowed the luxury of getting fresh air on deck or being sick over the side. During the voyage men and women alike sickened and died, their bodies quickly disposed of at sea. During the turbulent crossing on the *Medway*, Ellen Butler suffered with the other women battened down in the orlop and was soon putting her natural nursing skills to the test. When the *Medway* finally docked at Gallipoli she wept with joy when the orlop was unbattened and she saw the sun again.

From above the women, on the lower deck where the horses were loaded in slings in two rows facing each other to stop them slipping and sliding in the rolling seas, came the constant thudding of hoofs, biting and whinnying as panicking horses, their shoulders and breastbones crushed by the slings, injured themselves as the ships rolled and rocked. Such fine-bred and highly strung creatures as British cavalry horses would quickly weaken en route to Turkey. Some died from the sheer exhaustion of standing for weeks without being able to lie down; others wore themselves out panting wearily for days on end in the stifling conditions; many died in epidemics of glanders – a highly contagious disease causing swellings of the horse's jaw. Other horses simply went mad and raved themselves to death. Fanny Duberly spent most of her own sea journey in paroxysms of anxiety not for herself or her companions but for her three horses stowed below. Storms around the Bay of Biscay had made her violently ill and she had taken to her bed, from where she learned, at Malta, that her beloved grey horse had died – the fifth horse in the regiment to perish on the journey. No sooner had her horse been buried at sea than Fanny was enduring another fearful storm, being 'shot from the stern locker, on which I was lying, to the far corner of my cabin, and every box and portmanteau came crushing over me'.[5]

Many of the women who sailed with the troops were kept down below for the entire voyage, but some were fortunate enough, when the weather was fine, to go on deck and delight in the sight of swallows or stormy petrels settling on the yardarms and masts off Cape Finisterre, and see whales, porpoises and sharks circling nearby as the ship's hull cut through the water. The soldiers on board had a far better time of it; they spent their recreation time playing games of whist, chess and backgammon. The regimental band often played on deck in the evening, and there was time for conversation, singing, reading and laughter. War still seemed a very long way off.

The journey out to the Strait of Gibraltar could take anything from four to ten days, depending on the weather and the type of vessel, after which the troopships tracked the rocky North African coast en route to Malta in the southern Mediterranean. After five to eight days at sea, encountering the ferocity of the sirocco wind, the weary travellers would find respite in Malta. For five of the 4th King's Own women, who had become sick on the voyage, the campaign ended here, where they asked to be put on the next boat back to England. Another 24 women from the 33rd and 41st Regiments, already finding the sea voyage too much for them, also opted to return home on board the steamship *Himalaya* in April. Then there were those who soon found that staying in Malta and soliciting on shore among the thousands of troops crowding the streets of Valetta was a much easier option than continuing a gut-wrenching sea journey who knows where.

In Malta, where the ships stopped to take on coal, supplies and water, many troops spent days if not weeks waiting to embark for the next stage of the journey east. The 4th were disembarked here and camped at Fort Manuel for sixteen days; the Scots Fusilier Guards, with 25 women in train, were holed up in the stifling heat and dry sirocco wind for six weeks. Some officers had brought their mothers as well as wives with them thus far. The air of unreality about it all continued: socializing, picnicking and dining carried on among the officers as though they were in a barrack town in England. But the dream days eventually came to an end; the women hung on as long as they could, but 'heavy were the hearts as that day approached when Malta must be left, the troop-steamer declared in readiness and poor women, whether the wives of officers or soldiers, were left with streaming eyes on the Barraco, while the fine ship glided on towards her Eastern point, and those whom God joined were put asunder – when again to meet?'[6]

The journey onwards from Malta to the first major army encampment in the East, at Gallipoli in the Dardanelles, could have taken up to another ten days for the slower sailing ships. The *Golden Fleece*, with Elizabeth Evans on board, left Malta on 31 March, a dark and overcast morning, with the first portion of the British expeditionary force and soon headed into drenching tropical showers. They arrived off Gallipoli in 'black jolting seas' punctuated by 'furious gusts of wind' and were horribly buffeted as they attempted to drop anchor.[7] Here in early May they were joined by the Rifle Brigade, the 50th, 93rd, 28th and 44th Regiments.

Many of the women who had endured the difficult journey so far were soon to face bitter disappointment when they reached Gallipoli. They were told they were not allowed to land but had to say farewell to their husbands on board ship, to be sent back either to the main army base at Scutari on the same ships or to what was then only a smaller depot at Varna. The *Times* correspondent William Howard Russell, who had sailed with the forces on the *Golden Fleece*, boggled at what he considered the 'egregious folly' of the Malta authorities, who had sent 97 army wives on from Malta on board the *Georgiana* – to a place where even men 'were hard set to live'.[8] Commander Sir George Brown had taken one look at the boatload of sickly women and ordered them sent straight back to where they came from. French officers who had witnessed the arrival of the women had been astonished at the sight:

> 'Were they going out to the seat of war, instead of Sisters of Charity, to minister to the comfort of the sick and wounded?' 'Oh no!' 'As cooks?' 'Certainly not!' 'Where were they to live? What carriage had we for them? Who was responsible for their conduct? What pay had they for their duties?'

'What *could* I say?' wrote Marianne Young, wife of regimental surgeon William Henry Young of the 28th Foot. 'Could I lower the opinion held by the French of our army, our discipline, our religious estimate of ourselves as a moral and benevolent people, by telling the Colonel of the Fifth, and my friend the Staff officer of the Prince Napoleon, that our women were perfectly untrained in all habits of usefulness; that they were allowed to crowd out, to live like sheep upon the Turkish hills?'[9]

Many officers would commend Sir George's action in sending the women packing; in their opinion there were far more women on the strength than they would have liked and they were an annoying encumbrance. Other officers, however, disagreed, seeing the presence of women as an important boost to morale. They looked the other way and allowed women to slip through the net and disembark at Gallipoli. But there were no creature comforts to greet them. The men at least had tents; but the women were left to take shelter wherever they could, forced to lie down in ditches to sleep, 'with a soldier's blanket over them, houseless, starving'.[10] Some regiments such as the Royal Scots squeezed the women in with them, but the overcrowding and lack of privacy was appalling – a Mrs McKenna and her husband sharing one tent with 14 men and Mrs Frances Driscoll and her husband with the same number in another. At the end of May the army grudgingly allotted two tents per battalion to the women; but with their few clothes already threadbare they were made no allowances for clothing until the end of December, when an order was made to issue clothing 'on production of a certificate that the women applying were fit persons to receive it'.[11]

With many soldiers as well as women already suffering the effects of seasickness, heat exhaustion or disease contracted en route, the fallout rate began to rise, compounded as it was by a lack of supplies and medical provisions for the sick. As one captain in the 50th complained in a letter to The Times:

> Our encampment is very wretched and hardly anything except the men's
> rations to be got to eat . . . The commissariat is dreadfully managed;
> nothing of any sort. The French have everything – horses, provisions,
> good tents, and every kind of protection against contingencies . . . We
> are all obliged to sit on the ground and eat what we can . . . It is really
> more than a joke, and all owing to the very bad management of our
> commissariat department.[12]

The town of Gallipoli on first acquaintance looked picturesque enough, but on close inspection offered no comforts. With a mixed population of Armenians, Jews, Turks and Greeks, it proved a miserable, dilapidated little place. Its narrow streets were mean and squalid; what decent habitation there was had already been earmarked by the French, who had arrived in April. The French *tricolore* now flew at every corner, French street names were emblazoned everywhere and French efficiency and order dominated throughout Gallipoli, in sorry contrast to the badly organized British.

Having systematically taken possession of the town, with typical culinary brio the French had set up bakeries producing sweet-smelling fresh white bread – an object of desire to the long-deprived British. Marianne Young of the 28th found it highly amusing if not baffling that the English soldier was 'half-starved upon his rations, because he could not, with three stones and a tin pot, convert them into palatable food', whilst there was virtually nothing the French would turn their noses up at if it could be converted into food. They caught and ate tortoises and dug up their eggs (and, it is said, even made culinary delights out of rats); they turned a handful of wild herbs gathered from the hillside into *omelettes aux fines herbes* and used their chewy ration meat to make tasty ragouts.

On first arrival, the exhausted army wives had trailed through Gallipoli looking for accommodation in crude hovels made of clay, but they were soon driven away by the rats and vermin, preferring the open air and the night cold to being eaten alive. Many of the troops would comment on the numbers of snakes and centipedes, but Elizabeth Evans's most vivid memory of Gallipoli would be the swarms of locusts, 'so dense and innumerable as to look like black clouds'. Later, in old age, she wondered whether they had been 'symbolic of the shadow which came across the lives of so many of us'. Perhaps they presaged the coming cholera, 'that dreadful visitation which struck strong men down even as they worked and marched, and made their halting places their graves?' For ominous outbreaks of the disease began to sweep through the ranks at Gallipoli 'as mercilessly as locusts strip the land of its verdure'.[13]

Not long after arriving in Gallipoli a contingent of troops were ordered to march to a camp eight and a half miles north of Gallipoli at Bulehar (now Bolayir), a small town overlooking the Gulf of Xeros, where they were soon engaged in building defence works in anticipation of a Russian attack. For now and the rest of the campaign, it was 'tramp, tramp, tramp, for woman as well as man', recalled Elizabeth Evans, 'and I held up to it with a stout heart'. She considered herself one of the lucky ones for she was young and strong and loved her husband. 'My place was with him, at his side when that was possible, and always with my regiment.'[14] She would not be the only woman to carry with her throughout the war a profound sense of pride in the regiment; many of the army wives who doggedly followed their men to the Crimea were motivated by a loyalty to their husband's colours.

The early days on campaign were not without their moments of humour. The 1st Battalion of the Royal Scots, ordered to throw up earthworks on the Adrianople Road, were thrown into panic when the alarm was sounded that 'the Russians are coming'. As the words 'Loose ammunition!' were shouted out by Captain Neville, ordering the men to prepare their guns, Mrs Frances Driscoll rushed from her tent and grabbed her husband Patrick by the swallow-tails of his coat:

> 'Arrah, Patsy, you're going to be shot,' she screamed 'and what shall I do at all, at all.'
>   'Get out of that,' shouted Driscoll, as he struggled for his ammunition.
>   'Will you keep quiet, Driscoll, or I'll put you in the guard room,' called out Captain Neville, fifteen yards away.[15]

The laughter provoked by the anxious Mrs Driscoll and her husband, according to Sergeant Thomas Smith, defused the panic of the moment – which turned out anyway to be a false alarm. But for night after night afterwards the scene would be re-enacted in camp, with soldiers from the Driscolls' regiment mercilessly parodying both their antics and their rich Irish accents, to a point where the adjutant threatened to send them all to the guard room because of the noise they were making. Many months later, after the war was over, Sergeant Smith caught up with the Driscolls, now living contentedly in a hut at Balaklava, and could not resist remarking: 'Well Pat, you are not shot yet!'[16] By then,

Smith noted, Mrs Driscoll and the other women in the Crimea had become 'absolutely fearless'.

On 5 May the 50th, 93rd and Rifle Brigade were ordered to strike their camp at Bulehar, and leave for Scutari, their places to be taken at Bulehar by the 4th, 28th and 44th, who struck camp at Sulari, two miles from Gallipoli, the same day. Marianne Young had already seen many years of army service in India with her first husband and had written vivid accounts of her time in the remote Northern Provinces of western India in the late 1830s. She well remembered that morning. The bugles sounded for the tents to be struck at 3 a.m. and whilst the troops fell in and the bands played, the women in her regiment loitered, 'watching for the unlikely chance of a lightly laden cart to gain permission to ride'.[17]

Young was one of those lucky enough to ride on a cart and thus be able to enjoy the scenery en route as they made their way

> over the pleasant park-like slopes, past bright Turkish farms, and among perfect shrubberies of wild roses, the air vocal with the sweet carols of the newly arisen larks. Here and there some regiment of our brigade would be lost to the eye by the turn of a wooded knoll; then appear like a waving crimson line among the green barley, steadily, steadily moving without an apparent break – the distant melody of the band coming fitfully towards us on the pleasant morning breeze.[18]

William Howard Russell of *The Times* was also there that day. But he painted a rather different picture of the shambolic march from Sulari to Bulehar:

> The mass of baggage belonging to these regiments was enormous. The trains of buffalo and bullock carts, of pack-horse and mules, and of led horses, which filed along the road to Gallipoli, seemed sufficient for the army of Xerxes. For seven or eight miles the teams of country carts, piled up with beds and trunks, and soldiers' wives and tents, were almost unbroken, and now and then an overladen mule tumbled down, or a wheel came off, and the whole line of march became a confused struggle of angry men and goaded cattle.[19]

Those marching on foot – soldiers with heavy knapsacks and rolled-up greatcoats and blankets slung round them, plus 60 rounds of ammunition; women juggling large bundles of possessions, including tin wash tubs, pots and kettles – would have had no inclination to enjoy the view. Many dropped out with heat exhaustion along the way. For the army had been sent on campaign with no thought given to the need for transports, the government having seen fit to abolish them at the end of the Napoleonic Wars to save money in maintaining the forces in peacetime. Officers in Gallipoli now found themselves having to haggle with the locals for the hire of an inadequate number of bullock-drawn arabas and carts, while their well-equipped French allies looked on in astonishment.

The French had been far more judicious in leaving their women at home, although one or two senior French officers *did* in fact bring their wives with them to Gallipoli and even on to Varna. Madame de Saint Arnaud and her daughter had accompanied Marshal St Arnaud as far as Therapia, nursing him through his terminal illness until he bravely embarked for the Crimea, where he died in September. But these were rare exceptions. There was really only one officer's wife who attracted gossip and attention: Soledad Bazaine, the exotic Spanish-born wife of Colonel François Achille Bazaine. He had met her while serving with the French Foreign Legion in Algeria in 1848, when Bazaine had been seduced by the lovely seventeen-year-old flamenco dancer whilst lodging at the family's tavern in Tlemcen. The weary Bazaine, twenty years her senior, could not resist Soledad after years on campaign with the Legion; so besotted was he that he was determined to marry her. But Soledad had had only a rudimentary education and would hardly fit the bill as a colonel's wife. Bazaine therefore arranged to send the girl to a boarding school 60 miles away in Oran. Here she was educated at his expense, after which she went to the Sacré Coeur in Marseilles to finish her education, in the guise of the orphaned daughter of a general.

After facing down considerable opposition to the match from his senior officers, Bazaine married Soledad at Versailles in June 1854, just as his Legion received orders to sail for Gallipoli. He insisted on taking her with him and they rented a Turkish house in the town. The sultry dancing girl had now emerged from her chrysalis as a refined and cultivated *grande dame*, to the extent that she had insisted on having a piano in the house (probably brought from Constantinople).

Life at Gallipoli had at first had many attractions for Marianne Young of the 28th, for at this early stage of the campaign there was an air of unreality and 'all was energy and hope'.[20] In the mornings you woke to bright blue skies and the sound of larks; there was a fresh breeze and the perfume of flowers in the air. All around in camp men in uniforms of red and blue and gold drilled and marched and the bands played; in the balmy evenings there would be rides through the musky brushwood on the hillsides to admire the seashore and distant mountains of Rumelia. But as May turned to June and June to July, the grinding heat and dust of Gallipoli began to take their toll, as did the deteriorating quality of the rations. How the British troops envied the French, with their retinue of efficient *cantinières* and their well-stocked wagons of food. It seemed such a logical way of enlisting the services of army wives, many of whom were not motivated to do anything other than sit and burn in the hot sun. 'Why have we no *cantinières?*' would be the frequently heard complaint. Why, because it went against dyed-in-the-wool army regulations which vetoed the employment of army wives in any official capacity. Meanwhile, the inefficiencies of the Commissariat responsible for food and transport became ever more glaring, hardly surprising in view of the fact that it was under the control not of the Army, but of ageing bureaucrats at the British Treasury with no comprehension of the scale of supply needed for such a campaign.

And then someone in the camp of the 28th had a good idea: why should they not create their own *cantinière?* The enterprising Mrs O'Flanagan, who had demonstrated a talent for procuring the occasional chicken here and there, was chosen. The regiment provided her with a donkey and a tent for the purpose and she was sent out to forage for food as best she could in the local villages, with permission to sell her goods for a reasonable profit from a tent in camp. As if by magic, clever Mrs O'Flanagan produced geese, ducks, apples and other delights; her status in the regiment shot up and with it her confidence and her hemline. 'The flounced mousseline-de-laine dress of the energetic donkey-rider rose two or three inches,' noted Young. Mistress O'Flanagan now fancied herself a home-grown British *cantinière*. Sadly, the Irish entrepreneur soon wearied of her donkey-riding expeditions in pursuit of supplies. There were easier ways of making money – by cleaning out the supplies of local itinerant traders who came to the camp while the men were at muster and selling items on to them at an even more inflated price. But with the cost of her eggs, milk and onions rocketing, Mrs O'Flanagan was summarily ordered to give back her donkey and leave her tent. When she stubbornly refused, the army took matters into its own hands by burning the tent over her head. 'Mrs O'Flanagan became a sort of Suttee to her principles,' wrote Marianne Young,

> though, unlike the Hindoo widow, she yielded her confidence under the influence of green wood, and was very soon smoked out like a noisome insect, and remained seated under a neighbouring bush, leaning her arm on a barrel of Vin de Tenedos, and lamenting her destiny in a pathetic Irish howl.[21]

Some weeks later, the wily Irishwoman took her revenge on the officers who burned her out. Arriving back in camp one evening she claimed, whilst out washing at the river, to have met a group of veiled female slaves, working in a nearby vineyard under the supervision of an elderly Turk. Her curiosity had got the better of her and she had approached the women only to hear an English voice – that of a woman in the group who claimed to be the daughter of an Irish trader to Gallipoli, who had been sold into white slavery. Mrs O'Flanagan's eyes rolled as she told the assembled women how the poor girl was 'a sweet creature, with sich a hinnocent young face' but 'had been whipped horrible'. Having promised to procure the girl's rescue, she now whipped up British chivalry in the camp. At dawn the following morning a brigade of men descended on the vineyard and proceeded to rip the veils from the faces of the women workers in search of the Irish girl, only to find no sign of 'Erin's fair daughter'. This sparked a diplomatic row and the General of the Division was soon demanding explanations. Witnesses, rather too worse for the local Vin de Tenedos, were called from camp to give muddled evidence, after which it became clear that Mistress O'Flanagan had fabricated her story in order to avenge those who had smoked her out. She had also hoped to provoke the army into sending her back to Gallipoli, which they did, but to a prison cell. After due punishment, Young heard, the conniving Mistress O'Flanagan was to be shipped back to England 'to make the best use she could of her natural genius for romance'.[22]

But the opportunities for laughter soon receded when cholera broke out in camp in mid-July 1854. It got the better of even the best and strongest women on the strength, huddled together at night in the few tents made available to them and exposed to the broiling heat of the day 'either cooking for the men or washing on the hill-sides, with the skin peeling from their poor arms and faces'.[23] At Gallipoli eight women from Elizabeth Evans's regiment elected to be sent home. A makeshift hospital established by the 4th was given over to a husband and wife from the regiment to run, but, as Evans recalls, 'they were both victims, and both died, crying out for each other'. She recalled in particular one poor sergeant's wife who didn't make it home to England. When she succumbed to cholera, her heartbroken husband had improvised a small tent to protect her from the elements. With her natural nursing gifts, Evans was sent for:

> I joined her just as the sun was setting. I wanted a light, as darkness comes so swiftly there, and I told the sergeant to go and fetch a candle. Then I turned to the young wife.
>
> 'Look at the beautiful sun, dear,' I whispered.
>
> 'Ah me!' she answered. 'I shall never watch it rise again. Turn me round, so that I can see it for the last time.'[24]

Evans turned the woman towards the rising sun 'which so wonderfully flooded the skies in the west, towards home and England'. The woman looked; and then she died. Within an hour 'the Engineers had buried her, and everything belonging to her had been burnt'. Although Evans would see many more deaths from cholera, she couldn't help remembering the poignancy of this one: 'because, you see, it was the first, and she was a woman'.[25]

Another equally poignant death from cholera occurred in the French camp, this one attracting an enormous amount of publicity in the French press back home. In mid-July Michel Louis Félix Ney, duc d'Elchingen, the 50-year-old second son of the legendary Marshall Ney, got off his horse after taking part in a formal parade of his Cuirassier Brigade and collapsed. When Madame Soledad Bazaine heard that the duc was dying of cholera, she ordered he be given the comforts of her own home rather than suffer in his Spartan barracks. Here she soothed his dying hours, playing him Mozart and Beethoven. He died the same night, 14 July. In Paris the press soon made much of this romantic death, comparing it with that of Chopin, whose lover George Sand played the piano while he lay on his deathbed. Within three days, General Carbuccia, in command of the Foreign Legion Brigade, who had been organizing the duc's funeral, himself succumbed to cholera and died. By now, the French were said to be losing between 70 and 100 men daily.

As the cholera took hold in Gallipoli, other troop transports had meanwhile been sailing straight to Constantinople, where an army was massing for a campaign against the Russians, which it was thought would probably be conducted across the Black Sea in Bulgaria. With its mosques, domes and minarets the legendary city of Constantinople was an arresting sight, rising from the limpid blue waters of the Sea of Marmara, where 'not a vapour floated on the sky, and a peculiar atmosphere softened the scene – just as one might view bright colours shaded by the most transparent gauze'.[26] The route to Constantinople had taken the transports past many of the ancient and legendary places from Greek mythology: Troy and the island of Tenedos of Virgil's Aeneid, with the snow-capped Mount Olympus visible eighty miles in the distance and the beauties of the Bosporus ahead.

When the Turks had heard of the imminent arrival at Scutari of ship-loads of British soldiers, they had hastily withdrawn their women to more secluded neighbourhoods. But this did not prevent British officers able to afford the hire of a caïque from taking a trip along the smooth, cooling waters of the Golden Horn to get their first sight of Turkish women, some from the harem in the nearby Topkapi Sarayi, the great palace of the Ottoman sultans. Groups of them could be seen, with their soft milky skin protected from the sun, all but their almond-shaped eyes hidden behind white yashmaks, reclining on cushions and carpets on the grassy banks, eating sweetmeats and sipping lemonade, surrounded by their children. In their brilliant-coloured cloaks, their nails and eyelids stained with henna, and carrying colourful parasols, the women found it a pleasant diversion to sit and watch the '*Englese*', though fraternization was out of the question and they were guarded at all times by eunuchs. The British officers bowed as they passed, as they would to any lady, a fact which delighted the Turkish women, to whom such chivalry was completely foreign, but enraged the Turkish men watching.

Constantinople might have had its romantic attractions from a distance, on the approach across the Sea of Marmara, but at close hand these quickly palled. It lacked any comprehensive roads and was a maze of filthy, stony alleyways, pitted with holes, that twisted and turned up and down hill and in which it was very easy to get lost. The whole of the decrepit and rotting waterfront was infested with stinking green sludge and with the bobbing corpses of dead rats and dogs.

The troops were offered accommodation by their Turkish allies at the imposing barracks at Scutari, the other side of the Bosporus from Constantinople. At first sight the building seemed magnificent: 'backed by the hills of Asia, and looking like a marvelous erection made with a penknife out of white cardboard'.[27] When the Guards and the Light Division had first arrived, a brief attempt had been made to occupy the interior of the barracks, said to be capable of holding 10,000 men. But the stay was a brief one; the interior was dilapidated, filthy and running with damp, its water supply polluted by the corpses of dead rats. Within a day or two the troops had fled the barracks in horror at the insects, rats and other vermin with which it was infested, as well as the stench from its overflowing sewers. Yet this monstrous hotbed of disease was, within weeks, to become the British Army's major hospital for the war wounded.

The British divisions instead camped outside, to the west of the vast Scutari barracks, close to the wall of the famous Champ de Mars – the old Turkish cemetery. This had a lyrical beauty all its own, with the rich deep green of its ancient yew trees and sombre cypresses and gleaming white, intricately carved tombstones. At night you could hear the melodious notes of the nightingales and the eerie sound of the wind blowing through the rustling trees. It might have seemed the most romantic of settings, had it not been punctuated by the barking and howling of packs of hungry feral dogs in search of newly dug graves.

Fanny Duberly of the 8th Hussars and Lady Erroll of the 60th Rifles were among the officers' wives who had sailed straight on to Scutari. Fanny had enjoyed the lyrical splendours of the Dardanelles, feeling that she had indeed had a glimpse of Arcadia. But this soon ended when her husband returned from his first trip ashore and reported the filth and stench in the city of Constantinople to be 'indescribable'.[28] It was here at last, after thirty days at sea that Fanny finally induced her servant, Mrs Williams, wife of the regimental sergeant major, whom she had taken on as a favour, to attack the pile of dirty washing that had accumulated since their departure. Duberly tartly observes that this was 'the first assistance' her so-called servant 'has ever thought fit to render me since I left England'. Mrs Williams would have to go; and go she did, to be replaced by Mrs Blaydes.

One of the major topics of conversation in camp at Scutari was the green canvas marquee (as opposed to the standard-issue bell tent) inhabited by Lord Erroll and his wife, which had pride of place on the grassy plot in front of the Scutari barracks next to that of the commander-in-chief, the Duke of Cambridge. However, even a countess was obliged to make certain sacrifices on campaign. Asked in later life by a grandchild whether the bed she had slept in had been comfortable, Lady Erroll had replied: 'I don't know my dear. His Lordship had the bed and I slept on the ground.'[29] When the camp was hit by a rainstorm in May, the Errolls' marquee had been blown down, along with twenty other tents, and the camp was treated to the rare sight of her ladyship 'crawl[ing] from under the dripping canvas through the slush in a most sorry plight'.[30] It also soon became common knowledge among the men that if one were to approach the Errolls' lantern-lit tent at night, it might throw up an interesting shadowgraph of the good lady disrobing for bed. For all Lady Erroll's fortitude, most officers were highly sceptical of her intention of accompanying her husband throughout the campaign: 'Poor thing, she little knows what is before her,' they remarked.[31]

As the temperatures soared, the women encamped at Scutari would not just be enduring the heat but also the fearsome 'Turkish cannibals' – the mosquitoes which bred in stagnant water round the barracks and tormented them night and day. The lazy, slatternly women drowned their sorrows in whatever cheap drink – wine, gin or local raki – they could lay their hands on, but the more enterprising and hard-working ones, of whom there were several, established themselves as much-needed laundresses and set to work. But then the rain came, not just washing out the army tents but drenching the poor women who weren't under canvas like their menfolk, but who were living in an assortment of miserable hovels improvised out of mats and dried mud, which let in the rain at every angle. These wretched shelters 'more resembling the plasterings of mason-wasps than anything intended for habitation'[32] had been crudely constructed against the wall of the barracks, with a piece of matting for a door and one solitary small hole for letting in light and fresh air. They were so low that it was impossible to stand upright in them. In the heat of the day the women could therefore do nothing but stand outside in the sun and burn.

At Scutari, as well as at Gallipoli, the army wives would have to engage in the tortuous process of haggling for food in the local markets, struggling back with a chicken perhaps or a heap of potatoes twisted in their shawls. Such sights prompted Marianne Young to remark on the 'unchangeableness of the soldier's wife':

See her in Turkey, in India, in an English garrison town, or an Oriental bazaar, her manners, dress, and habits seem incapable of alteration; however long she may be in these lands, she never acquires a phrase of their language; however burning the sun, she exposes herself equally to its influence; however filthy the bazaar, there the English soldier's wife is still to be seen, scolding, and bargaining for whatever it produces.[33]

What particularly fascinated Young was the way in which the women always resisted being bullied or swindled. An Irish wife was observed in the market dealing peremptorily with a swindling stall keeper who had pocketed her shilling and pretended she had not given it to him. She bawled him out in the best of Irish brogues: 'Oh, you thieving rascal! Would you rob me of the shilling I got so hard, and me coming to defend your country? But for the likes of us, you tawny villain, the Rooshians would take the bed from under ye!' Her shilling was quickly and respect-fully handed back.[34]

Somehow or other the army wives always managed to make themselves understood, engaging with street vendors as though Turkish had been their mother tongue and buying vegetables without a single coherent word being said. When one woman lost her way returning to camp from the local market, she had enlisted the help of a local Turk, taking his arm and asking him in sign language to show her the way. When two veiled women passed and caught sight of the man in the company of an infidel woman they proceeded to attack them, spitting and screaming abuse. The army wife gave them short shrift: she blacked out the eyes of both her attackers and then calmly proceeded on her way.[35]

Once again at Scutari, as at Malta and Gallipoli, there was a 'natural wastage' of women, with the more enterprising ones deciding a life of prostitution in Constantinople was preferable to the hard grind of army life, or others opting to find work as domestic servants with the many European diplomatic families in the area. Marianne Young rued the loss of self-restraint among many of the now brutalized women in her regiment, forced to hang around outside their husbands' tents or take refuge in the infested dark cellars of the nearby barracks. Little wonder that suffering forced many into dissolution and drinking. This was what army life did to women, making them 'a burden, a disgrace to the army, instead of being, as they should have been, useful items in their camp machinery'. It made her angry that perfectly respectable women, as soon as they married soldiers, should have aspersions cast on their reputations and that they should be doomed 'to lose character, self-respect, and all that renders woman the safeguard of society, in whatever grade of it her lot may fall'.[36]

On 24 May orders came that the British at Scutari were now to rendezvous with French forces at Varna on the coast of Bulgaria. By now, many of the wives of the 28th were longing to be 'safe at home again'. According to Marianne Young, 26 women had been 'earnestly praying to be allowed to return to their native land' but had been left stranded because all the transports were heavily engaged in moving the troops on to Varna. Forced to take refuge in the cellars of Scutari, by the end of the year they would be joined by others sent back from Varna. Constantinople was also the final port of call for many officers' wives, who decided they had had enough of privation and opted for the home-from-home comforts of the Hôtel d'Angleterre, 'a charming little auberge' with the 'sociability of a boarding-house without its monotony' at Pera on the Bosporus,[37] or the even more overcrowded Misseri's, where high prices were demanded for dirty rooms and where the stinking effluvia from the waterfront, the heat, noise, dirt and the flies were just as bad as in Constantinople. Here, many naval wives also set up a community of grass widows who took refuge for the duration of the war in hopes of speedily being reunited with their husbands. Few of them were.

FOUR

The Disease That Walketh by Noonday Was Among Us

At the end of May 1854, a large contingent of 10,000 British and 12,000 French troops was ordered to mass at a vast encampment on a plain outside the seaport of Varna in Bulgaria, with other regiments setting up their tents fifteen miles inland at Devna. They had arrived in support of their Turkish allies' campaign against the invading Russians. In April, Tsar Nicholas I had ordered his commander, General Gorchakov, to take the Russian southern army across the River Pruth and into Wallachia and Moldavia on Bulgaria's northern border – a strategic military point on the main road south into European Turkey (Bulgaria at that time being under Ottoman control). But the Turks had surprised the Russians and fought back hard; led by Omar Pasha, they held out against a two-month siege at Silistria. On 23 June the Russians began to retreat.

The prudent French had once again got to the rendezvous point first. Their officers had already taken the best billets in town, so that by the time the British arrived they were once again greeted by an immaculately laid-out French encampment with an extemporized mini-Paris of cafés and hostelries and a contingent of chefs who could turn even the dullest of army food into something palatable. Here the easy-going French could smoke and drink and chat and while away the idle hours as they awaited the orders to march. In the open country of camp they fashioned themselves additional protection from the sun with bushes and ferns, they gathered brushwood and made fires to roast their coffee; their medical stores were well stocked, their transport system of baggage wagons, stretchers and ambulance vehicles for the wounded was all in good order.

All this activity fascinated the bemused inhabitants of Varna, who sat and watched ship after ship disgorge thousands of red-coated British soldiers onto the sandy seashore. Their eyes widened even further when they saw, trailing after them, a miserable gaggle of shabbily dressed soldiers' wives now arriving from Scutari and Gallipoli. For the correspondent of the *Daily News* who witnessed the excitement, the sights and sounds of the disembarkation, these women were the only sour note in an otherwise magnificent spectacle. He had never seen 'anything so woebegone, so forlorn, so helpless, hopeless, and miserable, as their appearance', he claimed, continuing:

> When I saw these unfortunates trailing their bundles after them along
> the quay, in the midst of all the hurrying, crowding, pushing, bustling,
> marching, swearing, yelling, and scolding, now thrust here, then there,
> wearied and exhausted by a long voyage and bad accommodation,
> wretchedly clothed, and many of them in an advanced state of
> pregnancy, I hardly knew whether to pity them, or feel amazed at the
> mock humanity or twaddling economy which won't pay for their
> subsistence in England.[1]

The old Muslim pasha of the town sat cross-legged sucking on his pipe, agog at the sight of so many women arriving with the army. He scarce knew 'whether he was on his head or his heels' when he saw Lady Erroll handed up out of the boat, for she rode into town 'with a brace of pistols hanging in a holster at her waist . . . followed by a Bulgarian porter with a shoal of reticules and carpet-bags, and books, and taking everything as coolly as if she were an old soldier'.[2] The Muslim town dignitaries puzzled at whether perhaps the British generals had brought their harems with them. It was an ominous sign. Having brought their women, the British it would seem had every intention of retaining possession of Bulgaria after the war was over. They were also exercised by the sight of so many young soldiers, for it soon became clear, from the surreptitious smiles and furtive glances they noticed their women directing towards the men, that Muslim women were 'quite as fond of admiration as English or any other women, and like to be looked at better by a dashing handsome young officer with a fine uniform, than by an old gentleman with one foot in the grave'.[3]

The poor British army wives had little to recommend them to the locals: they were worn down, hardened and sexless. And they seemed always to be toiling. 'I fear the picture many of our soldiers' wives presented of dirt and neglect, of bold rude manners, and of drunkenness, was not calculated to recommend Christianity to the Turks,'[4] remarked the nurse Sarah Anne Terrot later. In stark contrast was the sight of the magnificent Lady Erroll, resplendent in 'her habit with its long, bunchy, trailing skirt, its swallow-tailed coatee and rows of shining buttons, and her large plumed hat'.[5] The lady soon found herself adapting to being surrounded by men in often the most inopportune circumstances. One day she and her husband caught Captain Charles Glazbrook of the 49th on the hop. Having returned hot and dusty, he had stripped off at a fountain to refresh himself

> when up comes Lady Errol with her husband, I could not help it, she saw what she did see, and I immediately offered her a tin cup of water with a dash of sherry in it to hide her confusion, she arranged herself in the saddle, displaying two legs up to – never mind, this is all nonsense, and off she went, after coolly examining her revolver and long dagger which she always carries in an embroidered holster on the off side of her saddle.[6]

Fanny Duberly, meanwhile, was being her usual ruthlessly pragmatic self. She hated having to wear the bonnets and petticoats expected of women; they were an 'abomination' to her. From Varna she wrote home asking for a list of more practical items to be sent out: 'three strong and durable riding shirts, six pairs of doeskin riding gauntlets, six pairs of warm stockings, a fur cap and a riding whip' and, having learnt of the potential embarrassment of camping at night – a tent lining to protect her modesty.[7]

In fact, Fanny almost didn't make it to Varna. On 26 May, one of the divisional commanders, Lord Lucan, adamant that no women should accompany the troops from Scutari, had issued an order expressly for-bidding Mrs Duberly from travelling. Fanny was not to be thwarted, though her husband Henry was very down in the mouth: 'He looks upon the order as a soldier: I as a woman, and – laugh at it.'[8] She arranged to have herself hidden away in the hold, having boarded ship disguised as a downtrodden army wife. Lucan was enraged when he heard Fanny had defied his order, but his appeal to Lord Raglan to have her removed from her ship fell on deaf ears. Raglan rather admired the intrepid Duberly and had no intention of interfering. At 4 p.m. on 31 May, as her ship left Scutari, Fanny crept up on deck to watch the last of the lovely Bosporus fade out of sight. She admitted she would miss the sybaritic life she and her companions had enjoyed on board ship there, 'refreshing ourselves with strawberries, oranges and sherbet, lying lazily on the burning deck, and feeling as though excess of beauty overcame our languid pulses'.[9] But all such thoughts were suddenly dispelled by the filthy stench of coal smoke as the engines of the *Megaera* heaved and sputtered into life. The word was that at Varna it would be nothing but salt pork for weeks to come.

Whilst the town of Varna itself was squalid, dusty and fetid, much like Gallipoli, with dirty streets and ramshackle houses, and abounding in 'dogs, frogs and stagnant pools',[10] the surrounding countryside in Bulgaria was a place of great natural beauty. It was redolent with the sweet smells of flowers, rambling acacia, wild vine, clematis and aromatic herbs. Or so it seemed at first, for the great flat expanse of rolling countryside between the seashore and the lakes of Varna and Devna where many of the British and French troops were encamped was, it turned out, legendary in local folklore as a pestilential spot. The Turks had long been wary of the area; not for nothing had they called the Devna Valley the 'Valley of Death'. It was in fact a stagnant marsh, swarming with leeches and animalcula of every conceivable kind. Flies and ants infested the food and tents. Shortly after landing and camping for the night, Nell Butler and her husband in the 95th had unwittingly pitched their tent on top of an ants' nest and by morning had found the insects had made off with every morsel of their meagre ration of sugar. Fever and dysentery lurked everywhere, too, especially in the 'deadly exhalations' from the moist ground.[11] It also lurked in the sparkling waters of both the beautiful, inviting lakes and the streams that fed into them. Soon the heat, the clouds of dust and the diarrhoea began to do their deadly work; two-thirds of the army rapidly went down with enteric disease of one kind or another.

With locally bought food – eggs, chickens, meat – expensive and in short supply, soldiers had a field day foraging for wild food, though they did not have the equipment to go after the profusion of game birds, boars and deer. Nor could they exploit the fish that teemed in the lakes, for they had no rods and hooks. So they went about simply plucking apricots, green-gages, plums and cherries from the trees, gorging themselves, and then suffering as a result. As for drink, sour milk could be got here and there, but there was only one thing available to deaden the boredom of camp life: the rough local wine. At five pence a quart it was cheap compared to their own ale and porter, and so they inevitably drank too much of it and it made them ill. With rations running low, their digestive systems were further assaulted by acid-tasting bread (the colour of thick gingerbread) adulterated with dirt and corn, and sugar mixed with sand. Tough mutton, stringy beef and hard salt pork were all the British soldier got, day in, day out, and no vegetables, apart from any he managed to forage.

Meanwhile, the British army wives who worked as washerwomen, having arrived at Varna, had cheerily set to work once more, though the absence of their stock-in-trade – 'blue' starch, irons and ironing boards – made their work difficult. The logistics of drying and folding the washing in overcrowded tents were a problem, but working in the open air had its compensations. The war correspondent W. H. Russell noted that the washerwomen could be 'found in every shady nook and alley of the valleys round the camp, with extempore boilers fixed into the green banks' where they were always 'the *foci* of a circle of araba drivers, who seemed to think them witches engaged in some holy mystery'.[12]

At the beginning of July the 1st Division was ordered to transfer to a camp at the small village of Aladyn, eight miles inland at the head of the lower Devna lake. It was an exhausting eight-hour dusty march in intense

heat along a road that was little more than a cart track. The correspondent
of the *Daily News* was deeply disturbed by the sight of the soldiers' wives
he saw along the way, struggling in the broiling sun, carrying heavy jugs of
water as they toiled up the hill 'in attitudes of the greatest dejection, and
with words of complaint, scarcely audible from their parched and blistered
lips'. Their physical degradation was disturbing:

> their bonnets were gone – Heaven knows how long ago! Perhaps they got
> soaked in the violent rains which drenched the camp at Scutari, and
> then they were flung aside as worthless, half-rotten things, which only
> heat the head, but cannot protect it from sunshine, wind or rain. These
> women . . . went about with their wretched, seedy-looking shawls drawn
> over their heads, their faces were flushed with the sun, and perhaps with
> strong drink, and their features wore that settled expression of suffering,
> discomfort and despair, which at length, hardened and bronzed with
> depravity, stamps the face of the confirmed camp-followers. And what
> else can they become, these poor women, whom a cruel kindness has
> allowed to attach themselves to the baggage train of the army.[13]

Like Marianne Young, the correspondent could not understand the army's
folly in allowing women on campaign and then not providing for them: 'It
seems a strange inconsistency in a manner to legalise the women joining
the expedition, to let them draw lots for the privilege, to grant them a
passage out, and then all at once to treat them as strangers and persons
who have no business to be where they are.'

The dejected state of the army wives was now thrown into relief by the
presence in the French ranks at Varna of a considerable contingent of
cantinières. What a contrast these snappy little dressers in their smart
uniforms made to the raw-boned, weary women of the British rank and file
in their faded print gowns and old-fashioned straw poke bonnets. If it was
possible for women to be chic in a war zone, then it came naturally to the
French *cantinières*. The uniforms they wore were modified versions of those
of the soldiers to whose regiments they were attached: a tight-fitting blue
jacket with a 'habit shirt' of white linen over their neatly corseted waists
(even during the siege of Sevastopol there was a brisk trade among civilian

sutlers in the Crimea supplying corsets to the *cantinières*). The jacket had a turn-down collar and gold lace embroidery and was accompanied by Turkish-style red trousers with a broad black or green stripe down each leg, over which was worn a loose red petticoat and a broad shoulder belt. Right down to their well-polished boots and jingling spurs the *cantinières* were thoroughly feminine, despite the military garb. Topping the whole thing off was a fez with silver thread in the tassel, worn by women attached to the Zouaves (soldiers of the French Light Infantry), whilst the rest wore neat little glazed hats with ribbons flying from them.[14] Finally, there was the indispensable and 'gorgeously painted' tricolour brandy cask or *bidon* with the number of their regiment on it, which the women attached to their belt and used to carry wine or brandy to offer to weary troops. The British men had no doubts when they saw them: the *cantinières* were the 'best got-up' women they had ever seen on campaign or were likely to see till war's end.

The *cantinières* were the latest incarnation of the old camp follower or female sutler, familiar to all French regiments from the seventeenth century onwards, their role given the official title of *cantinière* in 1794. Before that women had served in the Royal Army of France as *blanchisseuses* (laundresses) and *vivandières* (sutlers), the latter name having been largely supplanted by that of *cantinière* by the time of the Crimean War (although British soldiers' accounts persistently confused the two terms). They usually were the wives of soldier-*vivandiers*, and on marrying into a regiment took the rank of corporal. Their husbands were at all times held responsible for their good conduct. Eight *vivandières* per regiment were originally allowed to follow the army with their wagons, selling food, drink and sundries, either from their mobile *cantines* or a tent, and for women born into military families it was often a logical progression to marry a soldier and remain in the regiment. The expanded French Army instituted by Louis Napoléon with the advent of the Second French Empire in 1851 had encouraged the enlistment of more *cantinières*, often the wives of non-commissioned officers.[15] In the Crimea, the chief activity of the *cantinières* would be providing drinks and first aid for the wounded on the field and selling alcohol from horseback or their mobile canteens. The only known female equivalent on the British side would be the extraordinary Mary Seacole, cook, doctor, nurse and herbalist, or 'pur-veyor to the British army' as she liked to think of herself, who would set up shop not far from the front lines and whose culinary delights were soon attracting many French customers.

Although Marianne Young asserts that the *cantinières* were not required to be very young or very pretty, 'but of a carriage, figure, and constitution suitable both for the due effect of her costume, and the due performance of her required duties',[16] their appearance at Gallipoli in trousers had caused a sensation, arousing an enormous amount of outrage as well as natural curiosity among the locals. British officers were appalled at the sight of women in trousers, finding fault even with the practical Fanny Duberly for riding around with leather trousers under her gown; wherever the *cantinières* went, polite English ladies would turn their heads in horror. But others took a more pragmatic attitude: British army women should be 'Bloomerised' *à la vivandière*, asserted Sir James Alexander in his post-war memoirs: 'straw bonnets and draggling petticoats are absurd in the field'.[17]

The rank and file and the sexually curious couldn't take their eyes off the *cantinières*. Inevitably, despite the fact that more than a few of them were fat and middle-aged – and were gaspingly tightly corseted into their uniforms – a reputation for being fast and loose would attach to them, if only because of their economic status and freedom of movement. But one thing was certain: where the downtrodden British wives often inspired contempt among the British officers, the *cantinières* were treated by their own troops with 'marked respect and consideration'.[18]

During the Light Division's march to Aladyn, Margaret Kerwin with the 19th was certainly feeling the exhaustion of it all. For after that, they had marched on another 40 miles inland to Devna, where she bought a little washing tub and 'carried the whole of my cooking things in it'. It was, she said, 'the whole of my baggage, and I carried it on my head during the march'.[19] Up-country, more and more men were falling out from the heat and she was kept busy giving them drinks from her water bottle. Arriving at Monastyr, fifteen miles further south from Devna, she found that the responsibility for all the washing for the men of No. 5 company had fallen on her – all 101 of them. She undertook her task with grit and stoicism, standing 'in the midst of the stream from 6 in the morning until 6 or 7 at night'. She kept no proper accounts of her labours; some of the men could afford to pay her, some couldn't, 'so that I was left with very little for my trouble'.

The dogged Lady Erroll was also on the march. Mounted on a pony, with her maid on a donkey, she brought up the rear of her husband's regiment, the 60th Rifles, and did her best to offer moral support by taking up and slinging on her saddle as many as she could of the rifles of the young soldiers too exhausted to bear them who would otherwise have fallen by the way on the road to Monastyr. As the weeks and then months dragged on at the camps in and around Varna in the sweltering temperatures of high summer, the troops became restless and discontented. Weakened as many men were by sickness and malnutrition, such a period of protracted idleness waiting in the breathless, oppressive heat for something to happen was interspersed with endless and unnecessary parades and drilling, which only served to further exhaust and demoralize them. It is no surprise that, depressed and despairing, many of the rank and file descended into hopeless drunkenness.

Fanny Duberly had been keen to ingratiate herself with Lady Erroll, her only serious rival so far on campaign, when the latter rode into Devna with the Rifles, for 'she and I are the only ladies'. But although Fanny found Lady Erroll's penchant for carrying pistols very infra dig, she could not disguise her envy of her lady's maid and cook. For much of the Varna interlude, Fanny seemed still to be on a foreign excursion, enjoying the benefits of her horse and the scenic side of campaigning like a lady tourist, failing to take any note of the exhausted women tramping along with her, her concerns mainly for the welfare of her horse, Bob.

In mid-July she was still waxing lyrical about the 'flute-like repose' of this 'land of herds and flocks' and the consolations of the natural world, when suddenly the cholera struck. It arrived on around the 23rd, at much the same time as it was decimating the French and British troops still encamped at Gallipoli, hitting the Light Division camp at Varna – and soon spreading among the rest of the British troops, at Devna and then at Monastyr.

The cholera proved to be an enemy far more terrible than the Russians.

'The disease that walketh by noonday was among us,' recalled Marianne Young, who was forced to watch the men and women of her regiment fall sick, 'terror-stricken and helpless', with alarming rapidity.[20] Elizabeth Evans too witnessed the suffering at Varna. What she saw there convinced her that cholera was 'worse, surely than battle itself – for, on the field, you did at any rate get the thrill and excitement of action and knew that you were fighting and suffering for your country'.[21]

The disease was thought to have been brought into the French camp by troops arriving on transports from Marseilles. The decrepit General Hospital in Varna, itself flea-ridden and rat-infested, could not cope with the sick; nor did the soldiers want to be taken there, knowing full well than any man going in would not come out again, except as a corpse. But the French at least wasted no time in mobilizing what they knew as the most effective help: the Sisters of Charity of St Vincent de Paul. For the past two hundred years they had taken these sisters on campaign with them as valuable battlefield nurses, familiar in their traditional, seventeenth-century-style peasant dress of grey serge and their distinctive stiff white peasant caps. These were sent for from the Maison Notre Dame de la Providence at Galata, outside Constantinople, a convent established in 1840 by Soeur Bernardine, who herself accompanied the first contingent. During the epidemic three of the nuns nursing at Varna would die of cholera.

This pitiless disease – in its most virulent form, *cholera morbus* – claimed its victims with ruthless efficiency and speed. Soldiers' letters from Varna relate endless stories of men being perfectly healthy in the morning, then succumbing and dying within hours and being buried that same evening. Margaret Kerwin recalled a Sergeant Murphy, a man hugely popular in the regiment. He came back to camp one day, tired and hungry after a long day's march. His wife, 'a nice respectable woman, came to me for the loan of my frying-pan, and before she had the beef-steak fried, her poor husband was dead'.[22]

Sailors on board ship were just as vulnerable: when cholera attacked the flagship *Britannia* in the Black Sea on 14 August, 50 men died within 20 hours. The troops at Varna were told to strike camp and change ground frequently, but the cholera relentlessly followed them. Curiously, however, the disease struck at random, felling men in row upon row of tents on one side of an encampment whilst sparing those a few yards away opposite. Regiments such as the 30th and 55th that had spent long postings in Gibraltar also seemed to fare better, acclimatized as they were to higher temperatures.

The bacterium that spreads cholera is water-borne, and no doubt the major conduits were the streams used by the troops at Varna both to wash in and launder their dirty clothing. This water was also drawn on for drinking and cooking and became the dumping ground for offal from slaughtered cattle. Once ingested, the bacterium rapidly infects the intestines, causing the sudden onset of violent nausea and stomach cramps, followed by constant and uncontrollable diarrhoea and vomiting. The shock of such rapid dehydration of the system – as much as a quart an hour (and no fluids can be retained by the stomach long enough to compensate for this) – can kill very quickly. Such dramatic fluid loss literally thickens the blood and, combined with a plummeting pulse rate, in some cases leads to cardiac arrest – perhaps a merciful release from their agony for some sufferers, who by now would be prostrated with exhaustion. For hours their bodies would be wracked with cold sweats and excruciating muscular spasms, their faces becoming pallid and distorted, their eyes sunken and their lips taking on a bluish tinge. The body surface would feel icy to the touch. For this reason it was considered important to keep the extremities warm with rubbing and hot compresses; but in a hard-pressed army on campaign, with virtually no medical supplies and only a handful of superannuated male medical orderlies, there was no time for such ministrations. Soldiers and women dropped and died where they lay and were given only the most rudimentary of burials.

The three-month cholera epidemic at Varna claimed the lives of a significant number of women as well as soldiers, but no record was kept of their deaths. Margaret Kerwin saw the men of the 19th go down with alarming speed – 20 dying in a single day. There wasn't enough wood or time for coffins: 'The men were dying so fast with the cholera and what they call the black fever that they had to be buried in their blankets,' she later recalled; but worse was to follow. When the order came to move camp, 'no sooner had we gone than the Turks opened the graves and took the blankets from around the dead men'.[23] The British returned to rebury the corpses, only this time with branches and brambles to cover them before the earth was thrown in.

In her memoir of the British at Gallipoli and Varna, published at the end of 1854, Marianne Young was saddened at having 'to recall to one's memory that beautiful spot which simply by a change of wind was altered from a paradise to a place where death in one of its most horrid forms reigned supreme'.[24] Too exhausted to empty the latrines, too weary to march; too weak even to carry their packs; the only occupation of many soldiers now was to bury the dead. Even the few horses they had were rapidly succumbing to the heat and lack of forage. Within three weeks 2,000 British soldiers suffering from cholera had been evacuated out of Varna to the military hospital at Scutari. By 19 August, 532 British troops had died of the disease, though the death rate in the French ranks was spiralling at 60–80 a day, taking the final death toll to around 7,000. The disease spared no one – from the rank and file to the most wealthy and privileged, among them Lord Frederick Leveson Gower, son of the Duchess of Sutherland, Mistress of the Robes and close friend to Queen Victoria. The letter of condolence the queen would write to the duchess would be the first in a 'terrible season of mourning and sorrow' and one of many hundreds of personal letters that poured from her pen during the course of the war.[25]

Fanny Duberly maintains a stony if not indifferent silence about the army wives throughout this terrible time. It was, surprisingly, the aristocratic Lady Erroll who did her best to help the women of the regiment at their new camp at Monastyr, one soldier writing home to say: 'She braves it nobly; she has been under canvas ever since she left England. She is a very benevolent lady. I don't know what the married women would do without her. She is the source of many comforts to them; not as regards money, but of articles that they cannot procure. She fears no danger; where sickness is, there is she.' The anonymous letter writer could also not resist passing on a message to his wife: 'Tell Sarah I think she would soon alter her story, if she knew the hardships that a soldier's wife has to experience.'[26] In his own dispatches, the Times correspondent W. H. Russell described how the women had managed to make the most of things at Varna, alleging that 'it must not be supposed for a moment that these women have undergone any hardships, save those inseparable from a camp life'. Many had managed to cadge a ride on an araba when the army marched and the men had done their best to build them 'snug houses of leafy branches' where they camped. Those who had worked as laundresses had made 'little fortunes'. But the pestilence when it 'smote the army' had, he admitted, fallen on the women with 'extraordinary fatality'. Till then, according to Russell, their courage and equanimity in adversity had been a bonus, for they had 'seemed the happiest and most contented beings in the camp, where their services as excellent foragers and washerwomen were fully appreciated'.[27]

Much to the surprise of the French and British, the Turks had proved themselves better troops than expected, when, unaided, they had driven the Russians away from Silistria in June. By early July the Russians were in full retreat and the Danubian principalities were once more secured. It might have seemed logical, at this point, for the war to be declared effectively over. But the allies were in no mood to conciliate. Still preoccupied with the power of the Russian Black Sea naval force and any encroachments it might seek to make on the Mediterranean, the British government now set its sights on the port of Sevastopol. With its fine dockyards and grand eighteenth-century admiralty buildings, it was a thriving naval and mercantile base, the pride of the tsarist navy and the jewel of the Black Sea. The war would go on, not in defence of the crumbling Ottoman Empire and its Christian subjects, but in pursuit of the suppression of Russian ambition and a more permanent, 'safe and honourable peace'.[28] 'We are all for one good fight,' wrote Fanny Duberly, 'to see which is the better man; all for one blow, struck so effectually as to crush all warlike propensities against us for ever.'[29] The honour of the British army was at stake; the public back home expected it to win its spurs and it had yet to do so. Sevastopol was to be the prize: its dockyards destroyed and Russian naval power neutralized.

In London, the British government had come to this conclusion back in April and was already intent on carrying it through; but on the ground Lord Raglan and his commanders were sceptical. The army as a whole was now sickly and malnourished; the cavalry had already been hard hit by disease and was not up to strength; militarily, the commanders were ill-prepared and ill-equipped for a campaign in totally unfamiliar territory and with no idea of the strength of the Russian forces in the Crimea. Furthermore, the campaigning season was too far advanced and soon the troops and animals would need winter quarters. Among the French, Marshal St Arnaud was by no means convinced that an attack on Sevastopol would bring the war to a swift conclusion. It seemed a mad undertaking, with little chance of success. To besiege a stronghold such as Sevastopol would risk high casualties and might go on for months.

But at home public enthusiasm for the war was still running high. Colonel Hodge of the 4th Dragoon Guards could only conclude that the prime minister Lord Aberdeen was 'crouching to public opinion and *The Times* newspaper' by agreeing to prosecute the war further.[30] Yet, strangely, for many in the rank and file it was a welcome decision to be on the move after months of idleness in Bulgaria and glad they were too to get away from the cholera, which in three months had killed or invalided out around 8,000 allied troops.

And so, at the end of August, the orders came to march to Varna for embarkation – 'destination unknown'. As a huge armada of 400 ships began to assemble at Balchik Bay, north of Varna, more women now wearily asked to be sent home, 26 alone from Marianne Young's regiment, the 28th. She herself would travel no further, her husband being assigned to escorting the sick and wounded officers of the regiment to Malta on the French vessel *Le Caire*.

By 6 September, the troops had finally settled on board their ships at anchor in Balchik Bay. But the allied commanders were still debating the best place for a landing in the Crimea. With deadening familiarity, they yet again seemed about to leave groups of grief-stricken women on the quayside – those forbidden to go further who had not managed to smuggle or talk their way on board. And then the army appeared to have a sudden change of heart – or, rather, its hand was forced. W. H. Russell witnessed the scene:

> At the last moment, ere we left, many an aching heart was made happy. The women of several of the regiments who had mournfully followed their husbands to the beach, and rent the air with their wailings when

they heard they were to be separated from those with whom they shared privation and pestilence, were allowed to go on board by an order from head-quarters.

The reason for the decision was born of the usual administrative short-sightedness and bungling:

> It was found when it came to be considered what was to be done with them that no provision had been made for their domicile or feeding. A camp of women! – the very idea was ludicrous and appalling, and so, as they could not be left behind, the British Andromaches were perforce shipped on board the transports and restored to their Hectors.[31]

In order to accommodate the women, a decision was made to reduce the numbers of horses and pack animals by selling many of them in Varna. But still the ships were overloaded. The sick women, however, had to be left behind.

Back in Gallipoli, the six companies of the 4th – the last regiment to leave the peninsula – finally embarked on 31 August, orders being that the three women, Elizabeth Evans, Mrs Chilton and Mrs Kelly, be left behind to take care of the sick. They were distraught. Faced with a parting that she dreaded, knowing full well she might never see her husband again, Evans refused to kowtow to orders: 'Stay behind, and our husbands marching off to war! It was more than flesh and blood could endure – certainly more than devoted wives could bear.'[32] Sharing the same perverse female pleasure in circumventing army orders as already displayed by Fanny Duberly, Elizabeth Evans and her two companions resolved to have their way. They managed to steal down to the beach and, drawing on all their feminine wiles, notably those of Mrs Kelly, the clever little Irishwoman who bewailed their lot in graphic detail, managed to impress the major in charge of the embarkation. He took pity on the three women and said they could go with the first troops in the morning. During their anxious night's wait they were befriended by some sailors on the beach, who gave them chocolate and biscuits and improvised a crude shelter for them out of old sacks, where they hid themselves till daylight. The following morning, eluding the quartermaster of the 4th who would have promptly sent them back, they managed to slip past him and board ship – albeit being separated onto three different vessels. Elizabeth Evans would not see her two stalwart companions again. During the entire two years she would spend in the Crimea, so she says, she never saw another woman: 'they were taken from me – and, indeed, in that ruthless land it seemed as if every-thing on which my heart was set was likely to be torn away'.[33]

These three were the only women of the 4th to make it all the way to the Crimea; of the 20 women of the 95th, only three – Mrs Polley, Mrs Crangle and Mrs Buller – reached the camp before Sevastopol; in the 93rd Sutherland Highlanders, army wives and laundresses Mrs Ross and Mrs Smith were among only four women of that regiment who now gathered on the beach at Varna for embarkation. Later they would witness their husbands take part in the Battle of Balaklava. But of the four, only Christina Ross would make it back to Scotland alive.

Meanwhile, Fanny Duberly had her own domestic preoccupations. She had lost her servant Mrs Blaydes to cholera on 20 August; the poor woman had not long recovered from an attack of fever and then had had a relapse 'from over-anxiety to attend to my comforts', as Fanny put it.[34] In passing she remarked in her journal that a woman of the 13th had died, but that is the only observation she has to make on the sufferings of the army wives at Varna. And now Fanny's other rival, Mrs Cresswell, wife of a captain in the 11th Hussars, reappeared on the scene on 24 July. Fanny critically eyed her from a distance and pitied the 'unnecessary discomforts' she was forced to endure, as she, Fanny, watched from the shade of her own 'pretty marquee and green bower'.[35] She looked upon the tough Mrs Cresswell with considerable scorn as a 'great *he* woman, who will kill her own buffalo and cut him up'. Fanny and Lady Erroll, with whom Fanny pronounced herself 'great friends', had gone over to inspect the new arrival and were horrified at what they saw:

After waiting some time a woman came from among the troop horses – so dirty – with such wretched scurvy hair, such black nails, such a dirty cotton gown open at the neck, without a sign of a collar or a linen sleeve. Oh, you never had a kitchen maid so dreadful![36]

Adelaide Cresswell had already been burnt berry-brown by the sun, thus adding to her 'common' appearance; her eating instruments and tableware left much to be desired, but the gutsy Mrs Cresswell was a hardened campaigner and whilst Fanny might think her no better than a kitchen maid, she was as good and knowledgeable a horsewoman as herself. She called the officers in her regiment 'boys' and acted like one of them. She took a pride in cooking her husband's dinner for him and emptied her own slop pail.[37] Mrs Cresswell was one of many officers' wives refused permission to sail to the Crimea on the army transports. Through grim determination she managed to find her own passage to Balaklava on board the *War Cloud*. But she arrived to find herself a widow. Her husband, sick with cholera, had died on the march south to Sevastopol and been buried near the Hussars' bivouac on the Bulganak river. Such a tragic loss, remarked Duberly, 'would crush me to my grave'.[38] Determined to keep watch over Henry, as though by some miracle she could fend off his death, she once again managed to defy orders that officers' wives were not to travel to the Crimea. She evaded the searching eyes of Lord Lucan at the quayside and crept on board the *Himalaya*, disguised somewhat unconvincingly as an army wife (her skin did not have that characteristic weather-beaten look), and hunkered down below decks and out of sight until the fleet sailed.

It would be four days before it did so, for the embarkation was an appallingly long-drawn-out process, as the men lingered on board ship in the harbour waiting for the right winds, during which time cholera carried off another ten men in Elizabeth Evans's regiment. But even at anchor, away from the cholera-ridden valleys of Varna, there were constant reminders of the recent epidemic, as dead and rotting bodies rose up from the bottom and 'bobbed grimly around in the water or floated in from sea and drifted past the sickened gazers on board the ships'.[39]

When embarkation day came, the weather was perfect, the sky cloudless and the sea smooth: 'Hurrah for the Crimea,' cheered Captain Edward Fisher-Rowe in a letter home, 'we are off tomorrow; fine country, people very friendly, take Sebastopol in a week or so, and then into winter quarters . . .'[40] His was a fatal and heartbreaking optimism.

By the time the 19th were ordered to embark for the Crimea, Margaret

Kerwin was lying dangerously ill with internal complaints, fever and rheumatism, the result, she was sure, of standing for long hours washing clothes in the river. She thought she was dying. Her husband was distraught at having to leave her behind. The men of his company did their best to construct a makeshift bower of branches to protect Margaret from the hot sun before leaving. But the agony and grief of separation were terrible. At the last moment, John Kerwin broke ranks and ran to kiss his wife: 'What must have been my feelings to see him going away from me, and I dying and thinking that I never would see him again,' Margaret later recalled. 'It was a hard feeling thing. The day my husband went away from me I was left on the beach of Turkeyland friendless.'[41]

FIVE

The Queen of England Would Give Her Eyes to See It

The allied fleet that left Varna on 7 September numbered about 400 ships, including a British flotilla of 16 three-decker men-of-war and 82 troop transports – 55 of them sailing ships – as well as an army of tugs to tow them into and out of shore. It was an awesome, fantastical sight, 'like some enormous city upon the waters', with, at its centre, and dwarfing every other vessel, the leviathan 3,438-ton British transport ship *Himalaya*. The world's largest ship when launched in May 1853, it could travel at a speed of 12 knots.[1] As it crossed the increasingly choppy waters of the Black Sea, the fleet dominated the horizon for miles – a great floating juggernaut with its moving forest of ships' masts, belching clouds of steam and coal dust. On board was an allied force of about 60,000 men, as well as an unidentified number of women – British Army wives, French *cantinières* and Sisters of Charity.

Of the British fighting force of 25,000 men, one in six would be dead within two months.

Cholera was still raging among the soldiers on Nell Butler's troopship and many died on the voyage, but she and the other women 'did our best for them', she recalled.[2] On board the *Himalaya*, Fanny Duberly tried to keep to her cabin and out of sight during the day, but the atmosphere was stifling. She crept out in the evening to dine with the officers in the saloon, but even here there was no escaping the relentless march of death, for on the other side of the screen from where they were sitting the assembled diners could hear the death rattle from cholera of Captain Longmore of the 8th Hussars. Feeling sick, Fanny nevertheless continued to sip her champagne. At sea she fraternized with Lord Cardigan, for he had taken a liking to her and had looked the other way when she boarded, disregarding orders from on high that Mrs Duberly should *not* sail to the Crimea. Fanny invited much criticism by openly showing her fascination with this notorious womanizer – a man with few friends and many enemies, including his own brother-in-law Lord Lucan, who was also serving in the Crimea.

It took a week or so for some of the slower sailing ships to make the 300-mile crossing, which provided a welcome period of recovery for many of the exhausted allied troops. The fleet arrived off the coast of the Crimea at sunset on 13 September, Lord Raglan and his French allies having gone ahead on the *Caradoc*, a Royal Navy paddle steamer placed at Raglan's disposal during the war, to reconnoitre Sevastopol at close quarters from the coast. They had quickly rejected a landing there as unfeasible and now agonized over the best alternative. It was Raglan who decided to land at Kalamita Bay, a four-mile-long stretch of sandy beach on the west coast of the Crimea, 35 miles north of Sevastopol and in sight of the town of Evpatoriya. Here the vast fleet anchored and by twelve o'clock midday on the 14th, 'that barren and desolate beach, inhabited but a short time before only by the sea-gull and wild-fowl, was swarming with life', according to W. H. Russell, the *Times* correspondent. 'From one extremity to the other bayonets glistened, and red coats and brass-mounted shakos gleamed in solid masses . . . the air filled with our English speech and the hum of voices.'[3] For the next three or four days a smaller fleet of rowing boats, launches, gigs, cutters and floats began the long process of disembarking both men and animals at the British landing point, known as the Old Fort.

Nell Butler, Elizabeth Evans and the other women on the troopships were told to stay on board whilst the men disembarked first. Seeing the troops being fired on by Cossacks, Butler borrowed a telescope and frantically tried to pick out her husband in the mêlée but was ordered below with the other women. Elizabeth Evans was frantic when she was told that she could not go ashore and rejoin the two other women from her regiment from whom she'd been separated. Neither she nor her husband would accept that she had to be left behind, so William Evans made a personal appeal to Lord Raglan to allow his wife to land, telling him: 'I would rather put a stone round her neck and drown her than leave her here at the mercy of foreigners.'4 The compassionate Raglan agreed she could go; Elizabeth Evans went ashore and back on the march again. Fanny Duberly, however, did not join them. Her horse had yet to be transported and whilst she was willing, she claimed, to endure the hardship, her husband considered her too delicate to trudge on foot with the other army wives. Ladies did not do such things. So Fanny reluctantly agreed to board the *Shooting Star*, in the charge of her friend Captain Fraser, and follow the army by sea.

On landing, the British soldiers were told to leave their knapsacks behind on board ship and carry everything they needed, including three days' rations of salt meat (four and a half pounds in weight), black bread and biscuit. The women carried their goods and chattels as best they could, the men weighted down with greatcoat and blanket fashioned into a kind of knapsack, inside which were rolled-up boots, socks, shirt and forage cap. They also carried a wooden canteen for water, rifles with fixed bayonets and 50 rounds of ammunition. But there was insufficient transport available; the men would have to carry all their equipment up the beach in the hot sun and on to their first night's encampment.

The Crimean terrain that confronted the British army and its women was comfortless. It was barren and stony, its undulating hillsides covered with patchy, withered undergrowth smelling of lavender and thyme, and only a few stunted trees and shrubs. There was virtually no visible shelter. And then the rain set in – a drizzle at first, but as the day progressed it got steadily harder. By the evening it was coming down in torrents and there were no tents in which to shelter, the huge army bell tents having been too big and heavy to land without transports. The well-organized French, of course, bedded down for the night nearby in their cosy two-man tents. For the first two nights the troops and their women were forced to huddle miserably together in whatever crude bivouacs they could fashion out of brushwood. They were chilled, hungry and thirsty, their clothes sodden, their single army-issue blanket offering no warmth or protection in the driving rain. It was impossible to light fires, even if enough wood could be found.

Five days later, with the troops becoming restive, the order to strike camp came at last. On 19 September, after a confused start, the allied march south to Sevastopol began. A vast double column, several miles long and four miles apart, of British and French, with Turkish troops in the rear, set out in blazing sunshine. The French took the safer, right-hand flank by the sea. As had happened at Varna and Gallipoli, the men's mood, and that of the women trailing after them, was lifted by the music played by their regimental bands, including the favourite marching song of the war, 'Cheer Boys Cheer'. But heat and thirst soon overcame many on the gruelling two-day march – as did cholera, which still lurked among them. 'The pain of weariness had begun,' a witness observed.[5] Normally strong men, constricted by their tight tunics, leather stocks and heavy shako helmets, fell by the wayside, ripping off their cumbersome uniforms, exhausted by even a couple of miles' marching, and begged the few overladen carts to allow them to ride. Many of the Rifle Brigade threw down their guns in despairing fatigue; once again Lady Erroll and her French maid were there to gather up their abandoned weapons and throw them across the saddles of their own mules.

Elizabeth Evans lost sight of her husband on the march; she remembered how hard it was for the women to keep up with the column, clambering over the obstacle-ridden stony ground and up and down through dense thickets in their long unwieldy dresses. 'I was to learn what it meant to tramp for a long weary day, without a drop of water to drink,' she remembered, for there was no food or water issued during the second day's march. Her feet were sore and blistered and every limb ached; so utterly exhausted was she 'that I could have fallen by the roadside, never to rise again'. Her husband did his best to rally her: 'If you fall out the Russians will have you, and God knows what will happen then.'[6] Their commanding officer also encouraged her to keep going, promising that he'd see to it that she had some good clothes when they got back to England.

Many of the troops were perplexed at why their landing in the Crimea had been unopposed. In such a deserted landscape, apart from the occasional sight of local, friendly Tatars or watchful Cossack outriders on the hillside on reconnaissance from Sevastopol, where was the enemy? The allies found out when they stopped to slake their thirst at the Bulganak river, in the heat of the summer now little more than a brackish stream. On a high ridge up above could just be discerned a Russian advance guard of 6,000 men – beyond it, on the road to Sevastopol and above the small town of Burlyuk, a far larger Russian force was firmly entrenched on the banks of the River Alma, in defence of the only approach road to Sevastopol.

Forty thousand Russians were encamped here in and around what seemed an unassailable gun battery – to be immortalized as the Great Redoubt – under the command of Prince Alexander Menshikov. So confident was the Russian commander that the allies would be easily repulsed and held off for at least three weeks that a party of Russian gentlemen and 30 ladies were invited out by carriage from Sevastopol to watch the engagement with their pearl-handled opera glasses, from a grandstand specially thrown together for the purpose.

After camping at the Bulganak overnight, the allies began their advance on the River Alma. It came in the broiling heat at one o'clock in the afternoon. A terrible silence fell upon the massed British troops. Margaret Kerwin's husband John assembled with his fellow soldiers in the 6,000-strong Light Division. He remembered the moment vividly: 'Comrades looked at each other and turned white . . . if a pin fell from the heavens you could hear it.'[7] There was 'no sound but the ramrods', he added – the rasp of metal against metal as ball cartridges were pushed down the long barrels of muskets. The French now moved off to cross the River Alma, with the British inland on their left, but when the British units came under heavy Russian shellfire, Lord Raglan ordered them to lie down and wait in the Burlyuk valley below. At about three in the afternoon, the British attacked after the French had requested support.

The rolling hillside was now a mass of moving men two miles across. As their advance took them to the Alma, some soldiers drowned through sheer exhaustion as they attempted to wade across; many, already severely weakened by sickness, were picked off by Russian gunfire. Having fought their way past Russian skirmishers in the vineyards on the northern side of the Alma, they then had to clamber up the high bank on its southern side towards their objective, the Great Redoubt. Such an arduous task in the heat of the day prompted more and more men to throw off their heavy bedrolls. Meanwhile, the Russians had set fire to Burlyuk making the disarray of the advance by the 2nd and 3rd Divisions at Bulganak even more confused. The smoke was choking; the collective noise from showers of grapeshot, shells, and musket balls deafening. The British had been forced by this onslaught to break ranks but now boldly pressed forward, launching a tornado of gunfire with their new Minié rifles. This forced the astonished Russians, who by now were sustaining heavy losses, to retreat, taking their precious heavy guns with them. The Great Redoubt was taken by the Light Division, who were then driven out, mainly by intense artillery fire; later the position was retaken by the Scots Fusilier Guards. On the slopes of the Kurgan Hill beyond, vast grey columns of the main Russian infantry force awaited the allies – about 33,600, holding a six-mile-long position.

Elizabeth Evans had watched her husband march away with the 4th as closely as she could until ordered to fall back. The compulsion to watch the battle despite the agony of fear she was going through as William made his way across the 'far-stretched field which was being ploughed by the merciless cannon balls and pitted with the rifle bullets' led her to take up her own position, 'a lonely woman', with the General Staff on a ridge nearby.[8] From here she saw William Evans's company go forward in the second line of attack 'to storm those dreadful heights' that 'frowned with the Russian guns and bristled with the bayonets', their regimental colours bravely flying and band playing. As she did so, one of the regiment's majors recognized her and gravely intoned: 'Look well at that, Mrs Evans, for the Queen of England would give her eyes to see it.'[9]

Evans may well have got a better view than the frustrated correspondent of The Times, W. H. Russell, who had been unable to find a decent vantage point. Offshore, the fleet had tracked the movement of the allied forces, and army wives were out on the decks straining to see what was happening. They had, so one fusilier claimed, 'a grand sight of the battle'.[10] Once the troops moved off and out of sight, all Elizabeth and the other army wives could see were the heights above 'breaking into tongues of fatal fire, and strewing the plains with dead and dying'.[11]

A courageous follow-up attack by Grenadier, Scots Fusiliers and Coldstream Guards in red coatees and bearskins and kilted Black Watch, Cameron and Sutherland Highlanders pressed forward toward the Russian lines in the late afternoon and broke Russian defences on the right flank. Meanwhile, the Russians had already begun to crack after French Zouaves, with covering fire from the French fleet offshore, had scaled the nearby cliffs that the Russians had left relatively undefended, dragging their guns up with them and encircling the Russians on their left flank. The Russians, taking heavy casualties from the superior British Minié rifles and some well-placed artillery fire, now retreated in disarray, throwing aside not just their arms but also their knapsacks and drums and abandoning most of their wounded. They had thought to meet with the British army, not these 'red devils'.

By half past four in the afternoon it was all over: the French on the right had taken possession of their objective, Telegraph Hill, two miles east of the British line of attack. Some 422 allied troops and 1,752 Russians were dead and at least 4,500 allied troops had been wounded. The few overstretched British army surgeons patched and sewed and amputated as best they could, on the spot in the battlefield or on makeshift operating tables made from doors torn from nearby barns and cottages. 'If God spares me again to see Old England, I shall probably never more witness as much practice in my whole lifetime as I saw there in two hours,' remarked one of them.[12] But, unlike the French, the British had no hospital transports, no litters or carts to carry the wounded away (lack of space on the ships had forced them to leave them behind in Varna), and woefully inadequate supplies of clean lint, bandages and much-needed chloroform.

The Alma was the first and last battle that Elizabeth Evans witnessed in the Crimea; having recounted her story many times, she said it was 'more than enough'. 'I do not dwell on its horrors,' she said, 'I try and keep them from my mind'; but even in 1908, when she told her story to the

Royal Magazine, she did not succeed. The images flooded back to her in all their graphic and agonizing detail:

> Even now . . . I see, just as clearly as I beheld it then, a brave officer lying where he had fallen, looking with wild eyes towards the heights of Alma. They were big, merry blue eyes, the most beautiful, I think, that I ever saw.[13]

After the battle, as the cold of night fell, the darkness was punctuated by the groans of agony from the still-unattended wounded and those whose death was a long slow lingering one, many of them calling out for water. The occasional shot rang out as British soldiers, slipping and slithering on the blood-soaked hillsides and tripping over corpses, were fired on by Russians as they tried to attend to the wounded of both sides. In the two days that followed 1,000 troops were deployed to bury the dead, for whom there was no time for anything other than rough and ready burial, 50 or 60 bodies at a time, in large pits. The wounded, thinking themselves lucky to be evacuated out of the war zone, were jolted off on crude wagons to hospital transports offshore. Many died on the way; those that survived found themselves crammed in with men suffering from cholera, dysentery and diarrhoea, their destination the deathtrap of the vast Turkish army barracks at Scutari.

When the first wounded arrived at Nell Butler's transport ship, she heard the blocks creak up on deck as they were hauled on board but noted that no one 'thought of calling on the women to succour the wounded'. Late that night she heard the captain shout: 'Just send up the live ones, you fool! There were three dead in the last batch.'[14] On board the *Vulcan* there were similar scenes, after 300 wounded men were crammed in with 150 cholera victims with only four surgeons to attend them all. The wounded seized the surgeons by their coats as they picked their way through the heaps of dying and dead on deck but the surgeons, over-stretched, exhausted and harassed as they were, shook them off.

Later that night, one of the women of the 4th, Mrs Kelly, was found alone on the battlefield, keening beside the body of her dead husband. As British troops searched among the dead and wounded on Telegraph Hill above the River Alma, they came across the remains of the picnic of chicken and champagne brought by the Russian ladies from Sevastopol and, scattered among it, the shawls, bonnets, parasols – and even a petticoat – that they had hastily discarded when it had suddenly become apparent that this was not to be a Russian walkover.

But there was one courageous young Russian woman who had been out there among the wounded with a cart and supplies, purchased at her own expense, and doing what she could to help. Darya Lavrentevna Mikhailova, or Dasha Sevastopolskaya as she has now gone down in Russian history, was the 18-year-old orphaned daughter of a Russian sailor killed at the Battle of Sinope the previous year. At the time of the British invasion she was living in her half-ruined home in the Korabelnaya district of Sevastopol, working as a laundress and needlewoman in the naval garrison. After the invasion, she had sold everything she had – her father's dinghy, her few chickens and her pig – in order to buy a shaggy Tatar horse and wagon from a local Greek and follow the troops into battle. She took her father's old navy cap and improvised a uniform, cutting off her hair and fashioning a disguise for herself as a naval apprentice. Having loaded her rickety wagon with two barrels containing water, she lost herself in the Russian supply lines in the rear and hitched her wagon to an oak tree. With only two Russian dressing stations to serve the thousands of wounded, Dasha took the unprecedented step, at a time when even the Russians had yet to organize a team of nurses, of improvising one of her own, handing out bread, fried fish, wine and water to the exhausted troops and tearing up her own clothing to provide dressings for their wounds, which she cleansed with vinegar. It was not long before sailors from Korabelnaya recognized her, but she was allowed to continue working as a volunteer nurse along with 30 or 40 other army and navy wives at the Russian dressing stations and on the batteries around the town throughout the siege.

Dasha's selfless heroism soon became legendary throughout Sevastopol. News of it reached Tsar Nicholas I in November 1854 and she was awarded 500 silver roubles and the gold medal 'For Zeal', becoming the only working-class Russian woman to receive the award. The following year she married and opened a tavern; imperial generosity responded with a dowry of one thousand silver roubles from the tsarina.[15]

Fanny Duberly, for all her eagerness to be in the thick of things and keep safe watch over her husband Henry, did not have a first-hand view of the Battle of the Alma. She was still out at sea on board the *Shooting Star*, being wined and dined by navy captains; but she could see the red glare of fires raging on the mainland and could hear the booming of the guns at the Alma even from there and had briefly pondered whether 'among the annals of a war, the sickening anxieties of mother, wife, and sister ever find a place', adding piously, 'Let us hope the angel of compassion makes record of their tears.'[16] When news came of the impending British move south towards Sevastopol and Balaklava Fanny was offered passage on the troopship *Pride of the Ocean*, and had the temerity to keep it and its shipload of troops waiting whilst she organized her luggage, her portable desk and her all-essential saddle, also ensuring she had a good ham and port wine to take along with her. On 21 September Duberly came ashore at Evpatoriya and heaved a sigh of relief when she was told that none of the cavalry divisions, despite Lord Cardigan's itching for a fight, had been sent into action at the Alma.

For Lord Erroll and his energetic and devoted wife, Lady Eliza, the war was already over. A hand wound and the loss of a finger at the Alma, though slight, had been sufficient for the doctors to send the fortunate earl home to England to recuperate. But the poor soldiers of his regiment, the 2nd Rifles, left behind in the Crimea, many already nursing far worse wounds than his, had nothing to look forward to but another bout of footslogging. For on the 23rd the army was on the march south again, crossing the undefended Belbek river and passing at last through a fertile valley of vineyards, orchards and vegetable plots. Grapes and vegetables, as well as any eggs and stray chickens, were grabbed en route, as was hay for the horses; even beehives were robbed of their honey. Many of the cottages and farmhouses they passed had already been abandoned and left open to plunder by 'a great hungry army, worse than locusts, and without compassion'; the fine summer villas of the nobility of Sevastopol, with their chandeliers, grand pianos and ornate furnishings, were quickly vandalized and pillaged of all moveable goods.[17]

It was shortly after the Battle of the Alma that the allied commanders made a fatal mistake that would soon cost their armies dear. The terminally ill Marshal St Arnaud (he died on 29 September) had vetoed Lord Raglan's desire to press directly on to Sevastopol from the north while the town was still relatively underfortified. The decision was taken instead to make a flank march and lay siege to the city from the Chersonese plateau to the south and east, using back-up supplies from French and British naval bases at Kamiesh and Balaklava. But once again the bureaucrats bungled, for the hopelessly overstretched British commissariat had also failed to investigate the ability of the limited and narrow harbour at Balaklava to cater for a huge influx of shipping and the removal from the quayside, seven miles up to the siege lines, of all the supplies needed to maintain the momentum of the siege.

At 6.30 a.m. on 17 October the allies, having dug in their own guns in a line of batteries on the semicircular heights to the south and east of Sevastopol, opened the siege with a massive bombardment from land and sea as 126 guns belched out their fire and destruction. But in the days since the allied landings in mid-September, the Russians had been as busy as worker ants, building huge defensive earthworks in the city, bringing up heavy guns and making it impregnable. Lieutenant Colonel Eduard Todleben, an engineering genius, had masterminded the enlisting of thousands of civilians – men, women and even children – to help soldiers and sailors work day and night in moving mountains of earth, women carrying it in their aprons, children helping to push loaded wheelbarrows. Logs and turf were carted, along with heavy sandbags and long bundles of brushwood known as fascines, to fortify the city's main defences. These comprised eight bastions, including the most impregnable, the Malakhov and the Great Redan. The great pounding match between the protagonists now opened in earnest as the Russian batteries responded with ferocious firepower, their resources and supply lines, still intact in the north, seeming limitless. At all times Russian women were there under heavy fire in the bastions to offer *kvass* (fermented rye) and water to the thirsty Russian gunners and help bind their wounds. The troops on both sides now settled down to a long, slow period of attrition, conducted in the mud and cold of the trenches – an experience to be repeated on a much larger and more tragic scale 60 years later in Flanders on the Western Front.

Out at sea on board the fleet, which had been engaged unsuccessfully in the early bombardment of Sevastopol, several army wives were still stranded, having refused to go home from Gallipoli and Varna. One of them gave birth to a baby on board the *Cyclops* just before the bombardment started and, being too exhausted to be removed to safety, had nursed her baby in its first hours in sight and sound of the gunfire. This experience had 'so weakened her constitution, that she sunk and died a few days afterwards'. A soldier of the 28th who witnessed her death wrote home matter-of-factly, telling his family how the woman was then 'thrown overboard in the bay of Varna', where the *Cyclops* was sent to bring in the reserve. 'This is war,' he shrugged.[18]

On board ship, Fanny Duberly had wondered after the battle of Alma: 'how can timorous, nervous women live through a time like this!' If she had acquainted herself with some of the army wives on campaign, she would have soon discovered something of the courage and fortitude with which they did so. Women such as Elizabeth Evans, who, with her husband on piquet duty in the siege trenches, kept herself busy during the day in earshot of the perpetual roar of the British and Russian guns, organizing the men's laundry and spending many an hour carefully patching and mending the Colours of the 4th, which had been torn and tattered at the Alma. Once dusk fell, if her husband was still on duty, she crept out beyond the British lines to join him until he completed his watch. Some of the officers tried to stop her, but in the face of Evans's dogged persistence, eventually turned a blind eye. When the time came for sleep, she did the best she could to preserve a modicum of privacy and dignity in the tent – which was full of weapons, kit and cooking equipment – by screening off a small section for herself and her husband. Fanny Duberly, however, took one look at the tent her husband Henry was obliged to share with three colleagues in camp and thought better of a life in the outdoors. She opted to stay on board the *Shooting Star* for the time being, making regular visits to camp to catch the thrill of the siege and the shot and shell that 'came hissing every two minutes'. She admitted to a 'high degree of excitement' at the sight of Sevastopol under fire and to hearing the 'magnificent din of war'.[19] It was, she wrote, 'a moment worth a hundred years of every-day existence'.[20] With her two female 'rivals' in camp – the widowed Mrs Cresswell and Lady Erroll – now departed, she could once more hold court as the only lady of quality in the Crimea; until December at least, when the first intrepid lady tourist arrived.

For the anxious public waiting back home, the full power of war had finally been 'unchained' in the Crimea with the Battle of the Alma.[21] When news of the victory reached Britain on the evening of Saturday 29 September, the nation was preparing for a special thanksgiving service for a bountiful harvest – the best in years. Word spread by telegraph to every major town in the country and people crowded into the newspaper and telegraph offices for further news. The following day the churches were filled to capacity as their bells pealed out across the countryside: 'Wives, mothers, and children trembled at the news, and waited with mingled hope and fear for the further intelligence, which would make them either the sharers in a national glory, or the heart-stricken mourners for the loss of those dear ones who have bravely died at Alma.'[22] The news, however, rapidly became totally garbled, with *The Times* on 2 October boldly proclaiming the 'Fall of Sebastopol' – a fact which was soon disappointingly contradicted.

Queen Victoria, who had received the news of the battle at her Scottish home at Balmoral, considered the noble sacrifice of her troops as having been made, by all accounts, 'with a *courage* and *desperation* which was beautiful to behold'. 'Never in so short a time has so strong a battery [the Great Redoubt], so well defended, been so bravely and gallantly taken,' she pronounced in positively Churchillian tones.[23]

With this first British victory in the Crimea, queen and country were now 'entirely engrossed with one idea and one anxious thought, namely the Crimea'.[24] However, with her characteristic impatience, Victoria was still very frustrated by the time it took for news to reach Britain. She felt the official dispatches arriving by courier and telegraph to the War Office were often 'meagre and unsatisfactory'. 'If only one knew the details!' she wailed,[25] now soliciting copies of letters sent home by officers and summoning and interrogating any commanders returning from the Crimea, including Lord Burgersh in early October.

To satiate her desperate need to know, Victoria pored over maps, becoming intimate with the lay of the land in the Crimea and the positions of the allied troops. She impressed her entourage with the accuracy of her knowledge of the Russian defences at Sevastopol, 'more than anyone I found at home knew', as the war illustrator William Simpson noted on his return.[26] She voraciously read the reports sent back to *The Times* by its special correspondent, William Howard Russell, and swooned and sighed over every detail of the heroic male fighting spirit, regretting 'exceedingly' that she was not a man and could not be at the front fighting alongside her beloved troops. There was, she felt sure, 'no finer death for a man than on the battlefield'.[27]

The carnage of the next two battles might have told the queen a different story, for when they were over the number of letters of condolence she would be writing would rise dramatically.

On Wednesday 25 October 1854, the second major engagement of the war took place when a large force of 25,000 Russians, commanded by General Pavel Liprandi, attempted a counter-attack from the north across the River Chernaya, in an attempt to cut off the British supply base at Balaklava, advancing on the plain through which the Vorontsov Road to Balaklava passed. The allied position at the time was defended by four redoubts along the Causeway Heights, which were armed with ten 12-pounder guns and manned by Turkish troops (in fact mainly inexperienced Tunisians). Liprandi's force first attacked Redoubt No. 1 ('Canrobert's Hill'), furthest to the east, and, after a brave resistance, the Turks were forced to abandon their position, with heavy casualties. In succession, the Turks manning Redoubts 2, 3 and 4 lost their nerve, turned and fled in terror. Rushing back down into Balaklava in confusion, past the camp of the 93rd Sutherland Highlanders, they were seen and jeered at by many of the army wives, including two washerwomen – Mrs Smith, wife of the soldier-servant to Lieutenant Sinclair, and Mrs Ross, wife of a sergeant, and personal laundress to the regiment's commander, Sir Colin Campbell. As they hurtled past, the Turks trampled the washing that the women had laid out to dry in the sun by a stream. In a towering rage, the women berated them, Mrs Smith seizing one by the collar and giving him a good kicking. When she realized the Turks in question had deserted her own regiment up on what was later called Sutherland Hill, she jeered contemptuously: 'Ye cowardly misbelievers, to leave the brave Christian Highlanders to fecht when ye run awa!'[28]

When the Turks tried to placate her and apologize, addressing her as 'Kokana' (a polite form of address), Mrs Smith became even more enraged: 'Kokana, indeed! I'll Kokana ye!' Hearing the kerfuffle, Lieutenant Sinclair came running to the rescue, but Mrs Smith needed no defending for, together with Mrs Ross, she was chasing the besmirchers of her regimental washing down the road, brandishing a large stick. After the war, Surgeon General Munro of the 93rd remembered Kokana Smith with great affection as being one of that rare breed, 'a stalwart wife' with a 'tender, honest heart'. Years of hard army life had left their mark: she was 'large and massive, with brawny arms, and hands as hard as horn'. But her face, 'though bronzed and weather-beaten and deeply freckled, was comely, and lighted up by a pair of kindly hazel eyes'.[29] Kokana Smith survived the war to carry the nickname home with her.

After his wife's disappointment at not seeing the Battle of the Alma, Henry Duberly was determined that Fanny should not miss the coming engagement and dispatched a hurried note to her: 'The battle of Balaklava has begun, and promises to be a hot one.' He sent over her horse Bob from camp so she could get to the front lines to watch, exhorting her: 'Lose no time, but come up as quickly as you can,' and adding, 'Do not wait for breakfast.'[30]

As the Turks fled south, down to Balaklava, the Russians now moved 2,000 cavalry troops forward onto the Causeway Heights with the intention of leading a probing attack to pave the way for a major assault on Balaklava, presently being held by the British. The resulting engagement proved to be a classic demonstration of the tough fighting spirit of the British soldier, and one graphically described and defined by W. H. Russell in *The Times* as 'that thin red streak topped with a line of steel', soon popularized as the 'thin red line'.[31] It came when 550 Sutherland Highlanders of the 93rd Regiment, in defence of the head of the inlet leading directly into Balaklava, took up position two-deep in a line facing a detachment of some 400 of the oncoming Russian cavalry. 'You must die where you stand' had been the order of the redoubtable Sir Colin Campbell; and so they did, with great courage – backed by the full power of their Minié rifles. Fanny Duberly had galloped up on her horse Bob, taking a circuitous and safer route around the French lines, in time to see it all through her lorgnette:

> Presently came the Russian Cavalry charging, over the hillside and across the valley, right against the little line of Highlanders. Ah, what a moment! Charging and surging onward, what could that little wall of men do against such numbers and such speed? There they stood. Sir Colin did not even form them into square. They waited until the horsemen were within range, and then poured a volley which for a moment hid everything in smoke.[32]

It took only two volleys from the Highlanders to disconcert the Russians, who, in the thick smoke of the rifle fire, suddenly came to a stand, wheeled about and retreated.

The Heavy Brigade, meanwhile, was still waiting to be called into action. When their commander General James Scarlett, in battle for the first time in his military career, saw the Russian cavalry advancing from the Causeway Heights, he courageously led his 900 men into what seemed like an illogical and piecemeal uphill attack. Once more the British fought like men possessed: 'I hope God will forgive me' wrote one dragoon, 'for I felt more like a devil than a man.'[33] The Russians, astonished by British discipline and resolve and by the sheer impetus of the attack, moved slowly and took its full force in a near-stationary position, after which they turned, were hit by British artillery fire and retreated in disarray. In the space of eight minutes, the vastly inferior numbers of the Heavy Brigade had executed an astonishing rout.

In the North Valley the Light Brigade, under the command of Lord Cardigan, was getting increasingly restive. Disappointed at not having seen action at the Alma, it was still awaiting its own moment of glory. The brigade was further frustrated when Lord Cardigan chose not to take decisive action and order them in pursuit of the retreating Russian cavalry. This missed opportunity rankled with many of them, including Captain Louis Nolan of the 15th Hussars, a courageous and skilled horseman who had served in the Austrian and Hungarian armies as well as in the British service in India. The author of a manual on the training of cavalry horses and a book on cavalry history and tactics, he was a fanatical advocate of the aggressive use of cavalry in battle.

The tragic events that followed would soon be laid down in the mythology of war and ensured that, whatever else happened during the Crimean conflict, the legendary Charge of the Light Brigade at the Battle of Balaklava would be engraved in the hearts and minds of the British public for ever. The Charge came about due to the misinterpretation of hasty and confused orders from Lord Raglan, who had been trying to organize a counter-attack by his infantry against the Russians taking the captured guns away from the redoubts on the Causeway Heights. The order itself was highly ambiguous: 'Lord Raglan wishes the cavalry to advance rapidly to the front, and try to prevent the enemy carrying away the guns. Troop of horse artillery may accompany. French cavalry is on your left. Immediate.'[34]

Captain Nolan, who had been assigned the task of taking Raglan's order to Lucan, in overall command of the British Cavalry Division, galloped off to deliver it with a flourish, but there was genuine confusion over the order's intentions: it made little sense to Lucan and he asked Nolan which guns Lord Raglan had in mind. Nolan, 'in the ardour of the moment' as his friend Fanny Duberly put it, is reported to have flung his arm out in the direction of the Russian cavalry lined up behind a range of guns at the end of the North Valley and to have contemptuously declared to his senior officer, 'There, my Lord, is your enemy! There are your guns!'"

Misinterpreting Raglan's directive as referring to the main Russian guns facing them straight ahead at the end of the valley below the heights, and no doubt influenced by Nolan's arrogant assertion that *he* for one knew which were the guns in question, Lucan passed on the order to charge to his brother-in-law, Lord Cardigan, even though he thought the action insane without the support of infantry. Cardigan too questioned the military logic of such an attack, but Lucan ultimately overrode his own and Cardigan's doubts without attempting to double-check Raglan's precise intentions, the word 'immediate' clearly being taken at face value.

Thus it was that Alfred Lord Tennyson's immortal 'six hundred' (more accurately, about 670 in total) were sent on a suicidal charge along a narrow valley straight into the terrifying firepower of the Russian guns, as well as cannon fire from both flanks. The British command, as well as news reporters and army wives, could do nothing but watch in horror from the hillside. Two thousand yards and seven and a half minutes later, having broken the line of the Russian guns – in itself an extraordinary tactical success – 103 cavalrymen lay dead (seven more later died of wounds), 130 were wounded and 58 had been taken prisoner. Other, horseless men were attacked by the rallying Russian cavalry, as they straggled back, wounded and tattered, to their lines. Dozens of crazed and riderless horses charged about in all directions in this ghastly field of carnage, not just strewn with the bodies of soldiers but with those of at least 340 fine cavalry horses; another 30 or so severely wounded ones were shot later that day.

It was a sight to break the heart of the horse-mad Fanny Duberly, who had watched the charge from the heights overlooking the North Valley, where some of the other army wives had gathered in fear and apprehension, huddling together in groups so they could hold each other's hands and share in both the fear and the exhilaration of the last few moments. It had all seemed so awesome, so romantic – the flying pennants, the jingling spurs and chomping on bits of the horses; but minutes later the Light Brigade was no more and some of the finest Hussars, Lancers and Dragoons in the army had galloped off to their deaths. Nolan – who had been given permission to ride in the front of the charge with the 17th Lancers – never lived to give his own version of events: as he turned in the saddle, his sword arm outstretched, a shell splinter had split open his chest in the first 100 yards of the charge; his body froze in spasm, and then fell forward in the saddle (an image later to be immortalized in Tony Richardson's 1968 film *The Charge of the Light Brigade*).

One of the Russian observers of the Charge later described it as being that of 'valiant lunatics'.[35] After the attack, Lord Cardigan, who led his brigade beyond the Russian guns – but then abandoned them to ride back up the valley – could only rasp that it had been 'a mad-brained trick, but it was no fault of mine', after which he is said to have blandly ridden back to camp for a bottle of champagne with his dinner and then bed. With Cardigan passing the buck for the debacle of the Charge back to Lucan, and Lucan in turn to Raglan (who did not live long enough for the blame to stick), the bitter rivalry between Lucan and Cardigan rumbled on. Lucan was sacked by Raglan and recalled to Britain, but he was soon joined by Cardigan, who went unwillingly before a Medical Board and was sent home sick. Nolan, whatever the motives for his actions, was meanwhile enshrined as a hero with the British public, though the true motive for his actions on that day remains the subject of fierce controversy among military historians. Meanwhile, the Battle of Balaklava, at which the Russians had had overwhelming superiority in numbers, was, strategically, a defeat for the allies. They lost control of the only hard-core road in the Crimean peninsula – the Vorontsov Road from Yalta in the south to Sevastopol in the north – and one essential to their own supply lines. During the treacherous winter of 1854, these would have to take a longer, more circuitous route through increasingly impassable mud. But such were the romantic heroics of the Charge of the Light Brigade that of nine Victoria Crosses subsequently awarded to participants in the Battle of Balaklava, six were to men who took part in it.

After it was all over, a stunned Fanny Duberly returned to her ship in what she described as a state of 'suspended animation'.[36] She had experienced no fear whilst watching the engagement at close quarters; it was only after she was once more safely on board ship that she was overcome with the significance of the day's events. 'What a lurid night I passed . . . Even my closed eyelids were filled with the ruddy glare of blood,' she wrote as she closed up her journal, remarking that the Battle of Balaklava had been fought on the anniversary of another, now mythic, British engagement – against the French at Agincourt in 1415.

. . .

W. H. Russell's account of Balaklava had yet to be published in *The Times* before the final battle of 1854 took place at 6 a.m. on 5 November. An early-morning surprise attack from Sevastopol by 35,000 Russian infantry and 4,500 gunners caught the British near the village of Inkerman, already hungry, tired and many just returning from a rain-sodden piquet duty, off their guard. In camp with the 4th, Elizabeth Evans was awoken by the firing and the calling of the alarm but was not allowed to accompany the soldiers. She watched in dismay as the 4th marched out of camp, leaving her alone with the drummer boys to watch over the sick.

The Russians had been rapidly reinforcing since the Alma. Galvanized by a welter of propaganda from the Bishop of Sevastopol against the ungodly and depraved English, and fired up by liberal issues of vodka and brandy, they emerged from the city to the peal of its many Sunday-morning bells and attacked the 3,000-strong British 2nd Division at Inkerman Hill east of Sevastopol. This led to a series of savage infantry engagements, later known as the 'Soldiers' Battle'. It lasted eight hours and was fought hand-to-hand with rifles, fixed bayonets and, when necessary, swords, revolvers and stones, in heavy brushwood on a narrow hillside. For most of the time thick fog and a continuous drizzle made it impossible for the allies to accurately gauge the Russian pattern of attack. Because of this they were forced to fight at such close quarters that the battle turned into a confused and bloody mêlée. Infantry units became mixed up and detached from the army's senior commanders and fought side-by-side in small companies: 'colonels . . . fought like subalterns, captains like privates. Once engaged every man was his own general'.[37] Eyewitness accounts describe how the men 'went like tigers at the enemy', ferociously thrusting and hacking and cheering for 'Old England'.[38] As the day wore on the troops were running out of ammunition and had to salvage it from the dead. Yet despite the odds being against them, once again the British, with French help later in the day, managed to force the Russians back, with heavy Russian losses of 10,729 wounded, killed or taken prisoner. Allied casualties totalled 3,220. The heaps of dead and wounded were piled within a very confined area, in the most tragic and contorted of positions. Such a sight, remarked Russell of *The Times*, would for ever cure a young gentleman of his 'love of arms' or romantic young ladies suffering from 'scarlet fever':

> If they could have gazed into the burial pits at those who were about to be consigned to the worm, they would feel the horrors of their hero worship and would join in prayer for the advent of that day, when war shall be no more.[39]

A journalist fresh out from England watched the women go out among the mutilated bodies afterwards, crouching down in the fading light looking for their own men. He found one of them, Mrs Polley of the 95th Foot, sitting cradling the head of her wounded rifleman husband George in her lap. She looked up at the journalist in astonishment: 'Oh, sir, you're a strange gentleman to stay here, when you could get away as soon as you like,' she sighed, as though the strange unspoken ritual of attending the dead and wounded was something the women alone shared in.[40] In amongst the corpses on the hillside, the unmarked body of a young *cantinière* was found – she had ridden into battle with back-up lines of French Zouaves, as the *cantinières* often did, but the cause of her seemingly peaceful death in the midst of such carnage was a mystery. Sadly, there were also human vultures on the field of battle at Inkerman – searching the corpses of the allied and Russian dead. Some may well have been hardened women camp followers now widowed and destitute, left stranded with the army and falling into disrepute; others, locals out from Balaklava, all of them looking for valuables such as the silver crucifixes, medals of saints and talismans worn by so many Russian soldiers.

During the Crimean War, no single battle did more than Inkerman to restore the reputation of the British fighting man from his age-old reputation of licentiousness, drunkenness and brutality. Britain was now priding itself on its 'people's army' as it never had done before. Inkerman, for which fifteen Victoria Crosses were awarded, had demonstrated the common soldier's courage, stoicism and solidarity with his comrades. It also further galvanized efforts back home to do something for 'all the wretched wives and mothers who are awaiting the fate of those nearest and dearest to them' and with whom the queen so passionately commiserated.[41] Many of them were now living in a state of extreme destitution and the Central Association, founded in March to help them, was rapidly becoming financially overstretched. In mid-October the queen therefore gave her sanction to the establishment of the Royal Patriotic Fund to raise money to assist the Central Association in its support of the widows, orphans and destitute parents of soldiers and sailors serving in the East. The response of the public to the suffering of its army was unprecedented.

However, a somewhat rose-tinted view of what life was like on campaign was being painted back home by, of all people, the novelist Elizabeth Gaskell, in a letter to her sister:

> Lady Errol, Mrs Daubeny [Duberly] & Mrs Galton the 3 officer's wives who are with the Camp in the Crimea, dress as Vivandieres & wash their husband's shirts, cook {each other's} their dinners &c., & say 'they never were so happy in their lives'.[42]

Fanny Duberly would have been appalled by such an assertion, for she had army servants to do both her cooking and washing. What is more, she was already priding herself that, having ridden through the French camp one morning, the soldiers there had been 'astonished at the apparition of a *lady* in their lines'. Fanny failed of course to note that the French had female *cantinières* with them. But, not being 'ladies' like herself, they were therefore invisible. Victorian social snobbery was alive and well, even in a war zone.

By the time Henry Duberly excitedly arrived to tell her all about the Battle of Inkerman and invited her to ride out to see the battlefield, even Fanny had had enough of carnage. 'I could not go,' she wrote. 'The thought of it made me shudder and turn sick.' The queen, meanwhile, was gratified to receive 'with pride and joy' the news of the 'glorious, but alas! bloody victory of the 5th' – and rather more quickly this time than previous reports. It came by telegraph, thanks to the recent laying of cables on the sea bed from Constantinople to the Crimea.[43] She sent her thanks and those of the nation for the victory to Lord Raglan on 27 November, asking that the rank and file should be assured that the country 'sympathises as deeply with their privations and exertions as it glories in their victories and exults in their fame. Let not any Private Soldier in those ranks believe,' she added, 'that his conduct is unheeded. The Queen thanks him – his Country honours him.'[44]

The weather in the Crimea was now turning bitter, with ominous signs of the long hard winter to come. Those army wives still out there had rapidly toughened up, the few now staying the course becoming as hardy and long-suffering as their men. Their clothing had, like the men's, endured the heat and sweat of summer, the dust of the forced marches and the drenching rain of autumn, and was now in tatters. Only a few, such as Mrs Munro, the sole officer's wife with the Grenadier Guards, were still the proud possessors of bonnets – and hers had lost most of its trimmings when a musket ball whizzed by her head one day. With their husbands absent during the day on long and wearying periods of trench duty, the women settled into a routine at camp: sewing, washing, cooking and helping where they could with the wounded in the nearby makeshift regimental field hospitals.

It was rapidly becoming clear that the army was here for the winter. But the fine force of fighting men that had left Britain in the spring was now exhausted, malnourished and undersupplied – and, furthermore, had by now been reduced by disease and battle to fewer than 15,000 active men. It was desperately in need of reinforcements and a systematic method of caring for the sick and wounded. In Britain public opinion on the army's plight had been dominating the pages of the newspapers since the Alma, and the women of England in particular were now 'thoroughly aroused' and begging to be of service to the troops.

At long last, the authorities were stirred into action. On 23 October, the first party of 38 British nurses specifically engaged for service in the Crimea departed by train from London Bridge under the direction of a wealthy, 30-year-old gentlewoman from the English home counties – Miss Florence Nightingale.

SIX

Why Have We No Sisters of Mercy?

When the Crimean War broke out in the spring of 1854, Britain had been witness to a steady growth in pacifist sentiment in the 40 years since the end of the Napoleonic Wars, during which an active Peace Society had been at work. Women had been busily engaged in fund-raising behind the scenes for the society since the 1830s, yet such was the lack of public awareness about their activities that their silent, self-effacing contribution was overlooked, dedicated as it was to furthering the better known and more influential work of its leading male figures – Joseph Sturge, Richard Cobden and John Bright. The Quaker feminist Anne Knight had loathed this ghettoization of women and their continuing confinement to traditional, non-controversial philanthropic roles. Women, she wrote, were no longer content to '"sit by the fire and spin" or distill rosemary and lavender for poor neighbours', any more than 'prick [their] fingers to the bone in "sewing circles" for vanity fair peace bazaars, where health and mind equally suffer in the sedentary "stitch, stitch, stitch"'.[1]

With quiet determination, these modest women's circles had been forging and strengthening the international bonds that would later link women from Britain, America and the Continent in the broader movement for women's emancipation. After Britain declared war on Russia in

March 1854, the women's peace campaign found a new and unexpected international spokeswoman in the Swedish novelist Frederika Bremer, who, like Anne Knight, saw her sex as condemned to lives of idleness – making preserves and pickles, learning to speak French and dancing Swedish polkas – and longed to see women released from the stranglehold of patriarchal social conventions.

On 14 August 1854, distressed by newspaper reports about the war in the East, Bremer took an unprecedented step for a woman. She sent out a public and heartfelt appeal to women everywhere to do something positive. She enjoined them to unite under the Christian principles of love and charity in a 'Peace Alliance' that would speak out against 'the direful effects of war', which even now was threatening to 'spread over several of the countries of Europe like a large bleeding wound'.[2] Her message was published by newspapers in Sweden, Russia, France, Germany and the United States. It appeared in *The Times* on 28 August 1854, Bremer being convinced that 'no hearts and minds in the world will be more ready to respond to the proposal . . . than the benevolent and high-minded English people'.

But it was too late; the women of England were by now in the grip of war fever. Indeed, the satirical journal *Punch* was quick to deride Bremer's sentiments, claiming that warmongering was as much the fault of women as men, because of women's long-standing admiration for 'a man in a red coat'.[3] Even the editorial board of the pacifist journal *Herald of Peace* was somewhat belittling in its response. Whilst commending the nobility of Bremer's Christian sentiments, it was quick to warn her that she should not 'rely upon any sympathy or help whatever from the political press, in her benevolent aspirations' and that she should be prepared to be greeted by 'the most perfect apathy and coldness from such quarters'.[4] And this indeed was the case, with *The Times* deriding Bremer's appeal as 'the mere illusion of an amiable enthusiast'.[5] The Peace Society was equally dismissive, sternly declaring that its women members should not 'participate directly in the coarse conflict of politics'.

However, there was no escaping the onward march of that increasingly contentious issue, 'The Woman Question', and the challenge being made to the two very separate and entrenched spheres – the public and the domestic – which men and women had respectively occupied according to tradition. Men might try to keep women in their place, asserting their own monopoly on the worlds of fame and fortune and politics and consigning women to a private, inner life of the emotions – as eulogized on the pages of the *Englishwoman's Domestic Magazine*[6] – but the coming of the Crimean War would set in train much debate over nursing as a profession for women, with its figurehead, Florence Nightingale, becoming the most famous woman in Britain after the queen. Previously, despite women's natural inclinations to nurse, it had not been considered a profession for 'ladies', and the conflict between unpaid, voluntary nursing – which was seen as devotional and vocational and the acceptable realm of submissive woman – and paid nursing by working-class women with families to support would become one of the major public debates of the war.

By the mid-1850s there were many thousands of British women who, either by changes to their economic circumstances or by personal preference, were desperate to escape the enforced and monotonous seclusion of life at home and the only two options then open to them – of being schoolteachers or governesses. Thrown into an overcrowded, male-dominated labour market, women such as these saw the extension of their traditional role as carers and domiciliary nurses as being one of the few viable occupations for respectable Christian females – especially gentlewomen in reduced circumstances. The Victorian press was much exercised by these changing perceptions of the role of women, anxious to emphasize the safe and uncontroversial characteristics of woman as domestic goddess. But with the now urgent need for nurses, the image of gentle, loving, compassionate woman ministering to the sick at their bedsides played on the imaginations of young and idealistic women, full of romantic as well as spiritual aspirations, who yearned to play their part.

The whole moral, social and practical can of worms regarding women as nurses was finally opened up for public debate on 12 October, when *The Times* published the report – often attributed to W. H. Russell but in fact from its special correspondent in Constantinople, Thomas Chenery – that would change the whole course of the treatment of the sick and wounded in the war. That morning, the British public was stopped in its tracks as it took its tea and toast over the latest edition of *The Times*. For the paper contained the most horrifying account of the total lack of adequate care and medical supplies for the British sick and wounded now arriving at the old Turkish army barracks at Scutari – a place serving not just as the main depot for the many cholera victims from the army, but also for the casualties of the Battle of the Alma:

> Not only are there not sufficient surgeons – that, it might be urged, was unavoidable – not only are there no dressers and nurses – that might be a defect of system for which no one is to blame – but what will be said when it is known that there is not even linen to make bandages for the wounded? . . . why could not this clearly foreseen event have been supplied?[7]

There was more from Chenery the following day, describing how the few superannuated Chelsea pensioners sent out as a token 'ambulance corps' to Scutari were hopelessly overstretched and inadequate (and, as it turned out, frequently drunk). Far worse, though, was the absence of nurses – a fact all the more shameful in the presence of well-equipped surgeons in the French hospitals at Constantinople, who had at their disposal a team of Sisters of Charity – local Levantine Catholic sisters of the Order of St Vincent de Paul from convents in Constantinople, Smyrna and Pera, who had been drafted in and were busy organizing the supply of clothing, bedlinen and hospital supplies.

Religious orders of women who devoted themselves to the care of the sick had flourished on the Continent since the mid-seventeenth century, particularly after the establishment of the Hôpital Général in 1656 in Paris under Cardinal Mazarin. With the Catholic Church's strong sense of responsibility towards the sick poor, a network of 100 such hospitals was in operation in France by the early eighteenth century and other nursing communities of women were also encouraged, notably Vincent de Paul's Filles de la Charité. At Kaiserswerth in Germany a Protestant pastor, Theodore Fliedner, had instituted training for nurses at the Deaconess Institute, where Florence Nightingale herself studied for three months in 1853. By then Ireland had communities of Catholic nursing sisters, and there were English Anglican (High Church) communities at Devonport (known as the Sellonites after being founded in 1848 by Priscilla Lydia Sellon) and St John's House – both of which sent nurses to the Crimea – as well as the Institution of Nursing Sisters, founded by the Quaker reformer Elizabeth Fry. But the numbers of British nuns who nursed the sick were at that time nothing to equal the French Sisters of Charity, who had a network of 12,000 nuns across Europe – France, Poland, Galicia, Prussia, Spain, Italy, Belgium, Switzerland, Lithuania – as well as in North Africa and South America. Meanwhile, the British Army appears to have lost sight of its own tradition, dating back to the English Civil War of 1642–9, when the Parliamentary Army had organized and paid local women to nurse the wounded after the Battle of Edgehill and hired army widows to nurse at its three military hospitals in London, including the Savoy.[8]

An angry *Times* leader in response to Chenery's report, written on the 13th by its editor John Delane, prompted an inrush of cheques and donations and the establishment of a *Times* Crimean Fund for the Relief of the Sick and Wounded (soon to be rivalled by the even bigger Royal Patriotic Fund under the patronage of Queen Victoria). The letters now flooded thick and fast into *The Times*, one on the 14th from 'A Sufferer by the Present War', who pointed up not just the sufferings out at Scutari and the Crimea but also the agonies of distress being endured by the families back home on reading such reports. It felt like a betrayal of their patriotic sacrifice:

> We sit at home trying to picture the last moments of those dear to us,
> and our agony is increased by the fear that all was not done that might
> have been done to relieve their sufferings . . . The strongest man
> becomes helpless and dependent like a child in his hour of need, and
> we all know how, in such a case, a humble nurse, with no other
> recommendations than a kind heart and skilful hands, appears to the
> sufferer as a saving angel.[9]

On 15 October two important letters crossed in the post. One was from Florence Nightingale, the unsalaried lady superintendent of the Hospital for Invalid Gentlewomen in Harley Street, to Mrs Sidney Herbert (wife of the Secretary for War) offering to recruit a team of nurses for the East; the other was from Herbert himself, who, having known of Nightingale's work and her administrative abilities, had written asking her to do precisely that. Even as these two letters made their way across London, one from a 15-year-old English girl was about to make headlines.

The young girl in question was Janie Skene, one of seven children of James Skene, a British diplomat in Constantinople. From Constantinople, Janie and her mother had travelled across the Bosporus to Scutari to visit her midshipman brother George who was lying wounded in the hospital there, after which Janie wrote home to her grandfather in Oxford, who in turn had forwarded her letter to *The Times*:

> You cannot imagine anything so fearful; to think that there are 3,000 lying in the barracks, and there are not even doctors enough to take care of them, and no nurses, for the few Greeks they tried to have were either not strong enough to bear the operations and the dressing of the wounds (for it was only very old women who could be procured), or else they drank so dreadfully that there was no depending on them.

The condition of the wounded from the Alma was filthy and pitiable, many of them having been left with maggot-infested wounds during the several days it had taken to transport them from the Crimea. The French, Janie claimed in her letter published on 17 October, 'have sent out 500 Sisters of Charity, who have been and still will be invaluable'. Her claim, like Chenery's previously that the French had sisters in 'incredible numbers', certainly might have been extravagant but it posed the obvious question:

Now, would it not be possible for us to do something too?[10]

Nightingale was by no means the only woman prompted into action by the *Times* report. Several others were already offering their own private means to fund groups of nurses, well before the government swung into action. The wealthy philanthropist and Evangelical Lady Maria Forester, after reading Chenery's 9 October dispatch, had offered £200 to send out three nurses under Nightingale's supervision. From Scotland, Mrs Elizabeth Mackenzie, the daughter of a Dr Chalmers who was working at the naval hospital at Therapia 12 miles north of Scutari, had also written to Sidney Herbert offering her own services in putting together a team of nurses. The response from Herbert had been blunt: if anything could be done, then 'a lady well known to himself would be applied to'.[11] For Herbert was convinced that there was only one woman for the job – Florence Nightingale.

On 24 October *The Times* published a passionate response to the growing debate on nurses, which argued that the army had a ready-made untapped source out in the field – the army wives stranded at Scutari – several of whom had been cooks as well as sicknurses in camp in Britain or for officers' families before the war, but who were now living in an increasing state of degradation and inaction. The author of the letter was none other than Marianne Young, surgeon's wife of the 28th recently returned from Varna, who, despite the wall of prejudice she encountered against the 'propriety' of employing wives of soldiers as nurses, was still arguing the case for the women out in the Crimea to be 'trained into habits of usefulness'. Young also reminded the British public of the plight of the courageous women who had gone with the army to Gallipoli and Varna and who were still awaiting passage home and of which 'poor creatures the public hear nothing'.[12]

Young's suggestion was ignored, no doubt because the disreputable behaviour of some of the army wives at Scutari, who spent their time drinking and whoring, made them too much of a liability. But, nevertheless, several soldiers' wives (and some widows) who had not been selected to go on the strength now applied to be nurses – it clearly being a way, as they saw of it, of being nearer to their husbands on campaign. Mrs Cotterall of the 97th Foot, Catherine Davies of the 72nd Highlanders, Eliza Donaldson of the 4th Light Dragoons all tried and failed to be taken on. As did Matilda Norman, wife of a soldier in the 90th, whose touching letter to the selectors also fell on deaf ears:

> I am Soldgers Wife and my Husband is just gone out to the East . . . the Colonel been well satisfied with my Carertor [character] thought I should

be very useful in the Regt but having heard that was being Nurses sent out I would do any thing to go for I there might be able to help him in his dieing moments I am Young and Strong and do not mind what I suffer should Sir you not think me Experienced I will try and get into a Horespitll for a time I really do not recorse to fly to . . .[13]

Mrs Jane Harding, wife of Grenadier Guard William Harding and one of the 32 women on the strength at the Guards Camp at Scutari, was, however, engaged as a nurse in December, as were several other wives, but this was done informally and no official record kept. In general the army failed to organize its own soldiers' wives, which it could and should have done in Varna, where the British Army had had no nurses at all during the cholera epidemic.

By now, Britain's French allies had yet again stolen a march on her. Sisters of Charity had already been present at Varna, sent out in groups of 25 as and when they were required, and by early September the French government had asked the Order of St Vincent de Paul to provide another 100 sisters for the hospital service of the Army in the East. On 29 September, 50 nuns sailed on board the Gange from Marseilles, with more to follow. By 30 November, The Times was informing its readers that there were now 62 French sisters attached to the field ambulances and hospitals and that some had been sent to the Crimea and were already having to 'bear the hard life of the camp, without any other shelter than a tent'.[14]

By the time the government finally appointed Nightingale as Superintendent of the Female Nursing Establishment of the English General Hospitals in Turkey, with a budget of £1,000 for essential expenses and contingencies, the Catholic Church in Britain had already taken the initiative. Under instruction from the Bishop of Southwark, a party of five nuns from the Convent of the Sisters of Mercy at Jacob's Island, one of the worst Dickensian slums of Bermondsey, had been organized. Led by their superior, Mother Clare Moore, they had already left for France in hopes that this spontaneous act of Catholic public-spiritedness and charity might dilute rampant anti-Catholic feeling in Britain, much of which had been fomented by the Oxford (or Tractarian) movement, towards High Church practice in the Anglican Church. The nuns were under strict instructions to be cautious in matters of religion and only discuss it with patients of their own faith, but with Nightingale now officially designated as sole arbiter on the selection of nurses, the Bermondsey nuns were swiftly told, in no uncertain terms, to wait in Paris for Nightingale's own team to join them.

It would take a woman of considerable administrative genius, of supreme self-possession and ruthless iron will to cut through the difficulties of the selection process for nurses in the record speed that the desperate situation necessitated. Sidney Herbert was most anxious to underline the fact that Nightingale had been appointed by the War Office to act in 'the strictest subordination to the chief medical officer of the hospital', but in fact her whole career in the Crimea would run counter to that. The only way she could make the British hospital at Scutari function, and also prove to the public back home that female nurses could be effective in a war zone, would be by assuming dictatorial control and fighting British military bureaucracy tooth and nail to the bitter end – a position that she was ever after reluctant to relinquish.

But how to disassociate nursing, as it then stood, from its enduring bad press and the public perception of the professional nurse as that classic Dickensian incompetent, the gin-swigging Mrs Gamp, who for a decade had given hospital as well as domiciliary nurses a bad name? The basic problem confronting Nightingale was a major social one: there simply was no respectable body of professional, trained nurses from whom the Crimean team could be drawn. It was a fact noted by Dr Peter Pincoffs, who himself visited the hospitals in the Crimea:

> If some of the paid nurses were found less efficient, and in their
> behaviour toward orderlies and by their general conduct gave cause for
> complaint, the reason is simply that in the hurry of the moment the
> selection was not carefully made, or rather that a selection was
> impossible, as in England up to that period such nurses, as would have
> been desirable, did not exist as a class.[15]

Hospital nurses, such as they were, only had the most rudimentary training and duties, reduced to little more than domestic servants on the hospital wards – making beds, emptying slops, feeding patients. All the traditional duties of nursing as we now perceive it – changing dressings, taking blood pressure and pulse rates, dealing with bedsores, administering drugs – remained the preserve of male doctors and male medical students.

From the outset, in order to counter the problem of the many ill-suited but ardent would-be nurses from the middle classes who applied, Nightingale set strict rules on age (24 being the minimum) and experience. The selection process would be highly discriminating and nobody, however kindly their intentions, would be considered 'without evidence of their experience or fitness to perform the arduous duties they undertake'.[16] So candidates such as Emily Hall of West Wickham in Kent, desperate to do something with her 'worthless, useless' life, received a prompt rebuff to the effect that ladies were not suitable because, with their greater sensitivities, they were 'less manageable'; Miss Nightingale, she was informed, required women from the 'lower classes'. At her comfortable London home, the equally bored and idle 24-year-old Isabel Arundell, having been roused to a frenzy of good intentions by the *Times* reports, would also repeatedly volunteer:

> I have made three struggles to be allowed to join Florence Nightingale.
> How I envy the women who are allowed to go out as nurses! I have
> written again and again to Florence Nightingale; but the superintendent
> has answered me that I am too young and inexperienced, and will
> not do.[17]

With so many untrained applicants, the recruiting of nuns was favoured. It was also a way of keeping down expenses, as they would be unpaid; and it was a move that, politically, could not be avoided, bearing in mind that a good third of the rank and file of the British army were Irish Catholics. The letters and testimonials of some 617 women who applied to nurse, still preserved at the Public Record Office, bear witness to a very diverse range of women and the ruthlessness with which their applications were rejected. Daughters of surgeons, doctors, army officers and clergymen applied in their dozens and were all refused as too young or too inexperienced. All three daughters – Frances, Georgina and Louisa Elton

– of a Somerset rector volunteered together and were politely turned down. Even Mrs Jane Carnell and her two daughters, Mary and Martha, were not taken on, despite having experience as nurses at Bristol's Royal Infirmary. Mrs Eugenia Huntingford, wife of the Canon of Hereford Cathedral, didn't make it either, despite her glowing ecumenical testimonials. But one woman who epitomized the plight of middle-class women of her day *was* accepted: Eliza Polidori, maiden aunt to the painter Dante Gabriel Rossetti. Now 45, she had been consigned, as youngest daughter, to spending most of her adult life shackled to the home in dutiful service to her ageing and increasingly sickly parents. Thanks to her years of domiciliary nursing and her mature age she would be taken on, but sadly not her niece – the budding poet Christina Rossetti – who was desperate to go out to Scutari with her. As Polidori's nephew William Michael Rossetti would later recall, 'the Crimean affair' was, for 'Miss Polly Dory' (as she was comically reported in the press), 'about the only "adventure" of her long life'.[18]

In the early autumn of 1854, a group of women in Oxford had proved their worth as nurses during a cholera epidemic that had also struck London and the Irish community in Plymouth, where Sellonite nuns from Devonport, some of whom were later recruited by Nightingale, had devotedly nursed the sick. The cholera in Oxford had been made worse by a simultaneous outbreak of smallpox across the city's poorest districts. At St Thomas the Martyr, 'the black sheep among parishes' notorious for its rookeries of thieves and prostitutes, the nursing of the sick in segregated buildings (in fact three converted cattle sheds) had been organized and supervised by Dr Henry Acland with the support of his friend the writer and philanthropist Felicia Skene – aunt of the young Janie Skene, whose letter had just been published in *The Times*. Skene had helped recruit a group of women and trained them in the particular rigours of cholera nursing. With Nightingale about to depart for the East, Skene offered her team to Mr and Mrs Charles Bracebridge, friends of Nightingale's who were recruiting on her behalf before going out to Scutari to join her. The Bracebridges travelled to Oxford to inspect Skene's candidates, the women ranged before them in a long line in Skene's dining room. 'Kind-hearted as Mrs Bracebridge was,' Skene later remarked, 'her proceedings were somewhat in the "off with their heads!" style of the famous duchess in "Alice in Wonderland". If the sudden questions fired at each in succession were not answered in a way she thought quite satisfactory, – "She won't do; send her out," was the decided command.'[19]

Dr Acland himself had had no hesitation in recommending his hospital nurses, remarking that 'of all the nurses I happen to have known, the three persons I would rather have in my house, in the case of any grievous illness befalling me or mine, are or have been all of them hospital nurses'.[20] (Interestingly, Acland specifically ordered that his nurses be allowed only one bottle of porter per day and no brandy; Nightingale severely restricted the intake of brandy in the Crimea, it clearly being the ruination of many a good hospital nurse.) Despite Acland's recommendations, several of the Oxford nurses were rejected; but Mrs Susannah Faulkner, a widow with ten children, was one of those hired at 16 shillings a week.

Rejections had been equally summary for the three black women who are known to have applied to nurse during the Crimean War – Elizabeth Purcell, a Miss Belgrave, and Mary Seacole, the remarkable Creole nurse. The decision to turn down Miss Belgrave, despite her visible robustness, because a 'West Indian constitution is not the one best able to bear the fatigue of nursing', was a flaccid one.[21] West Indian nurses like her might well have had years of experience in nursing fever and cholera victims, as Mary Seacole most certainly had. Nor is there any disguising the blatant racism of Miss Belgrave's rejection, on the grounds that 'some English patients would object to a nurse being so nearly a person of color', nor that of the 52-year-old Elizabeth Purcell from Shepherd's Bush, the wife of a 'respectable soldier' at the Royal Hospital Chelsea, who, despite this, was turned down for being too old and 'almost black'.[22]

Mary Seacole, after sailing to England from Jamaica at her own expense to volunteer, trudged from the War Office, to the Quartermaster General's Department, to the Medical Department, to the managers of the *Times* Crimean Fund, and even laid siege to Sidney Herbert's home in Belgrave Square in her quest to be taken on. She made no bones about her own rejection: her references were first-class and her years of experience nursing sick British naval and army officers in Jamaica indisputable, yet the response was unequivocal – 'had there been a vacancy, I should not have been chosen to fill it'. 'Did these ladies [Mrs Herbert and her recruiters] shrink from accepting my aid,' Seacole wondered somewhat tactfully for her white Victorian readers in 1857, 'because my blood flowed beneath a somewhat duskier skin than theirs?'[23]

All nurses joining Nightingale's team were obliged to sign a contract agreeing to submit to her authority, as servants of the British government, a fact which created and fostered enduring problems. Nightingale had the first right of dismissal. The salary offered was good; for the working-class hospital nurses, many of them widows with families to support, the Crimean posting was fairly lucrative. They were offered a generous 12 to 14 shillings a week, which could rise to 18 shillings after three months' service, depending on good conduct. But there were caveats. Hospital nurses were collectively deemed to be morally unsuitable and unreliable for the delicate task of bedside nursing and would be consigned to largely subordinate domestic duties. (In the main illiterate, too, they would not of course be able to write letters for or read the Bible and other edifying works to the wounded at their bedsides.) It was the nuns, and subsequently the genteel lady volunteers who went to the Crimea unsalaried and untainted by mammon, who would be charged with the supervisory role of ensuring the nurses did their jobs properly – and without engaging in fraternization or promiscuous conduct with the soldiers.

In order not to provoke sexual tension between the male sick and wounded and female nurses, Nightingale and her recruiters had pre-occupied themselves with selecting older, fatter and more matronly women who looked as though they had the stamina for the work expected of them. But this was no failsafe: by January 1855 Nightingale had to qualify her directive: 'I must bar these fat drunken old dames. Above 14 stone we will not have – the provision of bedstead is not strong enough.'[24] Certainly, the uniforms provided by the government did nothing to enhance the female form and everything to minimize its attractiveness, their objective clearly to desexualize the wearer and 'ensure respect'. They comprised an itchy grey tweed gown, grey worsted jacket, short woollen cloak, check apron and black straw bonnet. The addition of flowers or ribbons to bonnets was strictly forbidden. A brown holland cloth sash was to be worn across the shoulder with 'Scutari Hospital' (or whichever hospital they were based at) embroidered on it in red. The gowns, made by contract and all the same size – long or short being the only options – were ill-fitting and uncomfortable to wear. Nuns were, of course, allowed to wear their habits; but even the soberly garbed sister Aloysius Doyle remarked on the ugliness of the nurses' uniform: 'That ladies could be found to walk into such a costume was certainly a triumph of grace over nature.'[25] For one hospital nurse the old-fashioned white caps of pleated lace were the last straw. Rebecca Lawfield, who had had some rudimentary training at King's Hospital and St John's House, complained loudly to Florence Nightingale:

> I came out Ma'am, prepared to submit to every thing – to be put upon in every way – but there are some things, Ma'am, one can't submit to – There is caps, Ma'am, that suits one face, and some that suits anothers, and if I'd known, Ma'am, about the caps, great as was my desire to come out to nurse at Scutari, I wouldn't have come, Ma'am.[26]

While the nurses were being selected, many of the male British public and especially the medical profession remained highly sceptical that women would be able to tolerate the work they would be expected to undertake at the British hospitals in Turkey. Respectable women should not be expected or even wish to deal with the drudgery of hospital work or of washing and dressing the filthy, half-naked bodies of wounded men. It was degrading for the women, and humiliating for the men – and in both cases unsexing. At the very best, the work should be left to nursing sisters with a religious affiliation, or failing that, male orderlies.

To counter such arguments, others stressed the moral courage and devotional motives of women going as volunteers – that they were not seeking so much to supplant the roles of men but rather to offer those unique feminine gifts and 'affectionate' and 'beneficent' ministrations which only women can properly perform, motivated by a profound sense of religious duty – in other words, they were demonstrating precisely those natural feminine sentiments which Frederika Bremer had attempted to draw on only a couple of months before. On 11 November, *Punch* weighed in with a satirical account of the recruitment of nurses, pointing out that attending soldiers was hardly an appropriate duty for 'young ladies of rank and fashion, who knew not even as yet what it was to nurse a baby' – nor, by association, what a man's genitals looked like.[27] 'How will it be with the lady-nurses,' asked another letter to *The Times*, 'to bear the sight of blood without fainting, and to refrain from joining in the patients' shrieks when under the scalpel and the saw?' Women from sheltered backgrounds, where they had been protected against anything that might shock female delicacy and taste, and who certainly would not have seen a dead or mutilated body before, will 'find their ability to endure fatigue and bear up against disgust sadly inferior to their anxious desire to do so'.[28] 'You do not know what soldiers are like' was the repeated argument used to dissuade women up and down the country. Heaven forfend that the women of England should expose themselves to the coarseness and profanities of the common soldier, who was very different from 'a lady's *beau idéal* of a *preux chevalier*'. As for the 'common run of nurses', no woman in her right mind should associate with a species who were 'accustomed to drown disgust in brandy'.[29]

Many officers in the Crimea shared in this sentiment and wrote home to the eager wives, daughters, nieces and sisters who cherished romantic ambitions to go out as nurses, pouring cold water on their aspirations, much in the same vein as Captain Campbell of the 46th: 'If you know any lady mad enough to come out here as a hospital nurse, use all your interest to put her into a strait-waistcoat as soon as possible'. The sending out of women was to some of the surgeons and doctors at Scutari a slight on their professional integrity and abilities: in their eyes it was an admission of failure. Far better, suggested one reader of the *News of the World*, to send out male medical students – in a very pointed swipe at the eager numbers of lady scripture readers, many in the throes of a fashionable flirtation with High Anglicanism:

> The tractarian ladies would do much better by staying at home, and
> giving what money they can spare to provide good assistance for the
> wounded and dying, than by personally going into the hospitals. Little
> Lady Fannypops, who fancies that her soul would have a better chance of
> being saved if she were to dress and poultice a soldier's wound, or assist in

the amputation of a member, should be instructed differently. Sensible
charity would send out a lot of medical students. We say it again, one
half-dozen of cigar-smoking, casino-dancing, insolvent medical students,
would be more good than a hundred women with heads full of tractarian
discipline and the doctrines of Dr Pusey . . . A few of the wildest harum-
scarum fellows that walk the hospitals, would do the poor fellows at
Scutari more good than the litany-chanting genuflexing women, that
Puseydom could send forth.[30]

Despite her many doubts about the suitability of women as nurses in
military hospitals full of men, Nightingale was a pragmatist, and the
urgency of addressing the problem overruled all the many arguments put
before her. It was, in her view, a temporary measure: 'though temporary
may be a long word – as long as the war lasts'. With her characteristic
exactitude she considered the employment of women to be 'not an
inexpedient principle, but . . . an unprincipled expedient'.[31] And an
unprincipled expedient which, much to the disappointment of her many
detractors, she later demonstrated had kept the hospitals running through
that first terrible winter.

The original number of nurses recruited for Nightingale's party had
been 40, but the day before leaving, Nightingale had had second thoughts
about Mrs Dorothy Travers and had told her her services were no longer
required. On 21 October, therefore, Nightingale left London Bridge
Station with six Anglican sisters from St John's House and 14
'professional' hospital nurses; two days later, five Catholic nuns from an
enclosed order, the Sisters of the Faithful Virgin at Norwood in Surrey,
and eight Sellonite Sisters from Devonport followed them in the company
of Charles Bracebridge and his wife Selina. This was the first of ten groups
of nurses who would sail from Britain to the Crimea between October
1854 and January 1856 – some 229 women in all, but the figure takes no
account of the number of army wives already helping with the sick and
wounded on transports in the Black Sea, or out at Scutari or in the Crimea
in camp and, later, the regimental hospitals – some of whom were paid.

The Nightingale team left, having been given strict instructions on
what luggage was allowed: one trunk of clothing and a few essential items

such as brush, comb, toothbrush and that ubiquitous British essential – an umbrella. The government wisely provided them all with India-rubber galoshes. In Paris the group met up with the five Bermondsey nuns who had gone ahead of them; but even here, although Nightingale would develop a close personal bond with the Catholic Mother Moore, the tensions were clear. The social divide between the nuns and the working-class nurses who liked a drink, had coarse manners and used bad language immediately made itself felt. And there were personal rivalries, too, between Rebecca Lawfield, who led the St John's House group, and Emma Fagg, who refused to submit to her authority. At Marseilles the group of 39 lost another member when Mrs Larscher, who had been hired for her experience as a family nurse to Sidney Herbert's brother, fell ill and had to be left behind.

On 17 October the women sailed on board the steam packet *Vectis*. One of the Sellonites was Sarah Anne Terrot. The daughter of the Bishop of Edinburgh, she had rejected her comfortable home life to dedicate herself to philanthropic work, going against her father's wishes in pursuit of a career in nursing. Joining the Sellonites at Devonport in 1847, she had become one of their most accomplished and respected nurses. In her diary she recalled the voyage in vivid detail. Even at the best of times the *Vectis* shipped water, which washed over the decks and came down the cabin stairs and soaked their cabins, despite the portholes being closed. The air below decks was thick and fetid; the smell of vomit was everywhere; some of the women were so prostrated by constant retching that they lay on the soaking-wet floors of their cabins. Terrot could not bear the coffin-like confinement and the rocking of her tiny upper bunk, nor the legions of bugs it contained, and spent her nights sitting on deck. But beyond Malta they hit a gale and were forced to retreat to the stifling atmosphere below. At the height of the storm, with the sea raging and the wind whistling, the nuns huddled together, praying out loud, one of them in Welsh, for a 'speedy and Christian end'. 'It was a dismal scene,' Terrot wrote, 'the dark wet cabin, with one miserable swinging light, just enough to show the sick lying about in every direction.'[32] Then the ship's surgeon sent down a pailful of warm negus. 'Hope revived, and life seemed worth living, and the waves did not seem so appalling.' But they were all exhausted, cold, wet and dirty and the constant exposure to salt water and sea spray left a fine crust of crystallized salt on their faces.

The waters were finally calm when they reached the Dardanelles and on 4 November the nurses found themselves 'lying, as it were, in the arms of the Queen of the East, in the Golden Horn of the great imperial Constantinople'.[33] Their new home, however, was not to be in the beautiful glittering city before them, but what Terrot considered the 'ugliest object visible' – the Scutari barracks. On arrival, they were served tea without milk and stale sour bread, but Terrot, for one, was thankful to be once more on terra firma and 'was not disposed to grumble'.

SEVEN

Every
Accumulation of
Misery

With Florence Nightingale's appointment and departure for the
Crimea effected with such speed, many of the British public were
still asking themselves 'Who *is* Mrs Nightingale?' as she left. The papers
and illustrated journals were soon awash with reports of her work and
mini-hagiographies of her life, the sanitized coverage all accentuating the
now clichéd image of the Crimean nurse as angel of the bedside, whilst
underplaying the horrifying sights with which the real nurses were having
to contend. Such evocative descriptions ensured the relentless march of
Nightingale's canonization as 'the Lady of the Lamp'. But in truth
Florence Nightingale was to spend much of her war – up to 12 hours a day
– not ministering to the wounded at all but stuck behind a desk dealing
with the bureaucracy of running such a vast establishment as Scutari.

In the interim, and before her arrival, British bureaucratic bloody-
mindedness in Constantinople had refused a generous offer of help from
American residents. Cyrus Hamlin, co-founder of the American Missionary
College there, had offered to organize a dozen or so of his male English and
American students as night watchers for the hospital. The offer had been
rejected by Chief Physician Dr Duncan Menzies and was again turned down
when it was made to Commissary General Conrad Potgieter, on the

grounds that the British authorities could not admit 'any outside interference'.[1] Nor would they admit either advice or help from the French, whose own orderly and efficient hospital service and ambulance corps, where system ruled and the Sisters of Charity worked with quiet and unchallenging dedication, was already in place. The French Sisters even cooked for the wounded officers and without complaint. Their dedication, wrote Cardinal Wiseman the following year, was 'an illustration of power, and organization'. Had the British government approached the French at the outbreak of war, so the superior in charge of the French nurses had told him, they would have sent out a group of fifty trained nuns immediately to tend the British sick and wounded.[2] For all the French claims, however, the sisters would not quite fulfill Nightingale's idea of a trained nurse; she saw them as *consolatrices* – the administrators of extras, their primary task being to organize the linen stores and offer Christian consolation at the bedside, without exercising any real, practical nursing skills such as dealing with bedsores.[3]

When Nightingale and her team arrived at Scutari after their exhausting 12-day journey – during which she had spent the entire time holed up in her cabin, violently seasick – everybody, including local correspondent Thomas Chenery and John MacDonald, sent to Scutari as administrator of the *Times* fund, predicted failure. And indeed the situation that greeted Nightingale was one of imminent catastrophe. The wards and corridors of Scutari were crammed with the sick – many suffering from cholera and dysentery, their bodies suppurating with sores, their clothes and bedding unwashed for weeks and even the most basic of supplies lacking: 'no mops – no plates, no wooden trays – no slippers, no shoe brushes, no blacking, no knives & forks, no spoons, no scissors . . . no basins, no towelling – no Chloride of lime'.[4] With no cutlery available either, the unwashed sick and wounded were forced to eat their ration of meat with their bare hands. The stink was overwhelming. 'I have been well acquainted with the dwellings of the worst parts of most of the great cities in Europe,' Nightingale wrote, 'but have never been in any atmosphere which I could compare with that of the Barrack Hospital at night.'[5]

Yet despite the vastness of this place, where there was 'every accumulation of misery' as Nurse Fanny Taylor would later describe it, the atmosphere was strangely, eerily silent, like a catacomb.[6] Eyewitnesses would comment on the extraordinarily stoical and uncomplaining way in which the common soldier accepted and endured his suffering. Margaret Goodman, one of the Sellonites, observed: 'During the day scarcely a sound was heard in the wards or corridors (for the passages also were filled with patients) save the step of the orderly or the voice of the doctor.' It was only at night, in the dark, that there arose a strange, haunting 'moan of pain' and 'the murmurings of delirium'. It caused enormous distress to Fanny Taylor, too, on her first night-watch duty, for the saddest part was not so much hearing men's pitiful calls for 'mother' but the knowledge 'that there were many dying who might be saved if we could have given each the care we were bestowing on *one*'.[7]

On their arrival, the nurses were accommodated in the bleak, sparsely furnished north-west tower of the barracks. The nuns shared one room, the hospital nurses the largest and Nightingale and Mrs Bracebridge another. Here the washing facilities were nil, the access to drinking water extremely limited (less than a pint a day) and the food inadequate and inedible. The nurses had only a small copper basin each from which to eat, drink – and also in which to wash. Between eight of them in one room there were only two knives, two spoons and three forks. They had no fires and an icy wind howled through the broken window panes at night. Worse still, they now found themselves contending with another more personal war – against the 'heavy dragoons' of lice and the 'light cavalry' of fleas, not to mention the hordes of rats that came out at night. The levels of vermin throughout Scutari were 'past conception'.[8] For the nuns the lack of privacy and a quiet space in which to pray caused considerable personal distress too.

With only one doctor for every fifty or so patients, Nightingale assigned 28 of the group to the massive Barrack Hospital and the other 10 to the smaller General Hospital nearby. There was an urgent need to separate surgical from medical cases, but she was faced with terrible overcrowding, with four miles of beds, barely 18 inches apart, many of the mattresses laid on the bare floor, in rooms that let in the rain, wind and cold. With so many men not even having straw mattresses on which to lie, let alone pillows and blankets, the nurses were immediately commandeered to make crude sacking palliasses stuffed with chopped straw. Medical supplies of the most basic kind were in very short supply, especially lint, bandages and dressings, as well as clean linen and shirts for the wounded. The wooden floors were filthy, rotting and crawling with vermin; the sanitation was non-existent, with overflowing, unusable privies. With so many men suffering from diarrhoea, the only lavatory facilities were large wooden tubs standing in the wards and corridors, which created a stink throughout the whole hospital and were left to a handful of inefficient and querulous male orderlies to empty. The water supply too was almost at a standstill, its pipes old and broken and polluted with dead dogs and rats. The lack of proper heating made it impossible to keep the patients warm. Whichever way one looked everything contributed to the relentless increase in fevers, gangrene and septicemia and the spread of dysentery and cholera among the patients.

Nightingale immediately set about employing her skills as a 'kind of General Dealer', using her own money and the *Times* fund to obtain essential supplies – thousands of shirts, socks and drinking cups, for example – as well as organizing the cooking of special food for the wounded – arrowroot, broth, sago, eggs, jellies – in the nurses' own kitchen. Here Mrs Clarke, Nightingale's housekeeper from Harley Street, quickly proved herself invaluable, standing '23 hours out of the 24 at the great table in our great-room, cutting, cooking, ordering, tea making etc.',[9] and occasionally making an excursion to the nearest wards to give a teaspoon of warm arrowroot or chicken broth to those too faint to feed themselves. Sadly, Mrs Clarke soon also fell ill and was invalided home just before Christmas.

Within a few days of the nurses' arrival, Scutari was overflowing with hundreds of wounded from the Battle of Inkerman. They were in an indescribable state, the majority staggering in on foot though scarcely able to make the effort. Many had lost an arm or a leg and most had severe gunshot or shell wounds of some kind. But there was something else: they all had that peculiar, distanced look about the eyes which no amount of dirt or whiskers could conceal. It was the unmistakable outward mark of the inner suffering in which they all shared. A great many arrived in rags, the shirts of those that still had them stiff with blood – and lice. The first task of the nurses was to help the men undress and to unbind their 'ghastly and revolting wounds', many heaving with maggots, which had not been dressed since the day they had been inflicted, four days before. Then they gave them a wash – their first in weeks – and a clean shirt. Such ministrations came as luxuries to these exhausted mutilated men. Scutari seemed a haven of rest, even though, as Nurse Terrot observed, they lay 'in places such as no gentleman would allow any horse he cared for to be stabled'.[10] They died with alarming speed and in huge numbers. As fast as one man breathed his last he was sewn in his blanket, carried off and buried within hours. Another man soon took his place – the same bed filling and emptying several times in the course of a week with a succession of pale, ghastly, wasted men brought in to die, often spending their last hours in silence. One overworked nurse, writing home urgently requesting 'wine, and bottles of chicken broth, preserved meat for soup' and other things for the sick and wounded, seemed totally accepting of the fact that the nurses' work 'may lie for one year – it may be for ten'. That did not concern her; what did was the terrifyingly high death rate and the enormous task in stemming it that confronted her and her colleagues:

> You must be told again, that we do not complain of remissness of the authorities to do what they can, but even the necessary delays are fatal to the men, reduced as they are to the last stage of exhaustion. I expect to find two more dead on going round this morning; that will be a proportion of eleven to thirty in two days.[11]

The revulsion which some of the nuns and later lady volunteers must have felt when they first encountered the wounded is hard to imagine; it must have been a shock to the system to discover that the horrific wounds inflicted on the battlefield were a far remove from what their limited life experience could ever have conjured up. In time some learned to love and respect the nobility of the common soldier, but many nurses sent to the Crimea would prove emotionally and constitutionally unequal to the task before them. Miss Sellon had sent her party of sisters from Devonport with the exhortation: 'when you are attending the wounds of the soldiers, try and think of the wounds of our Lord'.[12] But the grim reality of finding wounds full of maggots, or removing linseed poultices for frostbite to find pieces of decayed flesh coming away with them, would have been nauseating in the extreme. One surgeon at Scutari noted that after only a few weeks, several of the nuns and lady volunteers who followed later were 'really disappointed at what they have come to, and wish themselves home again'. One had admitted to him that they had been 'carried away by the excitement at home and instead of coming out to attend poor noble fellows, they have to attend to poor miserable soldiers covered with fleas'.[13]

Meanwhile, in her efficient and businesslike manner, having discovered that the official army washing contract for the hospital with local Greek women (Turkish women, as Muslims, could not be hired for such work) had completely broken down, Nightingale set about addressing this urgent problem. It was also seen as a way of employing some of the army wives languishing at Scutari – 10 to 14 shillings a week was a princely sum to them. In a crudely organized wash house the women began dealing with the mountains of linen and clothing that had accumulated, a highly labour-intensive task considering that initially they had only a few basic utensils and some charcoal and had to bribe the orderlies with porter to bring up hot water.

...

Back in October, when Nightingale and her nurses had been enduring their stormy crossing, women in Russia had also been mobilizing. Having heard of the work of the French Sisters of Charity and of Nightingale's team of nurses now on their way to the Crimea, influential and high-born Russian women were just as eager to play their part. One of the best-known volunteers was Ekaterina Mikhailovna Bakunina (a cousin of the Russian anarchist Mikhail Bakunin). From a wealthy and privileged family, the daughter of the governor of St Petersburg and granddaughter of a Russian admiral, she remembered her horror the evening she first received news of the allied landings in the Crimea, a place popular as a holiday resort with the upper classes, where, as a young girl, she had spent the summers of 1849 and 1850 with her sister. 'I could not imagine that this beautiful little corner of our great empire could be turned into a brutal theatre of war.' Her response to hearing about the French and British nurses already out at Constantinople was a spontaneous one: 'And what about us? Were we really not going to do anything?'[14]

It was not only British bureaucracy and red tape that created delays in getting care to the wounded. In Russia too it had slowed down attempts to get urgent medical help to Sevastopol, argued for by the eminent surgeon Nikolay Pirogov. He had struggled against official obduracy for weeks in trying to get permission to travel south. Once again, as in Britain, it was the philanthropists who got things moving. In St Petersburg a wealthy aristocrat, Grand Duchess Elena Pavlovna (Tsar Nicholas I's German-born, widowed sister-in-law), had used her own money to found the Sisters of Mercy of the Community of the Cross in the Care of the Wounded and Sick the day after the Battle of Inkerman, in order to provide teams of nurses for the dressing stations and mobile hospitals being set up in the Crimea.[15] The women, who ranged from the lesser nobility and families with military backgrounds to a few humble but literate women (all recruits, unlike the British nurses, had to be able to read and write), were expected to commit for a year's service, without pay. As a semi-religious group, they wore a brown nun's habit and gold crucifix on a ribbon, with white nun's cap tied under the chin.

Meanwhile, in the Crimea itself, women from a local community of Sisters of Mercy in Odessa had been doing what little they could to nurse a few wounded officers; as had a contingent of Compassionate Widows (the *Frauen des Barmherzigen Wittwen Instituts* established during the Napoleonic Wars by the Dowager Empress, Mary of Württemberg) at the hospitals at Simferopol. Now a much larger, organized body of trained women was needed and Grand Duchess Elena Pavlovna wanted to appoint Pirogov to supervise this. Pirogov himself had an instinctive belief in the value of women volunteers as nurses, but despite his outstanding credentials as an eminent surgeon and member of five European scientific academies, he was faced with the same old social barriers and official prejudices against sending 'the fair sex' to a war zone. Genteel, high-born Russian women would not, it was felt, be able to endure the harsh conditions or the horrific sights of mutilation and death. Wild stories were put about by old diehards in the Russian army that it was all bound to end in immorality: women's presence among the troops would inflame male sexuality and lead to mass rape and pregnancy among the sisters – and a corresponding increase in syphilis. The Russian medical establishment, meanwhile, had its own agenda; much like its British counterpart, it did not want to see its own monopoly and authority challenged by women. Nevertheless, Tsar Nicholas I acceded to the grand duchess's appeal and issued a decree recognizing the work of the Community of the Holy Cross. On 10 November Pirogov finally set off for Sevastopol, with two doctors and one medical assistant. Much of his initial medical work in the Crimea – training and the provision of equipment, medication and dressings – was funded by his patron the grand duchess, who had accumulated and stored many supplies, including precious quinine obtained via family contacts in England, in the basement of her own home.

When he arrived in Sevastopol on 23 November Pirogov found 2,000 wounded from Alma, Balaklava and Inkerman all crammed in together, lying on dirty mattresses, their wounds infested with maggots and soaked with filth. All they had to protect them from the cold were their army greatcoats. The once grand and stately Assembly of Nobles – all chandeliers, pink marble and gilding – had been turned into a makeshift hospital. Over the next ten days, Pirogov's surgical powers and levels of energy seemed superhuman as he and his team operated almost non-stop, like a production line, sometimes on three patients at the same time.[16] He set up a strictly observed triage system for dealing with new arrivals in four basic categories: the mortally wounded or dying who were immediately entrusted to the care of priests and the devoted care of the sisters (when they arrived) at the Gushchin House; the seriously wounded needing immediate operations at the Assembly of Nobles; the less seriously wounded who could wait 24 hours or more for treatment; and those with slight injuries likely to recover and go back to the front lines who could be sent on to the Nikolaevsk Battery and other dressing stations. In addition, Pirogov ensured that at all times a couple of sisters were on call to provide the exhausted and thirsty wounded with wine, punch, tea or hot broth. In all cases requiring operations, extensive anaesthesia, by means of chloroform, was used, far more so than at Scutari.

A party of 34 Russian sisters of the Community of the Cross led by Ekaterina Stakhovich had followed Pirogov to the Crimea in early November, having undergone a brief induction course in the basic principles of nursing at St Petersburg's Army Hospital No. 1 before leaving; later groups were given two or three months' preparatory training before being sent to the Crimea. The women arrived in Simferopol, the administrative HQ for the war about 40 miles inland from Sevastopol, on 1 December after a tedious and difficult journey – much of it over 600 miles of dirt roads. On the road into the city, in the pouring rain, they were greeted by a vision of hell:

> on each of the wagons [conveying wounded from Sevastopol] lay two or three sick men and amputees, soaked to the bone and perishing with cold. Animals and men had equal difficulty moving through the mud, which was up to their knees. There were carcasses everywhere, swollen dead bullocks lay belly up, their stomachs bursting with load cracks. In one giant cacophony one heard the moaning of the wounded, the hoarse screeching of whole flocks of scavenging birds scenting out carrion, the cries of exhausted drovers, and the distant thunder of cannon fire from Sevastopol.[17]

For the time being, Pirogov decided to divide the sisters between the existing infirmaries in Simferopol, designating three groups: those who were to attend the wounded, make bandages, bind their wounds and assist in operations; those who took care of medicines and organized their distribution; and those who undertook the more general housekeeping tasks of washing, changing bedlinen and feeding patients and keeping the hospitals clean. The tasks were clearly differentiated and, unlike Nightingale's battles with the nurses at Scutari, there was no dispute over who did what among the Russian sisters. Not long after their arrival, however, many of the women were struck by an epidemic of typhus and their fellow sisters were obliged to nurse them as well as the wounded. Meanwhile, in Sevastopol, hundreds of unsung local women – among them Dasha Sevastopolskaya, as well as soldiers' and sailors' wives and daughters – had continued to use their own initiative, looking after the wounded at dressing stations and in their own homes, tearing up their own bedlinen and petticoats to make bandages. Dasha by now was also assisting Pirogov in operations. He was full of admiration for these women and ensured that their services were retained even after the sisters of the

Community of the Cross had recovered in sufficient numbers to travel on to Sevastopol in January, having lost four of their number to typhus. The second contingent of 13 nurses, led by Sister Merkurova, were already installed in Sevastopol when the first party arrived; the third group, led by Ekaterina Bakunina, who had overcome extremely fierce family opposition to join the Sisters of Mercy, arrived on 12 January. On 30 January the remaining 25 women under Sister Stakhovich (who herself had been seriously ill with typhus) travelled the slow, congested, muddy route to the south side of Sevastopol, where Pirogov greeted them in the mud 'in dirty boots with a greatcoat slung over his shoulder'.[18]

From the outset, Pirogov was convinced that the presence of women in his hospital alleviated much distress and suffering. He was impressed by the stoicism and adaptability of the sisters despite their youth and inexperience. They rapidly became 'absolutely indispensable' to him; Grand Duchess Elena Pavlovna, he was sure, 'had done mankind a true service'.[19] For the women not only braved the constant shellfire but also continued to face infection by typhus which was rampant among the wounded. Their working conditions during the constant bombardment were appalling:

> with the noise of bursting shells – groans and mangled limbs – the steam of the gore (which was an inch deep under foot) mingled with the fumes of chloroform – the doors opening and shutting – and wounded men continually carried in and out, with the short word of orders, 'on the table', 'on the bed', 'to this hospital', 'to that hospital', – the white mantles of the Sisters moving silently to and fro among the grey military cloaks of officers and men – and then at night the whole made more dismal by the light of candles and lanterns.[20]

Pirogov operated with the speed and precision of a man with a mission, claiming that it was entirely possible to carry out ten major amputations in 1 hour 45 minutes, 'even with the help of not very experienced assistants'. 'If operations are performed simultaneously on three tables by 15 doctors,' he added, 'it is possible to carry out 90 amputations in 6 hours and 15 minutes, and a little over 100 in seven hours.'[21] Most important of all perhaps, in terms of medical innovation, Pirogov was very aware of the exposure of wounds to 'contaminating vapours' from nearby latrines and other sources of infection. He made a point of separating post-operative patients into those with clean wounds and those whose wounds were suppurating and liable to gangrene – a highly infectious condition.

...

In England, meanwhile, Florence Nightingale's associate Mary Stanley (who had been privately preparing to convert to Roman Catholicism) had come increasingly under the influence of the Irish Sisters of Mercy from Kinsale led by Mother Frances Bridgeman. By 2 December she was ready to leave with a second contingent of 48 nurses: 15 of Bridgeman's nuns, 24 hospital nurses and nine lady volunteers. The hospital nurses departed with Sidney Herbert's exhortations to obedience and warnings that bad behaviour would prompt instant dismissal, sailing from Marseilles on the mail steamer *Egyptus* which was also conveying 250 French troops to the Crimea. Reverend Mother Bridgeman, keeping to her own and her nuns' counsel on board, tersely observed in her diary that by dressing the hospital nurses and ladies in the same unbecoming uniform the government had appeared to be nursing a 'utopian plan . . . to raise the moral character of the nurses by placing them on an equality with the ladies'. With hindsight, she grandly observed: 'It did not need much experience or foresight to conclude how ineffectual this experiment should prove, and what the result was likely to be.' On board the *Egyptus*, Bridgeman refused to allow her nuns to share the same dining facilities as the nurses and second-class passengers and thus be 'thrown into domestic contact with this class of people', and organized their dining at a separate time. Thereafter they determinedly 'lived as much apart as possible from our secular companions'.[22]

When she heard of the imminent arrival of a second party of nurses only three days before they were on her doorstep, Nightingale was incensed. To her it was a flagrant usurpation by Stanley of her authority and the stringent rules she had laid down on the selection of nurses. The Crimean experiment in nursing was *hers*, and she was determined to be sole arbiter of how it proceeded. She had particularly not wanted any encouragement of non-professional lady volunteers; but what was even worse, she was now faced with an imbalance between Protestant and Catholic nuns – with 25 of the total of 84 nurses being Catholic. She angrily fired off an accusatory letter to Sidney Herbert. He had 'sacrificed the cause so near to her heart . . . he had sacrificed her, and had sacrificed his own written word'.[23] She announced her resignation. Herbert ignored it.

When Mary Stanley's party arrived on 15 December, Nightingale refused to meet them, sending out a message that it was a 'gross mistake' on the part of the government to have recruited them without her knowledge and that she was, in any case, unable to accommodate them. Instead she sent them to lodgings at Therapia; here the Catholic nuns were taken in by the French Sisters of Charity at their nearby convent at Galata. A week later Nightingale relented and offered to take five of Bridgeman's nuns at Scutari under the supervision of Reverend Mother Moore of the Bermondsey nuns. The highly controlling Bridgeman refused point blank. She had no intention of relinquishing official or spiritual supervision of *her* nuns to another, even another Catholic. She took a boat across to Scutari for a meeting with Nightingale, conducted over a Spartan lunch consisting of a 'small remnant of musty cheese, dirty butter in a bowl, some sour bread . . . and cold potatoes'. There was 'something in a bottle' too, but Bridgeman could not identify what it was. She and Nightingale took an instant, frigid dislike to each other, Bridgeman observing with distaste the 'soiled and neglected' look of the Norwood and Bermondsey nuns at Scutari and the 'dirt and confusion' in which they lived. She was further appalled to hear that later that same day the Norwood nuns, whom Nightingale had deemed utterly incompetent, were to be sent home in 'the *most humiliating manner*', being marched through the hospital and down to the boat station like penitents. Later, Bridgeman offered by letter to 'co-operate *cordially* in agreeing the services of her nuns', but she would only allow them to come to Scutari to work under Mother Moore with herself as one of the party.[24]

On 8 January the Bridgeman nuns – plus their own priest, three lady volunteers and one hospital nurse – transferred to Scutari with Nightingale's agreement; later that month the other Bridgeman nuns were dispersed between a new hospital established in the Crimea at Balaklava, and hospitals at Kuleli four miles north-east of Scutari. But the falling-out with Mary Stanley over the second contingent of nurses and their dispersal outside Nightingale's aegis would mean she would systematically lose control over the nursing carried out in the other military hospitals during the war; her friendship with Stanley would be destroyed. The presence of so many Catholic nuns would be a continuing problem, with Nightingale and the British military authorities paranoid that they might spend more time attending to the souls, rather than the health, of the sick and wounded. To make matters worse, the strong-minded Bridgeman continually baulked at accepting Nightingale's authority. As far as she was concerned, Nightingale's responsibilities lay in organizing her nuns as nurses; their religious way of life in the Crimea would be maintained under her *own* despotic control. The two women would continue to exchange vituperative swipes, Nightingale privately nicknaming Bridgeman 'Mother Brickbat' or 'Manning's Nun', whilst Bridgeman would delight in learning that in the Crimea, the strong-minded Nightingale went under the nickname of 'Goddess of Humbug'.[25]

By the end of December all Nightingale's hard work, and that of her team of nurses, seemed, on the surface, to be paying off. Against the odds, Nightingale appeared to have effected something of a miracle, in the view of Chaplain John Sabin. 'Everybody,' he asserted somewhat optimistically, 'sees that Florence is like no other woman breathing and respect and admire her more than words can say.' In a letter to the Chaplain-General, George Gleig, on 27 December, he related how Nightingale, together with her 'efficient band of nurses' and the medical orderlies and clergy now working at Scutari, brought about radical physical improvements in just one month:

> One corridor alone contains 225 beds every one occupied and the wards leading out of the same corridor contain 313 beds. The whole of this corridor has been repaired, and every ward had new floors and windows within the last months, and now it is occupied from end to end. Surgeries are built on the wide staircases; boilers for hot water are erected at intervals; stoves are kept constantly burning in each ward, and down the corridor, which to lessen the cold is divided by wooden partitions; large tin baths are standing at the corners and entrances ready for use, and every man has a wooden bedstead, and comfortable bed and bedding . . .

There is now an air of comfort and enjoyment which I feared once never to see here.[26]

In reality, however, the death rates from infection and disease, which could and should have been contained, were escalating at an alarming rate, so much so that they far exceeded death from wounds inflicted in battle. In addition, Nightingale was having a hard job containing the growing discontent and troublesome behaviour of many of her hospital nurses. How could she, one individual, ensure 'female decorum' and keep control of forty women 'turned loose among three thousand men' who 'run scampering over the wards by themselves at night, feeding the men without medical orders'?[27] It was no trifling matter and she was forced to apply draconian rules, strictly curtailing the nurses' freedom of movement and fraternization. They could not work in the wards without a nun to supervise them. They were only allowed to walk out in the company of a housekeeper or in a party with at least three others – and even that only with permission. They were not allowed to accept gifts from any patients – especially alcohol, on pain of immediate dismissal. But it wasn't just infringements of the rules or professional incompetence that preoccupied Nightingale; her time and energy were also constantly diverted in keeping a watchful eye over the doubtful sobriety of many of the hospital nurses. Drunkenness would be the primary reason for dismissal during the war, with 18 nurses being sent home on this account.

The most vocal complaint voiced by the hospital nurses was that they felt they had been led to believe, on engagement, that they would be treated as 'ladies', i.e. on the same footing as the nuns. But the rules and regulations issued to all nurses were quite categorical: the nurses 'should understand that they will remain in exactly the same relative position as that in which they were in England'.[28] They grumbled at being given menial work – scrubbing floors, making bandages, sewing pillowcases. 'We are not come out to be cooks, housemaids and washerwomen,' they told Stanley at Kuleli.[29] Her response was to have recourse to a 'supervisor–penitent model' of discipline, her nurses there being treated along the lines practised with reformed prostitutes at St Mary's House Wantage, an establishment Stanley supported.[30]

At the end of the year came a sad and most unfortunate dismissal – that of one of the Sellonites, Elizabeth Wheeler. An ardent and rather impetuous woman, according to Sarah Anne Terrot, she had written home to relatives giving graphic details of the terrible neglect and suffering at Scutari. Without her knowledge, the letter had been forwarded by them to *The Times* and published on 8 December, one of many that had prompted an angry outcry in the press against the government's mismanagement of the war. When word of this reached Scutari, Sister Wheeler was hauled over the coals. Her letter, she admitted, had been incautious and an exaggeration. Worse, it was seen as undermining of public confidence and of Nightingale's work. Wheeler was summarily dismissed *pour encourager les autres*, Nightingale prepared to take the flak in her usual hard-nosed but courageous way, for the sake of her work at Scutari: 'till I am superseded, I shall carry it out at any expense to me of odium, tho' no human being can stand for two months what I am doing now'.[31]

It was a sad end to the year and to the start of Nightingale's mission, when on a dark, wet and stormy Christmas Eve ten of Nightingale's original party of 38 were sent home: the five Norwood nuns dismissed as incompetent, two Sellonites (including Wheeler) and three hospital nurses. Whilst Sarah Anne Terrot was profoundly disconsolate at the loss of a colleague and friend, Nightingale's banishment of the nuns brought on her head a 'blackguarding' from the Catholic Father Michael Cuffe, who damned her as being 'like *Herod* sending the Blessed Virgin across the desert'. Ever watchful for signs of Catholic plotting against her, Nightingale waited for the repercussions. Meanwhile, she was unqualified in her praise for the Catholic nuns from Bermondsey, who had rapidly become the mainstay of her team: they were 'the truest Xtians I ever met with – invaluable in their work – devoted, heart & head, to serve God & mankind – not to intrigue for their church'.[32]

But the discord continued: by the end of the year Nightingale was complaining that the 15 Catholic nuns were 'leading me the devil of a life'.[33] A heady atmosphere of sectarian bitterness was but part of the cocktail of insubordination, intrigue, intoxication, promiscuity, mutual antagonism, racism, bad language and quarrels to rival any soap opera. And all this at a time when the hospital at Scutari was about to receive its largest influx of sick and wounded: 4,000 of them, admitted between 17 December 1854 and 3 January 1855. The endless deathbed scenes and burials were, by the end of December, increasing with numbing familiarity. But at least by now, the rank and file soldiers had the comforting presence of women as they lay dying, often in their delirium mistaking the nurses for their own womenfolk. They told Terrot that seeing nurses on the ward was a great comfort, for it made them feel they had got home to their mothers. They were grateful too that the women were far gentler in cleansing wounds and more solicitous at the bedside than the male orderlies, whom the soldiers complained were rough and careless and stole from them. The ministrations of a nurse were, one soldier told Margaret Goodman, 'like the visit of an angel'; in their dying moments, 'like worn-out children sinking to rest', most of the soldiers spoke of England and the desperate desire to get home. One young country boy spoke of his little cottage back in his village, 'where a pleasant breeze is always to be felt' and where he could get plenty of eggs and milk. He was sure if he had them that he would 'get strong again immediately'. 'Never mind, sister,' said another young lad who had lost both his arms, 'we may be thankful, if, like the wounded beasts, we can only crawl back into our old, familiar haunts to die: we should all like to lay our bones in old England.'[34]

The rank and file who died at Scutari would be buried in mass graves at the rate of 50–60 a day in the burial ground nearby, with nothing to signify the lives ended in such suffering. So also the women who accompanied them on campaign. On 7 November, only days after her arrival at Scutari, Sarah Anne Terrot was called to the bedside of a soldier's wife dying of consumption. The poor woman had been consigned to die in a corner of a room set aside for army wives, where she lay on the floor unnoticed and alone while they sat 'rude and noisy, seemingly half-drunk'. The one thing they had in common was their filthy, worn-out and squalid state – 'not one bright fresh face to be seen', remarked Terrot. She sat with the dying woman till she was ordered to her quarters at nightfall. The following morning she returned to find the woman had died: 'She was already wrapped in a blanket and laid in her grave'; all there was to mark her miserable short life was the bald inscription 'A Woman' on a piece of wood used as a makeshift headstone.[35]

Death for the wounded officers at Scutari was somewhat kinder. Some were lucky enough to have their wives with them in their last days, for a few had followed their husbands on campaign as far as Constantinople and had taken lodgings there or at Pera nearby. But the additional strain of having to deal with the bereaved wives when they arrived was extremely distressing. Much of it fell on Nightingale's benevolent friends Charles and Selina Bracebridge, who had accompanied her to Scutari and had become indispensable in the day-to-day running of the hospital. In December Selina wrote home describing how she had been called to take the sacrament with Captain Charles Glazbrook of the 49th Foot, who was dying of lockjaw 'in a wretched room at the end of our passage'. His wife Marian and their son, she being pregnant with another child due within the month, were with him and 'a more heart-rending sight you cannot imagine'. 'What we are to do with the poor woman I can't imagine when he dies,' she wrote. At 5.30 a.m. on Thursday 18th, Charles Bracebridge recalled, 'the *expected* knock' came. 'I went to the kitchen-hall, and received at the door Mrs Glazebrook in the arms of Dr McGregor and Lieut. Gordon. She was brought to the bed room and laid down in hysterics.' While Charles went to close the corpse's eyes, assisted by the good Mrs Clark who had come to lay out the body, Selina comforted the widow, 'keeping her and her child all day in the bed room in agony'.

The following morning at 6.30 another knock came, this time to tell Bracebridge that General Adams, a much-loved commander in the 2nd Division, had died also, on the 17th; Mrs Adams too was carried in prostrate and again the women comforted the widow while Bracebridge went off to arrange 'the coffin for one and the funeral for the other'. 'These are only episodes of misery,' he concluded, 'every day comes some other . . . Oh if one had time to write pictures – every moment is one.'[36]

Over in the Crimea, a far bigger and more tragic picture was about to be painted. For the misery of the winter of 1854–5 was now upon the British army besieging Sevastopol.

EIGHT

This Little
Heroic Wreck of
an Army

In her journal for 11 November, Fanny Duberly wrote that the soldiers of the British army in the Crimea were now living 'in a state that few of our paupers in England would endure'.[1] The cavalry camp was like a knacker's yard, full of dead and dying horses; the sick and wounded men were suffering agonies as they were manhandled down from the front lines and then left for hours of protracted discomfort in the cold and the rain on the wharf at Balaklava waiting for transportation to Scutari. Everyone was dirty and covered in lice. The poor starved, worn-out artillery horses were now too malnourished to be able to drag the heavy guns; nor could the transport mules get much-needed supplies to the British siege lines from the ships that crammed Balaklava harbour. It meant that the soldiers themselves, already weak and exhausted, had to be commandeered to tramp the 14-mile round trip to Balaklava through virtually impassable mud to retrieve what rations and ammunition they could forage and carry. The supplies were sitting there, many yet to be unloaded from the ships at anchor, but such was the tedious bureaucracy, inefficiency and want of system in the British Commissariat that they sat for days if not weeks, rotting in ships' holds and on the quayside, before the requisite signatures were obtained to move them on.

Elizabeth Evans had been sitting in her tent near the front lines on the 10th when a heavy gale had struck and whipped away her cooking pots and camp furniture. She'd been making a new bonnet for herself but was knocked over by the wind and saw both her tent and bonnet, which she'd hung on the centre pole, disappear in the direction of Sevastopol. For her, the loss of this much-prized article at such a time of hardship was a major blow. Having survived the rigours of the march and the three battles of the autumn with her husband, Elizabeth was now doing what she could for the sick and wounded in the regiment's makeshift hospital, such as it was; for it really wasn't more than a rough covering, and inside it, Elizabeth remembered, 'our brave fellows were packed like herrings in barrels'. The three doctors they had with them could do precious little, lacking any medical supplies or equipment. All Elizabeth herself could offer was 'the help of a woman's sympathy'.[2]

In the Crimea, the care and nurturing of women was a welcome but rare respite for the men, for most of the army wives on the strength had not been allowed to travel further than Varna. Some – the sick and the widows – had already been sent home to England, but another 260 women had been collected together at Scutari from Varna and Gallipoli and abandoned there for the duration in appalling conditions. Some wives had managed to sail on the invasion fleet to Kalamita Bay but had not been allowed to land, leaving them still stranded on board the transports in the Black Sea weeks later, awaiting passage home. Even fewer women, Elizabeth Evans among them, by luck or sheer bravado had managed to disembark in the Crimea. Others like Mrs Crangle of the 95th had managed to conceal themselves in the baggage train during the confusion of the landings, following in the rear of the army and engaging in all sorts of subterfuge to make their way to the front and rejoin their regiments. Those women who had a little money of their own bought themselves a passage on French *pacquebots*, making their way to the siege lines via the French camp. Alone among French officers' wives, Soledad Bazaine had also travelled the Black Sea to the French base at Kamiesh, where she set up a modest home for her husband, now newly promoted to general in the Second Foreign Legion Regiment. The temptations to leave the freezing cold of the front lines for a night in the arms of his beautiful wife were great and rumour abounded that the general did so from time to time.

Once the British women had got themselves to the camp before Sevastopol, the officers were faced with a *fait accompli* about which they could do little. The women's unacknowledged, unofficial position in the Crimea meant that they were at the mercy of the regimental commanders and entirely dependent on their sympathetic response – or otherwise – to having women in the camp. Most put them to work washing or cooking for the men, often coming to prize the women as the regiment's most stalwart and loyal followers. But army regulations meant they could not be officially employed in any capacity, so much of their work was done by private negotiation. There was, undoubtedly, a strange kind of fierce and unspoken loyalty between these campaign-hardened women. They bonded in the same way that the soldiers did and would not be separated from each other. The regiment was their pride as well as their protector. They felt it would not desert them and so they uncomplainingly joined with the men in a share of their already meagre rations and a corner of a damp, cold leaking tent or an improvised shakedown made of barrel staves. Here they endured all the same miseries of frostbite, diarrhoea, gout, rheumatism, scurvy, dysentery and other camp fevers that were so prevalent – as well as the deadly cholera that still visited itself upon the troops.

But the sense of camaraderie was not universal: on one occasion, Fanny Duberly recorded being called out to visit one of the women of her own regiment, the 8th Hussars, who was suffering from fever and had been callously treated by the other women:

> I found her lying on a bed on the wet ground; she had lain there, in cold and rain, wind and snow, for twelve days. By her side, in the wet mud, was a piece of ration biscuit, a piece of salt pork, some cheese, and a tin pot with some rum! Nice fever diet! She, having failed to make herself popular among the women during her health, was left by them when she was sick; and not a soul had offered to assist the poor, helpless, half-delirious creature, except her husband, and a former mate of his when he was a sailor.

Sadly, Fanny fails to reveal in her journal whether she did anything to help the poor woman.[3]

At Varna, where she had had to be abandoned on the beach by her husband when the fleet sailed in September, Margaret Kerwin had been taken under the care of a kind and sympathetic doctor. In the town's makeshift hospital she had lain seriously ill until after the Battle of the Alma, when she received a letter from her husband John telling her he was safe and had only been slightly wounded. Such wonderful news speeded Margaret's recovery. The doctors were ready to send her home but she refused to go. She wanted to see her husband 'at the front' before she went. But the doctor was adamant, she recalled: 'if I went up there I would die, as there was nothing but hunger and hardship'.[4] After she recovered her strength, and having had some previous nursing experience in the army, Margaret was asked to nurse the sick men at Varna hospital and paid two shillings and sixpence a week. When the British camp there was broken up, she paid her passage over to Balaklava to meet up with John, who was now stationed in the Commissary Department. In the graveyard at Balaklava they put up the little marquee Margaret had purchased and soon she was back doing the washing, this time for men from the Commissary, scrubbing and pegging out her laundry among the tombstones – until the order came for her husband to go to the front.

Nell Butler was still stranded on a troopship in the Black Sea when news reached her that her husband Michael was sick with fever at Balaklava. She managed to get there partly by steamer and then by trudging the last stretch on foot. On arrival she searched among the many hundreds of sick and wounded in the hospital ships in the harbour looking for Michael. It was a hopeless and heartbreaking task, remembered Nell: 'The sights I saw blinded my eyes with tears.'[5] Whilst searching among the wounded, someone addressed her as 'nurse' and enlisted her urgent help. It was a doctor, 'knee-deep among the wounded'. The next thing Nell knew she was holding down a man's hands whilst he was given a swig of brandy before his leg was amputated: 'The doctor took a long bright knife and a saw. I lost all feeling and hung on to the man's hands as much to help myself as him. I could hear the grating of the saw.'

Nell fainted and came round to hear the doctor berating her: 'I can't allow that. You nearly spoilt all my work . . . I wasn't able to sew up that artery properly.'[6] Upon which the doctor snatched up his needle and carried on working, cursing Nell for her weakness. From that day on Nell found herself an unofficial nurse in the hospital tents at Balaklava harbour; she finally was reunited with Michael, who was now recovering from his fever (although he was never to enjoy full health again). But supplies during that winter were desperately short and Nell had to resort to tearing up her petticoats to make bandages; and she improvised poultices from old biscuit sacks. Even stocks of surgical thread ran out. Packthread proved useless as it rotted quickly and wounds reopened. Nell applied her practical skills by waxing the thread with a mixture of pitch and animal fat. Then, with the siege continuing, like Margaret Kerwin, she followed her regiment to the front lines for the final assault on Sevastopol.

As winter set in, the numbers of sick increased alarmingly. The Crimean landscape contrived to do everything it could to chill the body and deaden the soul. 'Imagine the bleakest common in all England,' wrote one soldier, attempting to describe it for his family back home, 'the wettest bog in all Ireland or the dreariest moor in all Scotland overhung by leaden skies as black as ink, lashed by a tornado, sleet, snow, drizzle and pelting rain . . . and roads turned into torrents of mud and water'.[7] Such intolerable conditions meant that the fallout rate among the rank and file was increased by long and exhausting trench duty, the men soaked to the skin in trenches full of water and paralysed with cold. It wore down even the strongest and left men dead at their posts by morning. Elizabeth Evans's husband would return from 'that awful work' shivering and almost entirely frozen. 'Time after time I would remove his boots and rub his feet, which were utterly numb, and likely to come off from frost-bite,' she wrote.[8] She implored him to go sick but he never would, for to do so would be to let down his comrades. All Elizabeth could do was to beg a drop of warm, weak coffee from the band sergeant for him. But the anguish every time he left for trench duty was terrible. She knew that the outlying pickets were 'no place for a woman', yet in the blackness of the winter night, time after time, she made her way out to where the British and Russians were only separated by a small stretch of ground, dodging the Russian sharpshooters and the fire from their batteries in order to be near William. In the dark she was guided by the trail of their missiles' fire and in the day by the hissing noise they made. 'I got many a terrible scare,' she wrote, 'it was a case of falling to the ground to wait for the crash of the explosion above your head, or the appalling burial of the shot or shell in the earth near you.'[9]

And then, four days after the gale of 10 November, an even more fearsome storm ravaged the allied camps in the Crimea. At five in the morning of the 14th a blood-red sun was the harbinger of a rushing wind of hurricane force, striking from the west and bringing with it torrential rain, which by late afternoon turned to sleet and snow. Within an hour, Fanny Duberly could see Balaklava harbour 'seething and covered with foam, and the ships swinging terribly'. By nine she could not keep her footing on deck as her ship plunged and crashed on its mooring. 'The spray, dashing over the cliffs many hundred feet,' she wrote, 'fell like heavy rain into the harbour' where many ships had come adrift and were now 'crushing and crowding together . . . all breaking and grinding each other to pieces'. Off the coast, the supply ships from England that hadn't been able to anchor in the harbour were going down in the storm and taking most of their crew with them, tossing many of those who had abandoned ship onto the rocks. 'Out of the whole, not a dozen people saved . . . Ah me! Such a sight, once seen, who can forget!' wept Duberly.[10]

By the time the storm abated, the harbour was a mess of crushed, dismasted ships, the water choked with wreckage, drowned men and animals, disgorged and sodden supplies. The screw-ship *Prince*, only just arrived from England with medical supplies, thousands of winter coats, boots and blankets, as well as 20 days' hay for the starving horses, had sunk in the harbour with all its supplies and 144 of its 150-man crew. It was one of 21 British ships lost that night, the French, in addition, losing 14. On land, tent poles snapped like matchsticks, the threadbare old bell tents and hospital marquees were torn from the ground or ripped to ribbons in the gale. Men and beasts were hurled into the air. Precious food stores were lost and bottles smashed. Chairs, beds, clothing, blankets, the horses' forage – all were tossed away. Elizabeth Evans saw the regimental band's bass drum carried off too. It ended up in the Russian lines two miles away.

In the aftermath, there was no food for man or beast; all stood or lay where they could, soaked and dejected amidst the wreckage in the piercing north wind. Morale among the troops plummeted further; their threadbare clothes and emaciated bodies made them look ever more spectral as sub-zero temperatures froze icicles to their beards, hair and eyebrows. The surrounding oak scrubland had been scoured and ravaged for every root, every stick of fuel and kindling; the salt pork had to be eaten raw, the green coffee beans were useless. The only water they could get was brackish and muddy. All that was left to protect the troops who had lost their tents were crude dugouts hollowed out in the mud, covered by whatever canvas they could salvage, but these rapidly filled with rain. Elizabeth Evans counted herself lucky that she had a beautiful great Scots plaid shawl; this and a share of her husband's greatcoat was all she had to warm herself all winter. Somehow she managed to preserve a modicum of dignity in the worn-out clothes she had, until, at the end of December, the army issued some new clothing to the women in the Crimea. In the camp of the 4th Dragoon Guards, Colonel Edward Hodge had no doubt that it was in fact the women of the army who were the 'worst off for comforts' and to whom few people had offered any consideration. He had given a pair of his flannels to 'poor Mrs Rogers', the much respected, hard-working cook and washerwoman for his troop.[11]

At Scutari a group of about 260 or so army wives, several with pale and sickly new-born babies, were also suffering. Some had been stranded when the Guards camp there had been ordered to the Crimea; others had followed their sick or wounded husbands to Scutari from the troop transports or the camp at Varna. Many were now widows. Separated from their regiments, they fell under no one's jurisdiction and no provisions had been made for them. Living, dying and giving birth in the same foul environment, many in their desolation and demoralization had abandoned themselves to drink and debauchery. It was a problem that Florence Nightingale did not need, for she had neither the time nor the resources to attend to their welfare; indeed, the women were a distinct nuisance as far as she was concerned. She called them the *Allobrogues* – a name given to the Celtic women who had followed the ancient Gauls into war. A lying-in hospital had been created for those of them who were pregnant in Corridor A of the Barracks Hospital, where their howling and railing in childbirth could be heard in the wards nearby and where they regularly besieged the hard-pressed Charles Bracebridge, in charge of the stores, for 'teas and flannel petticoats' or for mourning clothes for their dead husbands and generally 'deal[t] destruction round the barracks'.[12]

In mid-December the situation was saved when two dedicated philanthropists, the Revd Dr and Mrs Blackwood of the Evangelical Alliance (a movement supported by the pacificist Frederika Bremer and also, tacitly, by Nightingale), arrived at Scutari in the company of two young Swedish sisters and acolytes, Ebba and Emma Almroth. They had all travelled out to the Crimea at their own expense to offer their services, having been moved to do something after the terrible losses at Inkerman. James Blackwood soon was appointed as a chaplain to the Scutari hospitals, with the Swedish sisters assisting him in handing out tracts and prayer books – though under escort – on the wards. Meanwhile, Nightingale gave Alicia Blackwood the onerous responsibility of dealing with the *Allobrogues*.

Nothing could have prepared Lady Blackwood, daughter of a viscount, who had grown up at the family country seats in Hampshire and Somerset, for the indescribable pandemonium of the dark, airless cellars at Scutari. It was a Hogarthian hellhole of degeneracy, dirt and disease, of swearing and cursing and drunkenness that would have exercised even the pen of Charles Dickens. Many of the women were leading an animal-like existence, dressed in rags and covered with vermin; some dead drunk on poisonous arrack, a coarse spirit sold by local Greek traders, oblivious to the starving grizzling infants that clung to them. Some preferred brandy, procured at one shilling and twopence a bottle, and made any man welcome who'd bring a bottle or two in exchange for sex. Others fed their drinking habit soliciting custom in the taverns, shops and markets that surrounded Scutari hospital, often bringing their clients back with impunity, to drink, carouse and have sex openly amidst the jumble of boxes and bundles on the squalid filthy earth floors of the cellars, where the stench from blocked and broken drains filled the air. All that separated the piles of India matting and rags that the women and children slept on were a few old sheets hung up as improvised screens. With lamps in short supply the cellars were dark, night and day, with only an improvised rush light to eat by.

With brisk efficiency, Lady Alicia first reorganized the staff of washer-women set up by Nightingale, recruiting the more respectable and industrious army wives at wages of 10 to 14 shillings a week, and appointing a naval officer's wife, Mrs Keatley, to come out from England to superintend their work. By January an infirmary and lying-in hospital was established for 36 women and their infants (22 babies had been born by the end of December and many more would be born that winter) in a nearby house rented for the purpose, which was cleaned, repaired and fitted up from private funds. A few trustworthy army wives were employed here as sicknurses – all paid from private funds, not by the Army. A crèche was also set up to take care of the infants, and a Sunday school for the older children, well supplied with Bibles and tracts for their edification. A civilian surgeon, Dr Peyton Smith, sponsored by lady philanthropists, came out from England to care for the pregnant and sick women. Application was made to the Central Association to urgently provide money for the purchase of flannel cloth, tea, soap, boots and all the supplies so urgently needed, which soon came flooding in to Scutari.

But keeping control of such a group of wily and wilful women was a constant challenge. They were forever complaining, quarrelling and on the scrounge for goods from the Free Gift Store set up with donations from England. It was decided, however, not to simply give these goods away, for many of the women would immediately have sold them (especially tea and soap) to buy arrack. Instead the goods were sold for very low prices, Alicia Blackwood being of the characteristic Victorian mind that the women should be encouraged in 'industrious habits' and earn what they spent.[13] When a supply of flannel arrived there was a scrum to obtain it, especially to make clothing for the babies; but cambric for dresses was also much sought after and there was a terrible rampage among the women for one of a consignment of 50 bonnets when they arrived.

Whilst conditions for the army wives at Scutari might be improving, on the Crimean peninsula, Colonel George Bell watched in anger and impotence as not just the men but also the women of his regiment, the 1st Royal Scots, suffered and died that winter. On 27 November he could not contain his pain and bitterness:

Look into this [hospital] tent and observe the household. You see it is in
rags all about the skirting, and the floor is a thick paste baked nearly dry
by the heat of the fevered patients. That bundle of a dirty, wet blanket
rolled up contains a living creature, once a comely useful soldier's wife,
now waiting for death to release her from such misery . . . That young
woman, once perhaps the belle of her village, now in rags, but in good
health, is eating her dinner, the broth a bit of salt fat pork, with broken
brown biscuit pounded into it; a tin plate and iron spoon is all her
fortune. I had ten or twelve women who stuck to the regiment
throughout the winter. 'What is that down the hill there?' 'O, sir, that
is poor Mrs H—, sitting on her husband's grave; she is always there
shivering in the cold.'[14]

Fanny Duberly could have no conception of such misery on the *Shooting
Star*; complaining instead about the lateness of the mail from England, the
cold and discomfort aboard ship. Once the hurricane was past she could
return to her fanciful literary meanderings, mindful of future publication:
the sky was serene and blue, nature 'weary of her hurricane of tears' had
'sobbed herself into quietness'.[15] A few days later she was cheered by the
loan of a white Spanish horse to ride, her own half-starved mount Bob
being a rickety moth-eaten sight by now. She worried continuously about
the state of the cavalry horses, reduced to a handful of barley a day for food,
and also the officers who resembled their own horses, 'equally thin, worn,
ragged, and out of condition in every way', but in general the suffering of
the horses seemed to move her more than that of the human beings,
particularly the rank and file, and she spent her time engrossed in making
a huge canvas protective sheet for Bob. Not long after, her third horse, Job,
died of starvation, having 'sold his life by inches', but once again, the loan
of a dainty white pony with 'black lustrous eyes' lifted Fanny's spirits.[16]
Meanwhile, she heard tell of the sick at Balaklava dying at the rate of 80
per day and being manhandled in the most brutal way on board the
steamships for Scutari. Balaklava itself, once a pretty Italianate seaport
with a picturesque Genoese fort, had become a stagnant dumping ground
for the sick, the maimed and the destitute – military and civilian – a
noisome stew of human suffering that was representative of the

accumulating evil, mismanagement and neglect of the Crimean campaign. It provides us with one of Duberly's most eloquent comments on the war:

> Take a village of ruined houses and hovels in the extremest state of all imaginable dirt; allow the rain to pour into and outside them, until the whole place is a swamp of filth ancle-deep [sic], catch about, on an average, 1,000 sick Turks with the plague, and cram them into the houses indiscriminately; kill about 100 a-day, and bury them so as to be scarcely covered with earth, leaving them to rot at leisure – taking care to keep up the supply. On to one part of the beach drive all the exhausted *bât* ponies, dying bullocks, and worn-out camels, and leave them to die of starvation. They will generally do so in about three days, when they will soon begin to rot, and smell accordingly. Collect together from the water of the harbour all the offal of the animals slaughtered for the use of the occupants of above 100 ships, to say nothing of the inhabitants of the town, – which, together with an occasional floating human body, whole or in parts, and the driftwood of the wrecks, pretty well covers the water – and stew them all up together in a narrow harbour, and you will have a tolerable imitation of the real essence of Balaklava. If this is not *piquante* enough, let some men be instructed to sit and smoke on the powder-barrels landing on the quay; which I myself saw two men doing today, on the Ordnance Wharf.[17]

By the end of December, only 8,000 men out of an original fighting force of about 25,000 that had landed in September, could be mustered for duty. The daily burial parties in camp, melancholy though they were, no longer raised a flicker of interest as they passed, the usual military firing parties and obsequies long since abandoned; nor did the death throes of the once fine cavalry horses, chewing each other's manes and tails in a last frantic effort to feed themselves. Everywhere you looked there was just too much suffering; the army had become deadened and brutalized by it. With most of the backbone of its old, seasoned soldiers now dead, wounded, sick or broken down in health and spirits, the raw young recruits – undrilled, undisciplined and having hardly ever fired a musket – were a 'mere mob of boys' in comparison, 'destined to encumber the hospitals or perish miserably'.[18] Physically incapable of enduring the fatigue of trench duty, 'they lie down wet on the wet sod, helpless, unattended and shiver away their young lives in silent sorrow', wrote Sir George Bell of those in his own regiment.[19] At the present rate of death and sickness many officers were predicting not just the annihilation of their own regiment – but of whole divisions. The British army was melting away and would soon effectively no longer exist, except in name. As for honour and glory and all the great British values for which the army had fought and died that autumn, these were 'empty bubbles'.[20] One thing was now clear: disease and the trenches were killing far more men than Russian bullets.

What on earth would the romantic young ladies of England think, mused Lieutenant Richard Temple Godman of the 5th Dragoons, if they were to see the gallant British soldier now – a squalid creature of rags and tatters with matted hair and long beard, covered in mud, unwashed for weeks; his worn-out boots replaced by sacking or hay bands tied round his feet; wearing tarpaulin fashioned into leggings, and with a cloak and a blanket tied round him with bits of string to act as a coat? 'I don't think they would ever care much about us soldiers again.'[21]

The fact was, though, that back in Britain the public cared passionately about what was happening to its army in the Crimea. Expectations of a speedy victory at Sevastopol had now faded; the siege was at a standstill and their men were going to have to endure the winter there. The whole campaign was an unmitigated military, political and economic disaster, and public opinion was now being whipped up in *The Times* and other newspapers, most notably in the damning editorials by the impassioned *Times* editor John Delane in response to his reporter Russell's dispatches. 'Incompetency, lethargy, aristocratic hauteur, official indifference, favour, routine, perverseness and stupidity reign, revel and riot in the Camp before Sebastopol,' Delane thundered.[22]

In the weeks leading up to Christmas the whole nation could think and talk of nothing but the war: 'Our literature at present is the War Column of the Newspaper,' observed the writer Arthur Hugh Clough.[23] Reports of the war and extracts from letters from the front dominated the press and nobody in Britain seemed disposed to think or talk about anything else. War had done the one thing which no amount of social reform could ever achieve – it had united the classes, making everyone feel a common bond, a union of human hearts.

It is not surprising, therefore, that on 18 December, when the commissioners of the Royal Patriotic Fund held their first meeting under the chairmanship of Prince Albert, they were gratified to learn that an astonishing £291,392 (the equivalent of £17.6 million today) had already been raised for the relief of the wives, widows and families of the army in the East. The committee promptly agreed a 'Provisional Scale of Weekly Relief' for soldiers' widows according to rank, the top rate being nine shillings a week, with 3s. 6d. the lowest, for the widow of a private. The establishment of the Fund and *The Times*'s Crimean Fund for the soldiers themselves had brought the widest range of donations from the public. One hundred adult male criminals in a London reformatory volunteered to abstain from a day's food in order that the proceeds – £3 13s. 5¾d. – should be donated to the Patriotic Fund. Lord Blantyre at his own expense sent a ship loaded with oatmeal and porridge for the Scottish and Irish soldiers, whom he felt sure missed it so much. H. Golston & Co. of Fleet Street, 'knowing how important it is to troops and sailors to have photographs of loved ones', offered to take daguerreotypes *without charge* of anyone 'bringing satisfactory evidence' of being the wife, sweetheart, son or daughter of a serving man. Fifteen hundred children in six schools in Shoreditch – many from very poor families – paid a penny each into the Patriotic Fund. In Ireland, those most dedicated of drinkers, the workers at a Guinness factory, donated a day's pay. Schoolchildren handed over the small sums of pocket money they had saved, which they wished to be sent to the 'ladies who nursed the sick soldiers'.[24] Such was the concern for the troops that even skilled and well-paid industrial workers in Britain signed up for the army. Elizabeth Gaskell wrote to Dickens on 17 December describing how 'some fine-spinners in a mill at Bolton, earning their 36 shillings a week, threw up their work and enlisted last week, on hearing of the sufferings in the Crimea, for they said they could neither sleep nor eat for thinking how the soldiers there wanted help'.[25] Even ancient rivalries came into play in the donation stakes: by the end of December Oxford University had collected £700, as opposed to a massive £1,200 at Cambridge, the *Patriotic Fund Journal* observing that 'the contrast is creditable to Cambridge, and . . . may promote generous rivalry in a good cause'.[26]

Other groups were busying themselves with the army's spiritual welfare: the Soldier's Friend Society and the Naval and Military Bible Society had been keen to ensure all troops going to the Crimea had New Testaments (smaller and less bulky than the Bible) and had been distributing them since the embarkations. They and the Army Scripture Readers Society were now busily recruiting readers to go out to Scutari to read the Bible and other edifying religious tracts to the illiterate sick and wounded. Pamphlets and religious literature were produced by the cartload for distribution among the men at the front and stuffed inside socks being sent out there. In England, too, scripture readers were actively employed at army barracks and depots, in visiting the wives and families of soldiers and sailors, and even catering to the needs of Russian prisoners of war brought back to Plymouth.

On 25 November a letter from Florence Nightingale published in *The Times* appealed for urgent supplies of lint and clean, old linen to be sent to Messrs Thomas and John Cuthbert of Paternoster Row, for dispatch to Scutari, where they would be made urgent use of as bandages and dressings. The public response was astonishing. When the bales of goods arrived at the Barracks Hospital, contributions ranged from 'handsome damask tablecloths and fine towels, and soft linen sheets, and shirts and chemises, hardly the worse for wear, all belonging evidently to wealthy sympathisers', to bundles of little more than rags which indicated by their 'threadbare, carefully patched, and scrupulously clean' state that they had come from 'some poor but thrifty household'. Many parcels were accompanied by laboriously written semi-literate letters from those who donated them. One such, from a soldier's widow, contained what she said had been her 'only cotton petticoat in the world' which she had made into bandages. Another from a 'servant of all work' contained a pair of knitted gloves with an old fourpenny piece stitched inside one of the fingers and marked 'to be given to one of the gallant defenders of her country'.[27] As *The Times* so rightly observed: 'One touch of nature makes the whole world kin.'[28] There was no doubting the sentiments that prompted such generous gifts, but ultimately they became a problem; the nurse Eliza Polidori in charge of the linen stores at Scutari later begged friends in England to stop people sending out any more parcels – for they already had 'more than they could house' and much of the old linen they were receiving was little more than '*dirty* rags and heaps of complete rubbish'.[29]

The war in the East cast a shadow over many British families that winter. The frequency of people in deep mourning on the streets was striking; even the shops were filled with black, so much so that it had become 'a sort of *mode* to wear black or grey', with many people adopting these colours 'from the mere force of sympathy'.[30] A plethora of sentimental poetry about the war sprung up in the approach to Christmas, in which many sought solace and comfort, certain in the thought that no matter what, the patriotic British soldier's determination to accomplish his mission and see the war through to the end would sustain him through every trial and tribulation. Books such as Henry Sewell Stokes's *Echoes of the War* offered up 'Christmas Night':

> A health to those far, far away,
> Toss'd in some wild Crimean bay,
> Or where the Bivouac's wavering ray
> Tells how the wind is blowing!
> For them to-night no Yule log flames,
> To-night they'll miss the Christmas-games,
> But we will not forget their names,
> With cups and hearts o'er-flowing.[31]

The men in the trenches had not been forgotten; for still the exhortations were going out for donations of warm knitted goods. Up and down the land, benevolent ladies in country mansions and poor stocking knitters in cottages in Yorkshire were all busy making strong knitted socks. The *Illustrated London News* invited ladies to send their offerings to the boardroom of the Charing Cross Hospital on the Strand, whence they would be 'transmitted to the seat of war', issuing detailed instructions that the yarn used should be 'six-thread fleecy' and be 'first shrunk by immersion in boiling water and dried'; size 10 knitting needles should be used, 60 stitches to a row, the length from leg to heel 10 inches and from toe to heel the same. 'Amicus' of Spalding, who had written to the *Patriotic Journal* soliciting advice on knitting for the troops, was advised that 'warm worsted mitts, of a dark colour without fingers, are the best for soldiers' and told specifically not to 'make any fingers on the right-hand mitt, as they prevent the soldier from loading his rifle with rapidity and accuracy'.[32]

The Times's own Sick and Wounded Fund had also brought in donations of goods and handmade gifts for the troops in the Crimea. Steamships were now being chartered to take out bales of warm clothing as well as vast supplies of tinned and dry goods, wine, spirits, beer, potted meats, tobacco; even sugar plums and acid drops for parched mouths were not forgotten. At Scutari, the gifts most valued were newspapers and books, pocket handkerchiefs, and pens, ink and writing paper. Here, the nurse Fanny Taylor recalled how overwhelmed they were by the public's generosity: 'we had but to write to England and say we wanted such and such a thing and it was sent by the first opportunity'. It was an often moving experience unpacking the boxes when they came, for many of the letters they contained expressed the desire on the part of the donor that they 'could see the pleasure their gift gave'.[33]

The queen especially was greatly exercised about knowing *precisely* who received her own personal gifts, for even at Windsor the knitting needles were clacking. Just before Christmas, Lady Charlotte Canning, now busy recruiting further contingents of Nightingale nurses, found the queen knitting a comforter for her cousin the Duke of Cambridge, whose 'tendency to low fever' Lady Canning felt had prevented him from pulling his weight in the Crimea (he would soon be invalided out suffering effectively from a nervous breakdown and was much frowned upon when he did not return to the front).[34] Victoria herself found time, even on Christmas Day, to write to the duke, informing him that 'The whole female part of this Castle, beginning with the girls and myself . . . are all busily knitting for the army.'[35] Soon a large consignment of 100 pairs of woollen mitts, knitted by the fairest aristocratic hands in the land, was ready for the queen to send out to the Crimea.

Sitting in his tent, watching the torrents of relentless rain falling and his men struggling in the muddy and slushy quagmire, Captain Henry Clifford of the Rifle Brigade could not have been aware of the growing empathy that was uniting his countrymen and women back home and of the home-front efforts now in full swing. He was one of the lucky ones. He had shelter enough to find time occasionally to read, having been lent a copy of Charles Dickens's latest novel *Hard Times*. But he could not help wishing that the author 'could sit, with my pen and paper, and write a book, "Hard Times" in the Crimea. Only just what is passing in front of the door of my comfortable little tent, would give him plenty of matter.'[36] It was the mud that they all wrote about – repeatedly, and at length – in their letters home. A harbinger of the terrible mud of Flanders in the First World War, the Crimean mud was of a grim, tenacious kind that soldiers of many years' campaigning had never encountered anywhere else. It got into everything: their food, their water, their beds, their clothes, their hair, and added to their collective misery:

> I look back on a dark and dreary stage in which men stand night and day in trenches full of water, holding their muskets in their cramped and half frozen hands, ready to repel the enemy, the rain soaking them through the only clothes they have in the world, which, I speak from experience, once wet will remain damp for ever in this climate . . . The wind howls across the plain and throws storms of rain and hail against the tents, which shiver and tremble as if in pain, and let through streams on the men inside; the mist and the clouds seem close to the tents, not a star, not a patch of sky anywhere. It is a dreadful sight: the floors of the tents are inches deep in mud, half the horses of the Regiment are lost . . . The road 2 feet deep in mud and covered with dead and dying animals.[37]

So wrote Edward Fisher-Rowe that winter in a letter home. With Christmas rapidly approaching, a weary and despondent Nicholas Woods, correspondent of the *Morning Herald*, turned his thoughts to England and to the 'glories of London' at this festive period: 'The game – the poultry . . . the shops, generally refulgent with brass and gas, bedizened with holly and mistletoe, with windows full of currants, cinnamon, candied lemon, and other rich and bilious compounds.' Such thoughts only made worse the 'cold, stern realities of dirty Balaklava, where there is mud instead of snow, want instead of plenty, misery instead of rejoicing'.[38]

How very different the bleak, treeless Crimean plain to the shops and stalls at Covent Garden market bursting with a mass of Christmas greenery. A monster Christmas tree hung with 'a variety of brilliant ornaments and knickknacks, a profusion of large and small elegant Chinese lamps, and a number of flags and banners of all nations' had been installed at the Crystal Palace, where a gaudy Christmas fair was in full swing.[39] Families were taking their annual outings to the traditional pantomime, where they could see *Jack and Jill or Harlequin and King Mustard* at Drury Lane, *Little Bo-Peep and the Girl Who Lost Her Sheep* at the Haymarket, or *Ali Baba and the Forty Thieves* at Sadler's Wells. Those still too preoccupied with the war at this festive occasion could view Astley's or Burford's panoramas of the Battle of the Alma, as well as a model of Sevastopol – all on show at Leicester Square; or go to the diorama of Balaklava in Regent Street; or marvel at the assorted effigies and tableaux of French and British generals at Madame Tussaud's. Everywhere, to deaden the gloom of war, engravings in the popular illustrated magazines reminded all good Englishmen of their traditional pastimes – 'Bringing in the Yule Log', 'Cutting the Ashen Faggots', 'The Mistletoe Seller' – of laughing children playing charades, their parents toasting each other with cups of mulled wine, warming their toes and roasting chestnuts before blazing log fires, and families feasting on turkey and the roast beef of Olde England.

At Scutari, the nurses did what they could to mark the Christmas festival, struggling against their own painful sense of separation from home and family and familiar comforts. They went among the wounded 'with voices as cheerful as we could command' and exchanged Christmas greetings with the wounded. But, 'How strangely the words "Merry Christmas" sounded in that corridor of suffering,' remarked Margaret Goodman, for it was a place where many men would, even on Christmas Day, 'cross the dark valley into death'. Yet the soldiers did the best they could to create some semblance of conviviality, producing from under their pillows their own small rations of dried fruit, flour and fat to improvise Christmas puddings of a kind, the pudding cloths 'courtesy of the ladies in England' who had so kindly furnished the bundles of linen to boil them in.[40]

For Florence Nightingale, however, the festival was just another day of endless paperwork and hectoring for supplies. She spent her time firing off

Queen Victoria bid farewell to the Scots Fuselier Guards at Buckingham Palace on 28 February 1854, marking the high point of public support for the army as it embarked for the war in the East.

'Lady amateurs' on board HMS *Hecla*. A surprising number of women made trips to the Crimea during the spring and summer of 1855, touring the battlefield sites in their bulky crinolines with parasols, opera glasses and picnic baskets.

Mrs Rogers, army wife and cook to the 4th Dragoon Guards. Colonel Edward Hodge thought her 'ten times' more deserving of a medal than many of his men for her loyalty and fortitude.

A rare photograph showing army wives (*far left*) in the Coldstream Guards camp at Scutari Hospital. Many of these women were abandoned by the British Army when it embarked for the Crimea.

Lady Eliza Erroll, intrepid wife of the commander of the Rifle Brigade, who roughed it with the army in camp at Varna, Scutari and in the Crimea and boldly wore a brace of pistols at her waist.

Fanny Duberly seated on her beloved horse Bob, which saw the Crimean campaign through with her. Her husband, Captain Henry Duberly, Paymaster of the 8th Hussars, is on the left.

Florence Nightingale receiving wounded soldiers at Scutari. The painting also shows staff members Revd Mother Clare, Mrs Roberts, Selina Bracebridge and Nurse Tebbut.

Florence Nightingale in old age. After the war she turned her back on the accolades, devoting her life to establishing nurses' training and reform of the army medical services.

Mary Seacole, the Jamaican nurse, doctor and healer who made her own way to the Crimea after being rejected by official channels.

Watercolour of the Barrack Hospital Scutari by Lady Alicia Blackwood, who did so much to help the destitute army wives there by giving them honest employment as washerwomen.

The familiar sight of the Sisters of Charity in their traditional seventeenth-century habits and starched caps was a great comfort to the French wounded, both in the hospitals of Constantinople and in the Crimea.

A contemporary engraving of French *cantinières*, who were much admired for their good humour, courage and snappy uniforms, but horrified the British officers' wives by riding astride.

Photograph commissioned by Queen Victoria of Jesse Lockhurst and
Thomas O'Brien, two of the many severely wounded men she visited at
the military hospitals at Chatham in April 1856.

The redoubtable Elizabeth Evans of the 4th Foot, seen here with veterans of the Crimean War, who
doggedly followed her husband to the front lines in the Crimea and proudly wore his Crimean medals
after his death. The British government failed to award any medals to army wives.

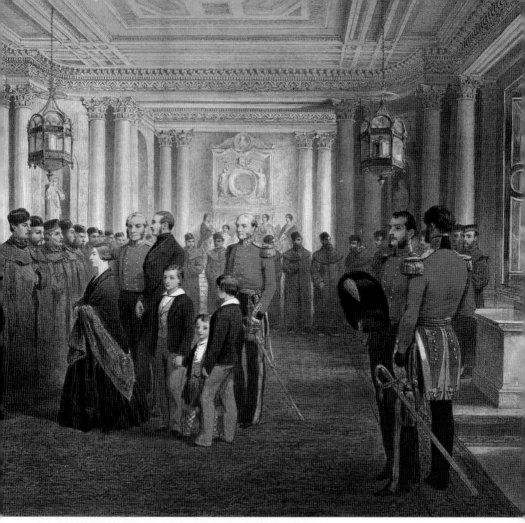

Queen Victoria, Prince Albert and their three eldest sons inspect one of the first contingents of wounded Guardsmen to return to England in February 1855.

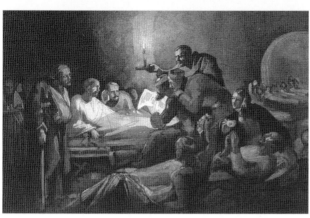

Wounded soldiers at Scutari gather round in December 1854 to listen to 'The Queen's Letter', a personal letter written by Queen Victoria praising the courage of the wounded. Deliberately leaked in the press, it did much to bolster morale among the troops.

Lady Elizabeth Butler's iconic Crimean painting *The Roll Call*. Although not painted and exhibited until 1874, it evoked powerful memories of that tragic campaign and attracted thousands of visitors when put on show.

The Field of Battle, a watercolour by Victoria, the Princess Royal, was exhibited and sold in 1855 to raise money for the Patriotic Fund to assist the destitute widows, children and mothers of soldiers and sailors killed in the war.

letters to Sidney Herbert in England, still angry about the problems created by the unwanted influx of nurses, the Catholic nuns in particular. It had endangered the efficiency of her nursing experiment; 'a tempest has been brewed in this little pint-pot as you could have no idea of', she asserted, warning Herbert that, in her view, Reverend Mother Bridgeman's objective was not to serve the sick but 'to found a convent, completely mistaking the purpose of our mission'. The appalling condition of the sick and wounded arriving at Scutari – 'frost-bitten, demi-nude, starved, ragged' – greatly concerned her. It was a stern warning to the government that if those in the trenches were not soon provided with warm clothing, then 'Napoleon's Russian Campaign will be repeated here'. The list of supplies still needed at Scutari alone was enormous: thousands of socks, slippers, flannel drawers, knives and forks, soap especially – the soap at Scutari was 'bad' – air cushions for bedsores, brushes, combs, razors. Nightingale was grateful that the queen, after hearing that eau de cologne was used for mopping fevered brows (and also to dab foul-smelling wounds), was sending out a consignment, but actually, she observed sardonically, she had no doubt that 'a little gin & water would do better'.[41]

In the camp before Sevastopol the relentless rain poured right up till Christmas Eve; then suddenly the weather changed. Christmas Day dawned bright and cloudless with a hard frost. 'How many hearts in our sodden camp must feel sad and lonely to-day!' wrote Fanny Duberly, 'How many pictures of home, and how many faces . . . rise before our hearts, all beaming with a happiness probably unpossessed by them, but in which our imagination loves to clothe them. Alas! How many assembled round the blazing fires at home drink no healths, but meet in sorrow to pour out the wassail as a libation to the many honoured dead.' Of the army wives in the Crimea that winter, Duberly was fortunate enough to be the only one to enjoy some semblance of a Christmas dinner – on board the *Star of the South*. Two days later she was complaining of the intense cold, feeling the 'want of a fire, of a carpet, of even a chair', noting only in passing that 'we should be worse off in the trenches'.[42]

The frenzy of effort to send comforts to the troops in the Crimea sadly did not ensure that they all actually ever arrived, or on time. 'Where were our presents, our Christmas boxes – the offerings of our kind countrymen and countrywomen, and the donations from our ducal parks?' asked W. H. Russell from the front.[43] 'We hear of huts, flannel, navvies, and potted meats, in yachts, all coming,' wrote Lieutenant Colonel Anthony Sterling. 'But Christmas is come and gone, and our men are nearly all without cover, except the tents.'[44] For most of the army and their women, Christmas in the trenches comprised the same basic rations of salt pork, mouldy biscuit, green coffee and a tot of rum – if they were lucky. It could not have been bleaker. Meanwhile, Balaklava harbour was awash with wood flotsam from the wrecked ships, which could, if the means and will had been there to organize it, have been used for much needed firewood to warm the troops in their dismally cold trenches.

In Britain Frances Anne, Lady Londonderry, was in agonies of worry over her son Adolphus, now at the front with the Scots Fusilier Guards. His letters home to her had described with considerable anger the neglect of both men and animals in the Crimea. The men, he wrote, were expected, in repeated platitudes from the mule-headed bureaucrats back home, to 'make the best of it'. The government's indifference to the state of the army and the 'brave spirits who seem tasked beyond human endurance' made Lady Londonderry's blood boil and she wrote to her friend the politician Disraeli in high dudgeon:

> Surely there must be an hour of reckoning for this hateful Government who go to war without providing an army. It is actual murder to let this little heroic wreck of an army fight these hordes and masses of barbarians who reinforce by tens of thousands while we hardly do so with hundreds. And that wintering in the Crimea, without comforts, habitations, hardly provisions, etc. it is all heart-breaking . . . I think of nothing else even in my sleep and if I were younger I am sure I should seize on the idea of The Times and get a yacht and go there. It seems so dreadful to sit at home and do nothing.[45]

One young woman with the nerve to do precisely what Lady Londonderry so longed to do was Ellen Palmer, the spirited 26-year-old daughter of a wealthy Anglo-Irish baronet of County Mayo. Ellen was, for her day, a highly unconventional and feisty young woman, who regularly picked herself up out of the mud on the hunting field. Touring Europe with relatives, she had hoped to visit her younger brother Roger, a lieutenant in the 11th Hussars, at Varna in Bulgaria before the embarkations in September. But she was not able to do so, and now, in the dead of winter, she persuaded her indulgent father to leave the others behind in Constantinople and take her to the Crimea – at that stage of the war a thing unheard of, the only *ladies* there being a handful of officers' wives including Fanny Duberly.

The imminent arrival of a 'female amateur' – effectively the first lady war tourist – soon reached the ears of W. H. Russell, who noted that Lord Raglan's steamer, the *Caradoc* was 'bringing a young lady of great fortune and personal attractions newly arrived in Constantinople to see a relative in the cavalry camp'.[46] En route, the ship's captain Samuel Derriman fell for Ellen's charms, as, soon after, did Captain William Peel of the Naval Brigade and his rather dull cousin Archie (himself visiting as a 'Travelling Gent' – as male war tourists were nicknamed). Ellen and her father arrived on Boxing Day. She clearly never got close enough to Balaklava to see its filth and misery or the wreckage from the hurricane, observing from the comfort of the *Caradoc* that it had a 'wonderful little harbour'.[47] Besides, she was soon otherwise engaged, surrounded by a circle of admiring officers, many of whom had not seen a woman in months. Taking care to cork her eyes and eyebrows to make herself look more alluring, she proceeded to flirt, swamped as she was with offers to dine and loans of horses – including Lord Raglan's finest – as well as willing escorts to take her to see the sights of the Crimea. This latter she did with alacrity, riding out for hours in the perishing cold. All those years of hunting in the mud and wet of Ireland had toughened her up.

On 5 January Ellen visited the immortal 'Valley of the Shadow of Death' near Inkerman (the subject of one of Roger Fenton's classic photographs), where the 'round shot & shell lay on the ground as thick as hailstones & one could hardly move without stepping on them'. But the highlight of her visit was a trip on 22 January to the siege lines, which she had insisted upon, much to the horror of all the officers including Captain Peel. Ellen found such objections 'comical'. Determined to have her way and see the batteries, she rode out under fire to the parapets where she had to crawl on all fours to avoid the Russian snipers, after which with utter fearlessness she walked 'through the whole of the battery regardless of the shot and our cannon balls flying about and shells bursting in all directions'.[48] The following morning she was up early again for a 13-mile walk along the coast to the Monastery of St George.

The indefatigable Ellen left the Crimea on 30 January, pursued by Archie Peel the lovelorn cousin of Captain William, whom she married soon after. The journal she kept of her visit is extraordinarily laconic for one privileged enough to witness what none of the anxious and grieving families back home could see; but few of the dreadful sights in the Crimea inspired this wilful, self-centred young woman with compassion. 'The men died of cold in the trenches last night,' she observed in her journal for 4 January, in the next breath adding: 'Capt. Peel & his cousin came in this evening & we played cards.' On 15 January after a long walk over the slippery, frozen landscape, which felt like walking on glass, she had again noted, 'the men are frequently brought in with their limbs frost-bitten, & sometimes they are frozen to death'. But again, 'Company in the evening' seemed equally of note.[49] Safely on board ship for home, Ellen recorded that the sea was rough and that she dined at half past five, noting in passing that there were 400 sick and wounded also on board, en route to Scutari.

NINE

Would a Guinea
Be Too Much?

Not long after Christmas 1854, in the midst of a snowstorm on a bitter January night, assistant surgeon John Ogilvy of the 33rd was called out to the Light Division Camp on an urgent case. His patient was an army wife, Mrs Burke, who, 'thanks to the booming of the Russian guns', had gone into premature labour with no woman or midwife to assist her. Only three weeks previously, 'despite remonstrance and reproof', Mrs Burke had struggled up to the camp from Balaklava to be with her husband. Ogilvy found his patient lying in a muddy hole which Corporal Burke had dug for her, this being her only shelter from the cruel Crimean winter. It was six feet long, three feet wide and two feet deep, and covered with a small pyramidal tent – little more than a dog kennel. 'Brushing away a foot or two of snow that almost buried the interesting habitation,' Ogilvy relates, 'I stooped and wriggled my head and shoulders within the door.' He observed with admiration the woman's fortitude during labour. In this make-do-and-mend situation Ogilvy delivered a baby girl, cutting the cord with his clasp knife and tying it with the mother's apron string. He was later happy to report that the commanding officer, Major General Codrington, had ensured that mother and child – 'the only females in camp' – wanted for nothing.

A day later, with a high north wind raking the Crimean plain and making the snow 'drift in clouds which almost blinded one', Mr and Mrs Burke received an illustrious visitor. Lord Raglan himself, accompanied by two of his aides de camp, rode out from the British HQ bringing food and drink and some warm things. Corporal Burke was 'so overcome by his Lordship's kindness that he had no words to express his thanks'. The next day Mrs Burke received a rubber sleeping bag lined with flannel that had been sent to Lord Raglan for his own personal use and which he now wished her to have.[1]

Mrs Burke's was by no means the only baby born in camp during the campaign. Ogilvy's view as a medical practitioner that Mrs Burke and other 'parturient females of the expedition' appeared to be 'retrograding towards the nomadic immunity from severe and long-continued labour pains' was shared by another medical officer writing to the *Lancet* the previous year, who had noted the birth of two or three babies in his regiment whilst in Varna and that they had borne up well against 'all kinds of exposure'.[2] Surgeon Edward Wrench had also been called to the lines of the 27th Regiment in late December, under fire of the Russian guns, where he had delivered a child in a bell tent, the mother no better off than Mrs Burke, with only the muddy earth on which to give birth to her baby.

Pregnant women in camp generally tried to conceal their condition for as long as possible, for fear of being sent home. Then, at the least expected moment, they would disappear without fuss or drama to give birth. One regimental colonel had noted that one of his Scottish 'soldiers' had gained an amazing amount of weight while the rest had got progressively thinner. The soldier had, so it was said, saved a comrade from being bayoneted at the Battle of Inkerman. Shortly afterwards the soldier in question disappeared, only to return five days later with a newborn baby in her arms – for it was a woman, who had undergone an extreme form of subterfuge in order to be with her husband at the front, by making her way to camp and pretending to be one of the rank and file. When her time came she had quietly gone to Balaklava and sought the help of Tatar women. 'They were a tough breed these soldiers' wives,' remarked Surgeon Wrench, 'prepared to follow their regiments to the ends of the earth!'[3]

And it was the same in the French lines too, for the *Times* correspondent W. H. Russell himself had heard tell of a buxom *cantinière* who had been busy supplying drinks to her regiment under fire in the siege lines when, towards the small hours of the morning, she had gone into labour and given birth to twins. Mother and babies were, so Russell heard, doing well. But whether any of these infants survived for very long in such harsh conditions is unlikely; nor did their mothers always recover. Army Chaplain Eade found himself called in to baptize a baby born to a woman who died in labour and whose sick father died soon after. The 'poor little mite', he reported, was being taken care of by another soldier's wife until it could be sent back to England.[4]

Other pregnant army wives, many widows of soldiers who had died in the fighting or of disease, were now being brought home to England. In the early afternoon of 2 January the great screw steamer *Himalaya* edged its way into Spithead off Portsmouth. On board were sick and wounded officers being invalided home from convalescent hospitals on Malta as well as 152 wounded men from the Crimea. But the majority of the 845 on board were the 225 women and 295 of their children, mainly from British depots in the Mediterranean. During the voyage, six of the women had given birth, the last on the morning that the ship docked at Portsmouth. One little girl, born to Mrs Rebecca Strange 'on the high seas' as a later census records, was named by her mother Himalaya in memory of her place of birth. It is doubtful that her mother's experience was a happy one.

During their journey on the *Himalaya*, the wounded, women and children, many in an extremely frail condition, had endured a succession of storms and gales after passing Gibraltar which even this state-of-the art ship had struggled through, so much so that there had been times during the voyage when the captain had doubted the *Himalaya*'s ability to make it back to England. For, after a year in constant service as a troopship back and forth to the Crimea, the ship's engines were already worn out and it was urgently in need of a refit. By the time it arrived at Portsmouth the stench on the lower deck, where the women, children and rank and file were berthed, was sickening.

At Portsmouth dockyard the officers and the most urgent cases were speedily disembarked. But the remaining wounded and the 520 women and children were left on board with no attempt to offer them medical or physical assistance. On the following morning, the wounded were left for hours lying upon the wet planks of the decks until they could be transported to the new Military Hospital at Portsea and from there by rail to the military hospitals at Chatham. Meanwhile, the women – many in a filthy, helpless state – were kept waiting whilst what constituted their pitiful baggage was ransacked by the Customs authorities on the open jetty. Many of them were totally destitute, with no homes to go to and no money to buy food when they disembarked. The correspondent of the *Portsmouth Times and Naval Gazette* observed that they had appeared so weak from the voyage that they 'could hardly be incited to exercise energy enough to select or look after their own trunks and clothing, so weak had the hardships of the voyage made them and this helplessness was evidently increased by fears that they would be thrown entirely on their own poor resources, without any one to help them on their way'.

In the Crimea, after months of delay, post-office facilities had finally been set up for men to make remittances to their wives in Britain of their field allowances. But the temptation to drink away what little money they had was always considerable. A man in the 48th wrote home to his wife, glad that at last he could send her money, 'for if it was gave to me you would not have it, for if I had money in my pocket I would spend it'.[5] But the problem remained for wives of soldiers sick and wounded in hospital: their pay was stopped all the time they were hospitalized and if a soldier's recuperation was a long one, his family remained destitute indefinitely. Take for instance the case of 'poor Mrs Armstrong', whose husband was invalided back to the Chatham military hospital in January 1855 but who had received no pay since the previous August and could thus give her no money. To all intents and purposes she was 'as badly off as if he were still in the East'.[6] The situation for these families was worse in many ways than that of the widows and orphans, who could at least be assured of prompt assistance from the Patriotic Fund.

Fortunately, thanks to the public outcry ten months earlier about the abandonment of army wives when the troops were ordered to the East, temporary accommodation had been set up for the *Himalaya* women by the Central Association with monies from the Patriotic Fund, at the nearby Clarence Barracks of the Wiltshire Militia. The women stayed here until they could be sent on to their nearest relatives, or, failing that, to the workhouses of their home parishes, to which devolved responsibility for their welfare. Within days, 40 women were sent on by train to London and another group of Irishwomen left by sea for Dublin; meanwhile, the Wiltshire Militia did what they could, providing comforts and material support. The Central Association was proud to announce that 15 shillings had been distributed among the women on their arrival, and the funeral expenses for three children who had died at the time were also defrayed. In all it had cost the CA 80 shillings to ensure that the women landed were forwarded to their homes. 'We can only hope and trust,' concluded the *Portsmouth Times*, 'that all the wives and children of our brave troops may fare equally as well as those who have come by the *Himalaya*.'[7]

Similar efforts were made soon after for the women and children on board the *Orinoco* and the *Mauritius*, the majority of them the families of soldiers ordered to the Crimea from bases at Gibraltar, Malta and the Ionian Islands. Many of these women had several children, having been living at foreign stations with their soldier husbands for many years. A contingent of 61 mainly Irish women of the 89th Regiment and their 94 children arriving in early March were accommodated at the old workhouse at Devonport, where fires were lit for them and tea and bread and butter handed round on their arrival and lady philanthropists arrived with gifts of warm clothing. Soon the women were sent on their way to Dublin and Cork and elsewhere. Those arriving friendless back in London – never having before 'seen the great capital of the empire' – were met by officers of the Central Association and taken to lodgings before being sent on to their home parishes. The officers of the association, now having had practical experience of the 'poorer classes', were gratified to see 'the amount of distress that has thus been saved to people, who, in the greater number of cases, are strikingly helpless'. The speedy expedition of the women back to the Board of Guardians of their home parishes also, of course, spared a greater burden being placed on the poor rates of the metropolis.[8]

At Scutari, too, the soldiers' wives rescued by Alicia Blackwood were being encouraged to take passage home, the Central Association having provided money for adequate clothing for them to make the journey. They would now have to prove 'their usefulness as washerwomen or servants' in order to be permitted to stay. Writing on 12 January, army chaplain C. E. Hadow bemoaned the 'mistake' it had been in bringing women out with the army: 'Physically and morally' the Scutari women were 'the worse specimens of Human Nature in the Barracks' and he for one would be very glad when orders were given to send them all home.[9] At the end of February, Charles Bracebridge reported that of 180 women left, 18 were widows and six were going to be sent home; 11 were now employed in the wash house, another 20 were doing freelance washing for soldiers and officers. But as for the rest, they were 'doing little or nothing', still whoring and getting drunk, and with the sick women lying among them in deplorable conditions, where no self-respecting surgeon could be asked to go and treat them.[10]

At its first-anniversary meeting held in London on 7 March 1855, the Central Association reported to its eminent patrons, including the Duke of Cambridge and the social reformer Lord Shaftesbury, on the extraordinary liberality of the public: £104,000 (the equivalent of nearly £6.5 million today) had been raised, of which £35,000 had already been spent on relief. Widows and orphans were now being supported directly by the Patriotic Fund, whose rules specified that only families of dead soldiers could be assisted; the destitute army wives and children, meanwhile, were being supported by the CA to the weekly tune of £1,000. Three hundred women had already been helped to find employment but the association now had 5,000 women and 8,000 children dependent on it for financial support, not to mention numerous aged, sick and widowed mothers of soldiers. The Central Association had plenty of stories of its munificence to tell to its meeting: of the 10 shillings given to Mrs Lane, whose two sons, Sergeant Joseph and Sergeant Nicholas Lane of the Scots Fusilier Guards, had both been killed at the Battle of the Alma; of Mrs Patterson, 'the widowed mother of six soldiers in the 44th' who was deemed worthy of 7 shillings a week for a year; or Mrs McCann, the 'widowed mother of four sons in the 14th', who was granted 3 shillings and 6 pence a week for a year.[11]

A small dent in the numbers needing relief was made by unsung private acts of philanthropy, when those with the homes and the means took in orphans and even widows, though generally on a temporary basis. Lord Shaftesbury had adopted three orphans of a sergeant of the Dragoons; the Countess of Ellesmere two daughters of a sergeant in the 28th; the Revd Dr Baylee had taken in two sons of soldiers and Mrs Codrington of Swindon three children of soldiers from the 17th Lancers. Relatives of

Mary Stanley's took in a widow of the 33rd who was about to give birth, together with her three children, though they warned friends that it was better to take in the children rather than the mothers. Mothers could be troublesome and a drain on resources; the mother in this instance was only to stay 'till she recovers & then seek her own livelihood, leaving the children to the care of a cottager who has a particular taste for children'.[12]

During the winter of 1854–5 a disappointed and frustrated Isabel Arundell, who had been refused three times as a Nightingale nurse, organized a group of 150 like-minded idealistic young women from leading Catholic families into a group she called the Stella Club, its object 'to do the same things as those we would have done if we had the chance out yonder among the soldiers themselves'. Together they set up a soup kitchen and a collection point for donations of clothing, using their own money and soliciting private donation, Isabel herself raising 100 guineas in shillings and sixpences from wealthy friends inside ten days. From the barracks of five local Guards regiments they obtained lists of the women and children of men who had married without leave, and for whom the army took no responsibility, and – ensuring there was no preferential treatment by reason of religion – organized lodgings, food and clothing for the families. They also offered words of comfort to all, 'teaching the poor creatures to trust in God for themselves and their husbands at the war'. Twice a week, soberly dressed for the occasion and carrying whistles for summoning help in an emergency (the club had originally been named the Whistle Club), Isabel and her friends went out into the slums of London handing out charity to the families.

'I know the misery of London,' she later wrote, 'and in making my rounds I could give details that would come up to some of the descriptions in The Mysteries of Paris or a shilling shocker.' Her own beat took her to 100 women and 200 children 'of all creeds and situations', for whom she read and wrote letters, visited the sick and dying and offered her own very Catholic words of comfort. Such work was decidedly risky for a young lady of privilege. The police warned Isabel and her club to stay away from the cellars, garrets and courtyards they visited, where thieves and ruffians loitered, fearing she and her companions would be attacked. But, as she recalls, on her arrival at such dens of iniquity, the waters parted at the sight of the Good Samaritan and she was allowed to pass, the dubious and the criminal doffing their caps to her. Her acts of charity brought criticism from her peers for offering the same assistance to 'fallen women' as to the virtuous ones. But it was worthwhile, for later she had the satisfaction of knowing that many of those she had assisted were now earning an honest livelihood, their children were being brought up 'in the fear and love of God', and that, when they returned from the front, the soldiers blessed her, saying, 'but for you I should have found no home on my return'.[13] Six years later, the fearless Isabel Arundell married the equally fearless explorer and Orientalist Sir Richard Burton.

Since the turn of the year, the queen had taken on an increasingly public profile as the focal point of the nation's compassion and concern for its army, and particularly its sick and wounded. Her popularity had received an enormous boost on 5 January when the British press had published a private letter she had written to Sidney Herbert in which she had begged that Mrs Herbert would 'let me see frequently the accounts she receives from Miss Nightingale and Mrs Bracebridge' from Scutari. She was deeply frustrated, for she heard '*no details of the wounded*' about whom she was so desperately anxious for news. The letter went on:

> Let Mrs. Herbert also know that I wish Miss Nightingale and the ladies would tell those poor noble and wounded sick men that no-one takes a warmer interest or feels more for their sufferings or admires their courage and heroism more than their Queen. Day and night she thinks of her beloved troops. So does the Prince. Beg Mrs. Herbert to communicate these my words to those ladies, as I know that our sympathy is valued by these noble fellows.[14]

Although the press had breached royal protocol in publishing the letter, its effect at Scutari especially had been extraordinary. Just to have nurses come out from Britain to care for them had in itself made the men feel much more 'homely and comfortable', as they put it, but the personal care and concern of their queen was something greatly to be prized. Copies of the letter were posted on the walls of all the wards and read to those who could not read. Many soldiers begged for their own copy to keep as their 'greatest treasure'; others vowed to learn it by heart. It gave an enormous boost to morale, prompting shouts of 'God Save the Queen' even from the dying as they heard it. The *Illustrated London News* gushed out a paean of praise to the queen's tender-heartedness and concern for her troops, seeing her letter as prompting 'an admiration and sympathy worthy of a great sovereign to receive, and of a great nation to bestow'. The *Morning Chronicle* lapsed into toe-curling sycophancy, lauding the queen's matriarchal sentiments as a 'well-spring of illimitable tenderness, goodness and grace'. Now, more than ever, Victoria was seen as the incarnation of modest, tender, retiring womanhood and there wasn't 'a heart in the country that would not throb, nor any eye that would be dry' at the words of her letter.[15]

In the Crimea, however, the overriding preoccupation was not with sentiment but with sustenance – supplies. 'We receive letters by every mail,' wrote the Deputy Surgeon General, John Ashton Bostock, 'intimations from brewers, bakers, pork butchers, etc. that ale, biscuits, hams etc., are coming out to the regiment . . . The whole of England indeed appears to have become a vast committee of supply.' As spring drew nearer the army in the Crimea was receiving everything it wanted. Everything, that is, 'except men – and where can we find again such an army of old, disciplined soldiers as left England last spring?'[16] At Scutari, the supplies were now pouring in in abundance, though Surgeon George Lawson noted how much more valued was the ton of butter that arrived than 'the amount of rubbish anxious old ladies are daily sending out here . . . a rag merchant might make a fortune from the surplus'.[17] Such remarks would have been wounding to the kind-hearted soul who sent out a pair of socks from England, stuffed inside which was a letter from 'The Women of England', expressing the collective grief of her sex at the hardships being endured in the camp before Sevastopol. 'There is not one woman amongst us who would not gladly give up everything she has to promote your comfort,' the writer asserted, 'we long to give up our seats and to crowd you all into our houses this severe winter . . . night and day you are in our thoughts and your sad state makes us quite miserable.' There were, she insisted, ladies of her own acquaintance 'who daily weep when the paper comes in detailing your suffering and exposure in the trenches'.

But hope, according to 'The Women of England', was at hand and with it a change for the better: 'wise men are now being chosen to advise our beloved Queen in this dreadful war'.[18] For in Britain, the winter of mounting protest and recrimination in the press had galvanized a shake-up of the conduct of the war. After an intense and heated debate on 28 and 29 January 1855, the House of Commons voted to appoint a Select Committee to look into the condition of the Army in the Crimea and also to appraise the failures of the Commissary and other departments; it left for Scutari at the end of February. Immediately after the debate the prime minister Lord Aberdeen resigned, taking with him his Secretary at War, Sidney Herbert, and his Secretary of State for War, the Duke of Newcastle. Queen Victoria loathed change. She had tried to resist the imposition of a new prime minister after the amiable Aberdeen but was forced to accept the return of 'Pam' – Lord Palmerston – a man for whom the British public, whipped up by the press, had been baying for some time, as the only politician capable of leading Britain to a military victory. Victoria and Albert had dreaded what new trials the irreverent, high-handed and fiercely independent Palmerston would put them to, having already had numerous run-ins with him as Foreign Minister. Yet they soon found themselves concurring with his aggressive promotion of British interests abroad and, most particularly, the conduct of the war in tandem with Lord Panmure, now appointed to the newly consolidated position of Secretary of State for War.

Throughout the winter, the queen's gifts to the sick and wounded in the Crimea had been generous. For despite the huge amounts being raised by The Times's Crimean Fund for the Army in the East, she had wanted to make her own personal gestures, unstintingly providing money from her own funds to send out every kind of comfort – concentrated beef tea, preserved milk, Windsor soap, cold cream, aromatic vinegar, sodiac powders, Cavendish tobacco, air cushions, tins of mock turtle soup and jars of raspberry jam – to the wounded at Scutari.[19] (In August, the queen, thoughtful as ever, ordered a shipload of American ice to be sent as well.[20]) She had also ordered supplies of books and newspapers, everything from The Times – the most sought after – to the Dublin Evening Mail (a necessity with so many Irish wounded), through the highly popular Punch and

Illustrated London News and Dickens's *Household Words*, to more esoteric literary and art journals.[21] Although the chaplains at Scutari were pleased to note that the book most often at a soldier's bedside was the New Testament, there was in reality an endless demand for 'amusing' books in the cheap library editions published by Routledge and others. All over Scutari groups of illiterate men could be seen collected round the stoves to listen while one of them read.

In the letters she wrote to Lord Raglan at the front Victoria had complained regularly and bitterly about the privations suffered by the army; the constant and escalating sickness was of the deepest concern to her, as was the plight of the wounded. As ever, she wanted to see things for herself and finally, on 20 February 1855, her opportunity came when she met one of the first groups of wounded to be invalided home: 32 men of the Grenadier Guards, who were brought to Buckingham Palace and lined up for her inspection. As she walked down the line, Victoria was told each man's case history. She noted how dreadfully pale some of them were, how very young some of the amputees; no details of their visible wounds escaped her inquisitive eye and she noted them down in her journal later, along with her determination to help those able to work to obtain employment, knowing that once discharged from the army, they would receive only very small pensions that were not sufficient to live on. Despite the careful selection of the walking wounded for the queen's benefit, she could not fail to be profoundly moved: 'I had meant to make some kind of general speech,' she wrote of that day's events, 'but I was so agitated, that it all stuck in my throat and I could only say to Col. Wood, that I hoped all would soon get their medals, which they well deserved.'[22] Two days later she inspected another 26 men – this time of the Coldstream Guards – who she thought looked 'worse than the others', noting carefully that 'A Private Lanesbury, with a patch over his eye, & his face tied up, had had his head traversed by a bullet, penetrating through the eye, which was gone, – through the nose, & coming out at the neck!'[23]

Victoria's curiosity was, however, still far from satisfied. She sought something more immediate than this orchestrated and rather sanitized line-up, a more visceral experience of the marks of war and the true suffering of the wounded – for it was only in this way that she felt she could really share, as a woman, in what they had endured. She therefore set off to visit the wounded in larger numbers after they arrived at Fort Pitt and Brompton military hospitals in Chatham. On 3 March, accompanied by Prince Albert, the Prince of Wales, Prince Alfred and the Duke of Cambridge, she made the first of three visits to Chatham that year. During her inspection she made a point of asking the staff surgeon Dr Parry to send to her a detailed return of the names of every patient in the hospitals at the time that she had visited, the nature of their individual wounds, where they had been injured and how their treatment was progressing. As she met the men, who sat, lay or stood holding cards giving their personal details for the queen's perusal, Victoria did not blanch when confronted with the worst kinds of maimed and mutilated bodies and asked the men questions about how their injuries were inflicted. The sight of 'such fine, powerful frames laid low and prostrate with wounds and sickness on beds of suffering' was, to her as a woman, 'indescribably touching'; if she could have expressed it so, it was also a shock to see them emasculated by their disablement.[24] She felt that her own sex were much more predisposed to suffer (in childbirth) and for this reason they were able to bear pain more easily than men.

After her departure Victoria ensured that a consignment of handmade gifts – handkerchiefs, muffatees (woollen coverings for the lower arms) and comforters made by herself, the Princess Royal and Princess Alice among others – be sent from Windsor, and distributed to those most worthy of receiving them. At the queen's specific request, a detailed return of who received what was dutifully sent, informing the sovereign, for example, that Sergeant Major Alexander Shields of the 6th Dragoons, suffering from 'drop sabre cut of back of head and right arm, lance wound of left side', had been presented with one of her own handkerchiefs; Sergeant John Breeze of the 8th Hussars, who had lost his right arm at Inkerman, had one of her comforters; and Private William Cunningham of the 7th, who had had part of his foot shot off at Inkerman, had been duly gratified by the queen's personal gift of 'two drawing books, 24 pencils and [an] India rubber'.[25] Despite the inadvertent irony of the queen's personal gift of a handkerchief to William Boyce of the 34th Regiment – a man who had had both hands blown off in battle – he dutifully dictated a letter of thanks.[26] Nor did the queen have any inkling of the discord and disgruntlement that the distribution of her favours caused for the officers delegated to hand them out; for how were they to decide who was most deserving and how to placate those left out – and, in respect of the gifts Victoria sent to the Crimea, which included neatly embroidered arm slings made by her own fair hands, how to find time to sit down and compose long, detailed copperplate lists for the sovereign of who received what in a leaking tent in the middle of a war zone?

The queen ensured that her later visits to Chatham in June and November 1855 were much more informal, and she took time to converse in detail with men such as Private Thomas Walker of the 95th, a tall, good-looking lad whose head, bound in rags, 'had an unnatural sinking', the top of his skull having been blown off. Poor Walker had found himself tongue-tied in response to the queen's questions but later told curious reporters, fascinated by the sight of the linen on his head 'moving with the pulsation of his brain', that he should get sixpence a day extra pension for his wound. However, unable as he was ever to go out in the sun, he would have to 'send in a requisition for an umbrella or a large brimmed hat'. His only complaint was that the queen herself had not given him his Crimean service medal for 'it makes it better, don't it?'. But the queen had, nevertheless, asked him to send her a detailed description of his wounds and how inflicted, for she 'wanted so as not to forget me'.[27]

And Victoria did not forget, for she had an extraordinary memory for faces and stories. Whilst at Chatham, she had also made a point of conversing with one old soldier of 21 years' service in the Royals, who had seen the whole Crimean campaign through from the start, receiving a severe arm wound during the assault on Sevastopol for which he had now been invalided out. In the Crimea soldier O'Brien, because of his loyal and brave service, had been a recipient of a handkerchief embroidered by the queen. But alas this had been lost with his knapsack after he was wounded, which 'caused him the greatest distress' so he told her. The morning after her visit, O'Brien received a parcel containing a black morocco leather arm sling from the queen and a silk handkerchief from the Princess Royal.[28] In similar fashion, after her visit, the queen reiterated to her secretary Colonel Phipps that 'if . . . amongst those who *were* or *are* at *Chatham* there are *any* who from their poverty or suffering she could help by the gift of *a wooden leg*, or arm, or any such sort of thing, or by getting them into any sort of situation, or in the way of business or employment, she need *not* say how *truly* happy she should be – the Queen feels *she* can *never* do enough for these poor men'. And she continued to provide help for many years after the war.[29]

Busy female fingers had been just as actively engaged elsewhere in the war effort that winter, although with no fanfare and in rather different circumstances. In Northfleet, Kent, some 400 working-class women were employed at Schlesinger & Co's Ammunition Works, their small fingers being ideal for rolling slips of cartridge to be slotted over the brass tubes of ball-cartridges made of sulphur, saltpetre and charcoal. A manufactory in Islington too had become reliant on the dexterity of its female workers, mostly young girls of 16–20, in the manufacture of lint, where the quickest of them could earn as much as two shillings and sixpence a day working long hours. But much of this work was sent to outworkers – 'scattered amongst the dingy courts and alleys of London' – via dealers, whose exploitation of the women during the increased demand for lint even the *Illustrated London News* took pause to comment on.[30] The worst abuses of female labour, however, took place in the garment trade, where contractors working to a government order for 40,000 greatcoats hired an army of needlewomen – and children – to work 16-hour days in filthy rooms in the East End at appallingly low piece rates: five pence a coat was the going rate and the women had to pay for their own thread out of these meagre wages, leaving them with an average of two shillings and sixpence a week. Such abuses provoked even the sedate *Lady's Newspaper* to comment that contract needlewomen were 'wearing their lives out with hard toil, for a morsel of bread and a drink of water'.[31]

Most of the coats, like much of the other winter clothing sent out by a Commissariat Department reacting too slowly, too late, arrived in the Crimea after the worst of the weather was over, as did many of the knitted gifts from the public. Eventually there was such a glut of mitts, socks and comforters, as well as dried, potted and tinned goods flooding in, that officers like Captain Robert Portal were writing home: 'Pray don't send another box of any kind. I hear of seven more coming out. What in life I shall do with them I don't know.'[32]

Throughout 1855 Britain remained caught up in a frenzy of fund-raising and public-spiritedness and the year was punctuated by an endless succession of fancy fairs, auctions and charity concerts. At the end of March an exhibition of amateur paintings in aid of the Patriotic Fund was staged at Burlington House in Bond Street by one of the queen's favourite art dealers, Ernest Gambart. It included donations of drawings and watercolours from the five eldest royal children. One work in particular by Victoria, the Princess Royal, caused quite a stir. A semicircular painting, subsequently known as *The Field of Battle*, depicted a dying Grenadier on the field of Inkerman in the arms of his beautiful wife and occupied pride of place over the fireplace of the exhibition hall. It was, so the press concurred, by far the best work in the exhibition: 'The composition is artistic, the sentiment poetic, and the execution spirited,' enthused the *Illustrated London News*, 'the children will soon excel their parents – so careful has been their training.' But of all the royal offspring the Princess Royal was the one with an innate feeling for 'high art'.[33] The royal parents were praised for inculcating in their children a 'spirit of public usefulness' in the adaptation of their artistic talents to the war effort.

When asked what price she would like put on the painting, the Princess Royal modestly ventured, 'Would a guinea be too much?' Gambart naturally overrode this and opened an auction on the painting, himself bidding 75 guineas. It eventually sold for 250 guineas, with 55 guineas being paid for a drawing of a knight in armour by the Prince of Wales, and three drawings by Prince Alfred, Princess Helena and Princess Alice all raising 30 guineas each. A chromolithograph was also produced of *The Field of Battle*, which earned another £1,200, bringing the proceeds of the sale to over £13,000 (£788,000 today).

The nurse Martha Nicol remembered how thrilled the patients were at the new civilian hospital at Smyrna, three thousand miles away, to hear of the Princess Royal's painting and the others donated by her brothers for the Patriotic Fund: 'They never could be done speaking of it, saying, with tearful eyes – "God bless them", Her Majesty will never want soldiers while there are such princes.'[34] Without knowing it, the royal children had done more to promote the Army than any amount of recruitment campaigning.

TEN

Miss
Nightingale
Queens It with
Absolute Power

In February 1855, alarmed at the continuing high mortality rates at Scutari, which had peaked in January with 3,168 men dying – many unnecessarily from infectious diseases – the military authorities in the Crimea agreed to an experiment. A total of 462 wounded and sick were sent to an army hospital on the Greek island of Corfu on the HMS *Dunbar*, there to be treated under the supervision of one of the British army's most gifted but controversial medical officers – Dr James Barry. Much to his disgruntlement, Barry, a man of enormous ego, flaming ambition and unshakeable opinions, had been turned down for a posting in the Crimea as being too senior, having hankered after the job of Deputy Inspector General to Scutari under Sir John Hall.

As an outspoken critic of army mismanagement in the treatment of the wounded, Barry ordered a ruthless clean-up of the facilities to be used at Corfu before they arrived. A fortnight after their arrival, thanks to Barry's regime of cleanliness and good diet, 53 men were already fit and ready for duty; 63 able to carry out slight duties. By April, having only lost 17 patients – a 90 per cent reduction in the death rate compared to Scutari – Barry was ready to send 213 men back to the front, provided they had a few days' more convalescence on board a commercial steamship en route. Later that year, probably in October, Barry took his leave in the Crimea, spending three months with the fourth division before Sevastopol.

Whilst in the Crimea, Barry also managed to find time for an imperious inspection at Scutari where he crossed swords with Florence Nightingale, who was appalled by his high-handed, peremptory manner. 'I never had such a blackguard rating in my life – I who have had more than any other woman – than from Barry,' she later wrote; of one thing she was certain, he was 'the most hardened creature' she had ever met.[1] Despite the rigours he no doubt encountered in the army and at the front, and the duels he had sought and fought, the surgeon's true identity was never unmasked. For Dr James Barry, one of the most gifted and pioneering army surgeons of his generation, was in fact a woman. Despite all the many suspicious observations of his squeaky voice, his smallness of stature (he was only 5 feet tall and very slight in build) and his strangeness of manner, his identity was never questioned during his 46 years of army service. It was only after his death in 1865 that James Barry, a.k.a. Margaret Bulkley, was discovered to be female – or, as has recently been argued by Rachel Holmes, an intersexual.[2]

The run-in with Barry was but one of an endless catalogue of quarrels, conflicts and tantrums that plagued Florence Nightingale at Scutari during 1855. Whilst the sick and wounded undoubtedly revered her as a saint and miracle worker – in whose presence they would respectfully cease to cuss and swear – Nightingale herself was never cloyingly sentimental about her work as the press at home suggested. She was relentlessly driven at all times by the ethics of efficiency and clinical detachment; as Charles Bracebridge had so perceptively observed in a memorandum to Sidney Herbert, there was only one thing that preoccupied Nightingale and that was 'the fear of having her usefulness in her Vocation restricted or anni-hilated'.[3] Having banned her own nurses from the wards after 8.30 p.m. (fearful that they might succumb to improper advances from the soldiers), Nightingale herself patrolled the hospital corridors on her own. Thus was born, much against her will, the romanticized image of the 'Lady with the

Lamp', first published in the February 1855 edition of the *Illustrated London News* and later immortalized in 'Santa Filomena', an 1857 poem by Longfellow.

After conducting her ward patrols, Nightingale would often sit up well into the night over her statistical tables, preparing reports on the wounded to be sent back to England. Working herself to the point of exhaustion and refusing to delegate, she demonstrated almost superhuman powers of resistance against the toll of her work until she finally contracted fever in the spring of 1855 whilst visiting Balaklava. Meanwhile, she remained stubbornly embattled: at war with many of the male medical staff who despised female interference in their work; with the purveyors of the Commissariat, fighting to get enough stores at the right time, in the right place, surrounded by bureaucracy and struggling to retain her exacting and absolute control over her disparate team of nurses. Worse still, during January and February 1855, she had to witness a dramatic and unstoppable escalation in mortality rates at Scutari that would haunt her until her dying day.

Since her arrival, Nightingale had seen her great nursing experiment slowly disintegrate. In late January the Mary Stanley party had left their lodgings in Therapia and taken possession of a cavalry barracks converted to a hospital at Kuleli, five miles up the coast from Scutari. Here they were soon joined by Mother Bridgeman and her Kinsale nuns, who had had a frustrating time at Scutari. Deeply suspicious of their proselytizing tendencies, Nightingale had given them little to do other than serve out soup and unpack the bales of old linen arriving from England, the latter task reducing some of them to tears when they found they had to work alongside the often inebriated hospital nurses. Mother Bridgeman remonstrated with Nightingale, complaining that she and her nuns had come out to nurse the sick, not perform menial tasks, but when they arrived at Kuleli, they found the hospital and their accommodation in a confused and filthy state, the food even more inedible than at Scutari and themselves grossly overworked. Soon after, a second hospital was opened at Kuleli where the Kinsale nuns installed themselves in isolation from Stanley's secular ladies and nurses, intent on returning to their own familiar routine of 'holy poverty and mortification'.[4] But religious bigotry and mistrust of their work continued and with it regular complaints made their way back to Nightingale that the Catholic nuns at Kuleli were engaged in a conspiracy to win their Protestant patients over to Romanism.

At Kuleli, Stanley's leadership was muddled and ineffectual from the start and she had quickly submitted to the influence – if not interference – of Lady Stratford de Redcliffe. As the wife of the British ambassador in Constantinople, the good lady had been in the habit of visiting the sick and wounded at Scutari, crossing the Bosporus in her grand official caïque with her three daughters in tow. She now took up a personal mission of philanthropy and patronage at Kuleli, which led her to view the hospital as a personal fiefdom. It resulted in extravagance and mismanagement of the supplies, and it fostered bad relations with the hospital nurses who were looked upon as domestic servants by the ladies and nuns. The nurses would have none of it. Led by the vociferous Elizabeth Davis, a professional nurse of long standing from Wales and still an incorrigible rebel at 65, they threatened to go on strike. Davis complained that if she couldn't work on the wards at Scutari then she wanted to go home – and what is more, she'd tell the papers why she'd come back. Davis was promptly called to an audience with Nightingale at Scutari, where she was reprimanded for her insubordination. The two strong-minded women took a deep dislike to each other: 'I did not like the name of Nightingale,' wrote Davis, after the war. 'When I first hear a name I am very apt to know by my feelings whether I shall like the person who bears it';[5] nevertheless, with surprising even-handedness, Nightingale conceded and organized Davis's transfer.

At Kuleli, Stanley and Stratford's favouritism towards the pious lady volunteers, who took to walking the wards behind the doctors with note-books in hand, was anathema to Nightingale; such portentous behaviour was detrimental to nursing standards, their 'spiritual flirtation' with the patients nothing but time-wasting.[6] In addition, Mother Bridgeman did not disguise her withering contempt for Stratford, whose horror of 'Romanism' she saw as the outlook of 'a weak-minded silly bigot'. By March, Mary Stanley had succumbed to fatigue and the strain of holding together her team of ill-matched nurses, who she felt were like 'troublesome children'.[7] Announcing her intention of becoming a Roman Catholic, she returned to England.

Although she had hated relinquishing control over Stanley and the regime at Kuleli, Nightingale had found it expedient to wash her hands of this group. She had never had any authority over the 300-bed naval hospital at Therapia, 12 miles north of Constantinople, either. This was run by Mrs Elizabeth Mackenzie, a nurse trained at the Middlesex Hospital, with quiet efficiency and a team of three ladies and five professional nurses. Mackenzie was confident that hers was the 'only hospital with any degree of comfort'.[8] Nor did Nightingale have jurisdiction over the new civilian hospital at Smyrna, which opened in February to ease the overcrowding at Scutari, and which would be run by a civilian doctor with a team primarily of lady volunteers recruited in England by Lady Charlotte Canning; nor the state-of-the art civilian hospital at Renkioi, composed of clean and efficient prefabricated huts designed by Isambard Kingdom Brunel, which opened in May 1855.

What mattered most to Florence Nightingale was to retain strict control over Scutari where she could continue to work to her own plan – avoiding the use of lady volunteers and Catholic nuns and sticking, in the main, to the hospital nurses; for she now had high hopes that things might improve with a new batch of Scottish Presbyterian nurses, who seemed to be 'admirable, good plain homely useful bodies'.[9] Then, just as things were settling, Lord Raglan, considering Balaklava now secure enough to have its own hospitals, asked in January 1855 that Nightingale release eight nurses to assist in the General Hospital there. She reluctantly agreed, although, mindful of the temptations of so many soldiers on the Crimean mainland, she sent three of the most well-upholstered and matronly women in her team in the charge of Mother Langston, one of the Sellonites, as well as another four nurses from Kuleli.

One of the nurses at Scutari eager to escape Nightingale's dictatorship and assert her independence by going to Balaklava was the fiery Elizabeth Davis. Her seething resentment of Nightingale had continued to bubble, Davis alleging that whilst she and the other nurses dined on the stewed-up, tough old meat used to make soup for the patients, Nightingale 'had a French cook, and three courses of the best of every kind of food . . . served up everyday at her table'.[10] Once installed at Balaklava, Davis proceeded to bulldoze her own way, taking over as cook in the Extra-Diet Kitchen and challenging Nightingale's rules for the distribution of goods from the 'Free Gift Store'.

Another of the nurses sent to Balaklava, from the Kuleli group, was the enigmatic Martha Clough, whose motives for volunteering to nurse in the East seemed rather less altruistic and more to do with being able, once out there, to visit the grave of her officer sweetheart – Colonel Lauderdale Maule of the Highland Brigade – who had died during the cholera epidemic in Bulgaria. Arriving at Balaklava, Clough had gone into ecstasies of joy to find herself greeted by the sound of bagpipes and 'one of *his* Regiment'. Her first request, once installed in her tiny sparse rooms only seven miles from the roaring siege guns, was for 'men's boots to wade through the mud'.[11] Within a month, however, Clough, who clearly had had a close association with the Highland Brigade over many years through her relationship with Maule, took the unprecedented step of transferring to the Highland Brigade's own hospital on the Genoese Heights above Balaklava at the specific request of its Brigadier General Sir Colin Campbell and with the agreement of Lord Raglan. Clough's uni-lateral action had incensed Nightingale, who, having objected forcefully to Raglan, fired off a furious letter to Clough. The response was a cool one. Clough was unperturbed; she did not consider herself accountable to Nightingale, insisting (correctly) that 'according to my certificate her [Nightingale's] superintendence of the nurses of the hospitals of the Army extended over Turkey and the East only' – not to the Crimea itself. Clough felt that she was more than a match for Nightingale, and that both Campbell and Raglan resisted her rival as a 'martinet'. Confident that they would be on her side, Clough put her head down and ignored Nightingale's rage, certain that she would 'have a tough job to un-nest me'.[12] Up there in splendid, poetic isolation on the Genoese Heights with the wind whistling round her hut at night, Martha Clough found her own kind of heaven: a sanctuary where she could feed the unrelenting morbid grief of her loss, from time to time looking on Maule's picture, which she kept in a small leather case, and dreaming of making a pilgrimage to Devna to lay flowers on his grave.

Nightingale's optimism about her new batch of hospital nurses was, meanwhile, rapidly defused as it had been over most of them. The dismissals had in fact begun almost as soon as she had arrived in the Crimea: Mrs Margaret Williams, a 40-year old widow with seven children, had been dismissed for intoxication on 21 December. Nurse A. Faulkner had been sacked the same day, also for intoxication, despite being found to be a 'very good surgical nurse'.[13] In addition to the five Norwood nuns whom Nightingale had rejected, yet more women had been sent home as incompetent, such as Mrs Anne Higgins, a St John's House nurse, dismissed on 15 January. And then, in April, two of the Presbyterians from Edinburgh, nurses Thompson and Anderson, were summarily dismissed, with no free passage home, after going out with a male orderly and coming back dead drunk – a matter for considerable regret since till then Nightingale had considered them 'hard-working, good-natured women'.[14] Nurse Anne Sinclair, whom Nightingale had particularly liked, also disappointed her shortly afterwards and was sent home for drunkenness. It was no better at Kuleli either: of the 21 hospital nurses in Stanley's party, 11 would be dismissed either for misconduct or intoxication within eight months. The lady volunteer Catherine Hobson described with amusement their wily attempts at getting at the drink. The hospital nurses there would come to her storeroom, 'look at the brandy bottles, and, as if they were synonymous, complain how they suffer from "them spasms", in an attempt to obtain a drop or two'.[15] Florence Nightingale had similar problems with Nurse Hawkins, a 48-year-old widow and professional night nurse from Guy's Hospital, whose perennial drunkenness could only be controlled when she locked up the brandy kept in her sitting room, which Hawkins had regularly volunteered to clean. The offers soon stopped once the brandy was under lock and key.

At Scutari, with all but a few stalwarts among the hospital nurses baulking at Nightingale's iron discipline, the list of negatives stacked up in the great ledger she kept on their employment history: observations of 'bad nursing practise'; 'temptation to intemperance' – with nurses even being discovered dead drunk in charge of patients; 'want of propriety'; 'bad temper'; 'immorality'; 'bad language'; 'going out without leave in bad company'; 'vulgar manners'; 'impudence in conduct'; being troublesome, disobedient and unruly; 'too old for the work'; 'disorderly and lacking in discretion'. The complaints were endless, with Nightingale finding few to praise: Mrs Roberts 'worth her weight in Gold', Mrs Drake 'invaluable, kind, careful, modest', while Mrs Rebecca Lawfield – despite her early complaint about the caps and her lack of technical skill – was 'one of the most valuable nurses I have from her great propriety of conduct & kindness'.[16] Although she despised drunkenness, Nightingale did at least give nurses who attempted to control their drink problem the benefit of the doubt; she was a great believer in the power of reform. The worst sin in her book was dishonesty and she came down hardest on those who had indulged in subterfuge, signing on as nurses merely as an excuse for a free passage out to Scutari and the chance to be reunited with their soldier husbands in the Crimea (hence her deep hostility towards Martha Clough). A few clearly had mercenary ambitions and were out to find a husband, prompting Fanny Duberly to dub them the 'Matrimony-at-any-Price Association'. On one day alone, Alicia Blackwood recalled, six nurses collectively presented themselves in Nightingale's office announcing their intention to get married, closely followed by their prospective corporal and sergeant suitors.[17]

In the main, the hospital nurses appeared to be living up to the 'Mrs Gamp' image, a fact which added grist to the mill of Nightingale's detractors among the male medical staff at Scutari. By 22 April, Nightingale was sadly admitting that the hospital nurses only 'come out to get drunk'.[18] It was a battle she could not and did not win. Ladies, nurses and nuns could *only* work together if they were strictly faithful to their duties. Yet nothing could convince her that ladies were a better option as nurses. Their inefficiency through unfamiliarity with work, their lack of physical strength and endurance (several having succumbed to fever already at Kuleli), their indulged upbringings and predisposition to being waited on made them unsuited to the hard work and long hours. As for the nuns, sectarian rivalries and the risk of proselytizing made them undesirable in the long term too. There was no doubt in Nightingale's mind that the best nurses would have to be professional, trained ones with hospital experience. But for now, the continuing problem of having 40 women or so of varied tempers, religions and habits cooped up together, many of whom were new to discipline and routine, created endless management problems which constantly threatened to bring Nightingale's whole system of nursing into disrepute. And then, on 28 March, the British nursing contingent suffered its first casualty of the war, when Elizabeth Ann Smythe, who had worked herself to exhaustion on the fever ward at Kuleli, fell sick and died of typhus. 'We laid her on the green hillside far away from the old churchyards of England,' wrote fellow nurse Fanny Taylor, 'but we felt the ground was in some sense sacred, from the noble and brave who rested there.'[19] Nurse Smythe's death moved the lady volunteer Catherine Hobson to commemorate her touchingly in verse:

> . . . why is it too, that women grace
> The soldiers' lonely burial place?
> Is it that here, to-day, they bring
> The grave a gentler offering:
> No soldier hero now they bear,
> 'Tis woman claims their tender care.
> She is the first of that small band
> Who, from our dear own English land,
> Came forth, in trembling hope and fear,
> To work her woman's mission here.[20]

In contrast to the turmoil in the British nursing ranks at Scutari and its 'dull, silent and wretched' atmosphere, as described by one British correspondent, the eleven French hospitals on the other side of the Bosporus in and around Constantinople appeared to be havens of calm and order, of neatness and cleanliness, and harmony among the nurses. 'Instead of solemn silence, whispered words and footsteps scarcely heard, blank faces and melancholy routine, we have life and gaiety,' Cassell's Illustrated Family Newspaper told its readers. The ubiquitous Sisters of Charity of St Vincent de Paul were to be seen gliding about in their distinctive starched white caps in every direction where their services were required, 'bringing wine, jellies, soups, in fine, everything which could conduce to the comfort of the poor sufferers'. Nothing, it seemed, could exceed the zeal with which they devoted themselves to their self-imposed mission . . . there was no phase of human suffering with which they were not familiar, and which they had not tended to alleviate. Their voices must have sounded to many a poor fellow, with a lively imagination, like a foretaste of the glory and consideration he would meet with in his own village. Every word seemed to express such a true admiration for valour, such a gentle and special interest in the 'excellent enfant', addressed such a sweet readiness to listen, and such unwearied activity in ministering to the smallest of his wants.[21]

In contrast to Nightingale's views, Dr Peter Pincoffs, a British civilian doctor at Scutari, wrote later of his own 'leaning towards Catholic sisters as hospital nurses'. His experience of English, French, Irish – and eventually Italian nurses (who came in support of Sardinian troops) – was that they were 'intelligent and docile as assistants to the Physician, patient and uncomplaining under any accumulation of work, and invariably gentle in manner towards the patient, so thoroughly conversant with the practical part of their business, that all the help they gave was done handily and expeditiously'.[22]

It was noted that the French sisters also seemed to have particularly clear, bright complexions, an indicator of 'good conscience' argued the author of Pictures from the Battlefield and a quality he had often observed in the French religieuse. Yet there seemed something ineffably sad in the sight of such delicate young women doomed to harsh and often short lives of self-sacrifice and self-denial.[23] Admiral Sir Adolphus Slade felt that the male sex could not equal the sisters' uncomplaining self-sacrifice: 'In our unworthiness we have been unable to elevate our thoughts to that frame of mind which leads women, many of them fair and young, to devote themselves, uncheered by fame, their names and garb conventional, to the service of humanity in its most repulsive form.'[24] One thing was clear however: the French sisters, like their British Catholic counterparts, were also greatly preoccupied with the care of the souls of their patients. One Chasseur related to Captain Henry Clifford how he had been wonderfully cared for by a 'pretty little Sister of Charity', believing that 'her looking at the wound did it more good than anything else'. Indeed, he had thought of the Blessed Virgin whenever he saw her pretty face. As soon as his fever was over and he was recovering she came and asked him 'How is your poor soul?' and urged him to get to confession and take communion and never gave him a moment's peace about doing so until he left the hospital.[25]

The Russian sisters, too, although a lay order, seemed to share the same qualities of absolute obedience and dedication possessed by the French Catholics. They were later praised by Pincoffs for a strength of nerve and energy that 'borders on the marvellous; their self-devotion beyond all praise'. Typhus had hit the first contingent of nurses from St Petersburg very hard, as it would continue to strike later arrivals throughout the siege, and the first three groups were not finally assembled in Sevastopol until the end of January, just as the siege was once more intensifying and they were most needed. Of the 96 Russian nurses now in the Crimea, 63 were in and around Sevastopol and the rest inside the town itself.

It took the British press quite a while to wake up to the presence of the Russian sisters in the Crimea; their letters home, some of which were published in the European and eventually the British press, told of the carnage the allied siege was causing and of the relentless depredation and destruction of a once fine city. The sisters daily took risks escorting the wounded under constant bombardment out to the safer north side and had had to witness fearful scenes on 24 March when 600 wounded were brought in within 24 hours. The casualties were the result of a massive Russian sortie against the allied lines on the night of the 22nd, which had turned into one of the bloodiest engagements of 1855. Ekaterina Bakunina remembered how they prepared for casualties at the Assembly of Nobles: the immaculate parquet floor of the ballroom was now converted into a hospital ward with 200 beds, beyond it the old billiard room was used for operations by Pirogov and a team of eight doctors and eight *feldshers* (medical assistants). Bakunina and two other sisters prepared mountains of bandages and kept the samovar boiling, ready to serve tea laced with wine or vodka to the wounded in order to raise the pulse before they were chloroformed for operations. Once the wounded started flooding in, as Sister Alexandra Krupskaya recalled, the nurses were on their feet for two or more days and nights with no food or drink, yet managing to help ligature blood vessels with complete composure during the most difficult of operations. Bakunina herself assisted at 50 amputations non-stop over 36 hours. She and several of the other sisters proved so skilful that they were considered capable of operating themselves, had they been allowed to. Within weeks, so confident was Pirogov of Bakunina's abilities that she was entrusted with overall supervision of patient care and control of the linen stores.

With the siege dragging on and no resolution in sight, all sides were now praying to their own particular God for an end to the conflict. In Britain, on 21 March a solemn day of fasting and national unity in prayer had been called at the suggestion of the Archbishop of Canterbury. It had been supported, before his resignation, by Lord Aberdeen, but Queen Victoria had objected most strongly to his original suggestion of a 'Day of Humiliation'. 'We are not humiliated!' she had remonstrated. It was all the Russian emperor's fault for his selfish ambition and 'want of honesty'. Britannia's cause was just. When Aberdeen politely added that it had long been the custom to call such occasions a 'Day of Humiliation and Prayer', the queen had refused to budge. She was grateful for God's blessings and help, but it was her 'particular wish' that the day be called one of 'prayer and supplication'.[26] For many of the press, however, the decision to hold this event was misguided. Broadsheets with prayers specially printed for the occasion were being hawked about on the streets 'like mackerel, muffins, or hot-cross buns', all, alleged the editor of Pen and Pencil, to 'propitiate the God of Great Britain and ensure no more green coffee is served out to the troops'. The whole thing was a sham:

> Who believed in the efficacy of the fast? Who fasted? Who was humbled? Who, in cushioned pew, bowed himself down one wit less pompously than upon the latest festival? What was the Palace dietary that day? A Fast which was only fish-eating for the rich, and for the poor one day more unnecessary misery, a day of humiliation spent as a holiday, – was but the crowning sham of that great lord of shams, our deadly enemy – Routine.[27]

The worst of the sham was that the real culprits responsible for the army's suffering in the Crimea were the bureaucrats, bogged down in hidebound systems, who, despite the Commission of Enquiry into the State of the Army now in progress, were unlikely to be punished or their superiors impeached. Nevertheless, in the trenches before Sevastopol there were those who did wish to observe the National Day of Prayer, most notably Captain Hedley Vicars of the 97th. A devout Evangelical, he had led a typically sybaritic life as a commissioned officer in the colonies. In the Ionian Islands his high-spirited behaviour and sense of mischief was taken note of by a senior officer, as well as the fact that he had been 'not very particular about the propriety and the language he used, or about the quantity of stimulants he swallowed'.[28] He also enjoyed himself in Jamaica, where his regiment was posted in 1848, and where he had become acquainted with Mary Seacole. And then, suddenly, while posted to Halifax, Nova Scotia, in 1851, he had found God, upon which he had proceeded to convert the men of his regiment.

Before leaving for the Crimea in May 1854, armed with tracts and Bibles as an emissary of the Soldiers' Mission, Vicars had met and prayed with his devoted friend Catherine Marsh. Convinced he would not return from the war, he had asked her one last favour: 'When I am shot, write to my mother, and comfort her as God will teach you.' Once arrived in the Crimea, Vicars adopted the lifestyle of an ascetic, sleeping on a bed of stones and leaves, eschewing all special privileges granted him as an officer and reading the Psalms by his campfire when off duty. On the night of 21 March, Vicars, consumed by the fire of charismatic Christian militarism and anxious to win souls for God, gathered the faithful in his tent for a prayer and Bible reading. The following night, 22 March, during the mass Russian sortie from Sevastopol which had taken the British lines by surprise, Hedley Vicars had led his men *Boys' Own Paper*-style from the front in a counter-charge, and had been shot. He bled to death before help could reach him.[29] When word circulated of his heroic death, his grave in the Crimea became a place of pilgrimage – and a tourist attraction.

As it turned out, it would be his modest friend Catherine Marsh rather than the military or the press who would ensure Vicars's installation in the pantheon of the great and good. At the request of his family, Marsh brought together an account of Vicars's life based on his journals and letters, accompanied by testimonials from those who witnessed his death. Published at the end of 1855, this most sober and Christian account of the Good Soldier and the pious devotion of his mother and sisters behind the scenes epitomized for all self-respecting Victorians precisely what constituted patriotism and Christian duty in war. The book's publication surpassed all possible expectations. Commended by Tennyson and Charles Kingsley, *Memorials of Captain Hedley Vicars* became the most wanted book in every British household across the land, elevating Catherine Marsh to the reputation of a 'female Dickens of the Evangelical world' and selling 70,000 copies in its first year. Translated into French, Italian and German, it was endlessly reprinted and also published in versions for the juvenile market. As late as 1881 Lady Alicia Blackwood remarked that the *Memorials* were still the favourite book 'in many a village circulating library'.[30] In England, Catherine Marsh tirelessly spread the gospel according to Vicars among audiences of soldiers and sailors, offering his vital and vigorous form of evangelism as proof 'that a man of their own day could be a zealous Christian without being any the less good a soldier'. The disreputable British soldier of old was no more; the British Army was now the 'People's Army' and the Army itself an integral part of the Church Militant on earth.[31] In the welter of post-war books about the Crimean campaign published by male politicians, clerics, medical men, travellers and soldiers, Catherine Marsh's *Memorials of Captain Hedley Vicars* would outstrip them all.

Writing a letter home to her sister Selina in February 1855, Fanny Duberly remarked with amusement on the fact that her name had now found its way into the British press, she being one of the few ladies out with the army in the Crimea. Indeed the story had gone farther afield than that; even reaching the only newspaper in the frontier state of Panama, where the *Panama Star and Herald* reported in its 'Incidents of the War' that 'Mrs Duberly, the wife of an officer in the 8th Hussars, rode over the battle field after the action of the 25th [Balaklava] and witnessed without quailing, scenes of horror and blood that would make many a strong man faint and sick'.[32] Press reports about Duberly prompted the arrival of fan mail, with Fanny receiving letters from 'all sorts of people whom I don't know or have scarcely seen' asserting that she was a 'Crimean Heroine' and that her being out in the war zone made her 'the glory and envy of every English woman'. She found the idea rather preposterous in light of the terrible winter she had endured, during which she had undoubtedly demonstrated a degree of stoicism rare in her own class, adding, 'A fine squawking there would be if we had all the Englishwomen out here.'[33] Nevertheless, despite the privations and her repeated wish to see her less than robust husband Henry safely on the boat home, Fanny had taken a certain pride and pleasure in her position as uncrowned queen of the Crimea.

But all that was now about to change. Competition – for Fanny Duberly and Florence Nightingale too, as it turned out – was about to arrive in the most unexpected and idiosyncratic of forms: a mixed-race Creole doctor, nurse, herbalist and entrepreneur, who had also set her heart on serving and on becoming, as she put it, 'a Crimean Heroine'.[34] Since January, business cards had been in circulation among officers in camp, heralding the imminent arrival at Balaklava of a certain 'Mrs Mary Seacole, late of Kingston, Jamaica', on which she boldly announced her intention of setting up a British Hotel with a 'mess-table and comfortable quarters for sick and convalescent officers' in the Crimea.[35]

After her string of disappointments in trying to join the Nightingale nurses in London the previous autumn, the indomitable Mary Seacole had decided with her characteristic chutzpah to buck the system and do things her own way. There were plenty of officers and medical men in the British Army who could vouch for her good work, having known her or been nursed by her in Jamaica. Determined to make herself useful to her 'sons' in the British Army, Mary had raised the money to buy stores and secured a passage to Constantinople and thence to the Crimea, where she would set herself up not only as a self-appointed sutler and provisioner, but also, with an eye to posterity, as the military man's Everywoman – as 'doctress, nurse, and mother' to the troops.[36]

ELEVEN

···

The Iron House on the Col

Obtaining a passage to Constantinople as a lone female in a world suspicious of the virtues of any woman who went anywhere unchaperoned was not an easy matter for Mary Seacole. But as a woman who prided herself on her independence and free spirit, she was not the sort to let anything get in her way once she had set her mind to do her bit in the Crimea. Eventually she secured a place on a Dutch-owned, iron screw steamer, the *Hollander*, due to sail from London's East India Docks on 25 January. The bulk of her supplies were to follow in a separate vessel; at Balaklava Harbour she would be met by her British business partner, Thomas Day, who was involved in the shipping business and had travelled on ahead of her. In the event, Mary's departure was delayed by more than three weeks because the *Hollander* was requisitioned by the British Commissariat to take supplies to Scutari which had yet to be loaded. It is likely Mary was one of the few civilians on board and certainly the only woman of business when she sailed from Gravesend on 15 February. The voyage proved longer than Mary would have wanted, for the *Hollander* stopped off at Gibraltar and Malta, but having made the sea crossing from Jamaica to England on numerous occasions, she was at least a good sailor and was cheered en route to bump into soldiers from one of her favourite regiments – the 48th – being invalided home from the war.

Arriving in Constantinople on 5 March, Mary took the time to purchase more stores and see the sights, unflustered by being 'an unprotected Creole woman' despite the penetrating gaze of the curious who had never seen a black woman before, and certainly not one dressed as flamboyantly as she always was, in a gaudy dress and straw bonnet with red streamers.[1] Word from Thomas Day via letters at the poste restante at Constantinople was not good. Balaklava and camp life were grim and for a moment or two Mary had her doubts. But her desire to get to the Crimea was greatly reinforced after she took a caïque across to Scutari. The first thing she noticed on entering the great Barrack Hospital was the silence, the men quiet and subdued in their beds. That and the strange haunted look in the eyes of the nurses, who clearly had 'gazed too long on scenes of woe or horror', made her begin to register the true scope of the war's misery.[2] But even here one or two voices called out 'Mother Seacole!' in recognition and she could not resist stopping for a chat or to adjust a bandage and offer words of comfort here and there. Night was now approaching; tired and in need of a bed, Mary didn't want to risk trying to find her ship in the dark. She therefore took the letter of introduction she brought with her from an English doctor to Mrs Bracebridge in hopes that she might be given a bed for the night. Bracebridge assumed Mary had come to solicit a post as a nurse at Scutari. Miss Nightingale needed no more nurses, she told her bluntly. But Mary soon put her straight: oh no, she was bound for the front; she was convinced that she could be of far more use three or four days nearer to the seat of war.

A brief audience followed with an equally frosty Florence Nightingale, tall, slender, soberly dressed and quiet of voice, who (quite legitimately) was unable to accommodate Mary at the overcrowded hospital. She arranged for her to sleep in the washerwomen's quarters (probably those set up by Alicia Blackwood nearby), where Mary spent a restless night being eaten alive by fleas. Before leaving Constantinople, having arranged transportation for herself and her supplies on the Commissariat ship *Albatross* taking cattle to Balaklava, Mary recruited a young Greek Jewish boy, 'Jew Johnny' as she called him, to help at her hotel. At a dirty and chaotic Balaklava, it proved impossible to store the supplies unloaded from the *Albatross* (and the *Nonpareil*, which arrived with the rest of their stores soon after), or find decent lodgings. So Mary bravely took a berth on a merchant ship, the *Medora*, that had been hired by the Army to transport ammunition. Here, she clambered up its steep sides in her unwieldy gown and parked herself at night above tons of gunpowder and cartridges that would have blown her and most of Balaklava into oblivion had it gone off. Meanwhile, she wasted no time in sending out messages to officers of her acquaintance up at camp, announcing her arrival. Shortly before his own death, Hedley Vicars, whose 'kind face had so often lighted up [her] old house in Kingston', was one of the first to come down to greet his old friend from Jamaica.[3]

Like Nell Butler, Mary Seacole was greatly moved by the legions of wounded at Balaklava – a sight which she observed could 'unman' even 'rough bearded men', who stood and cried 'like the softest hearted women' at what they saw.[4] She did not wait to ask permission but as always used her initiative, striding in and doing what she could to help. As the wounded arrived, she gently helped them down from the mules and ambulances that brought them to the sick wharf, and brought them hot tea and coffee, refreshing lemonade, as well as her own special sponge cakes which she made in the galley of the *Medora* for them. The cakes, like Mary's motherly ministrations, were a great comfort and reminded the men of home. Every day for the next six weeks, while Mary waited for the construction of her establishment to be rubber stamped by the military authorities, she shivered out on the rain-lashed wharf under a makeshift awning from where she also sold provisions. The light-fingered Greek and Maltese boatmen managed to relieve her of some supplies when transporting them from the *Nonpareil*, and it was a constant struggle to protect her goods from Balaklava's turbulent population of crooks and grafters, whose thievery beggared belief.

Mary had wanted to build her hotel closer to the front lines, near the Light Cavalry's camp, but permission had been refused. So, up at a rather exposed and desolate spot known as The Col, on a cart track to Lord Raglan's headquarters about three and a half miles from Balaklava, she now chose to build her establishment. It would be located near the stationary engine of the railway line that supplied the camp before Sevastopol, Mary knowing that she would soon be happily attracting well-paid customers from the semi-civilian Army Works Corps and the Land Transport Corps, some of whom had already discovered her medical ministrations on the wharf at Balaklava. With a gesture of Jamaican sentiment at a time when the weather was still raw, she named the place 'Spring Hill', Jamaica being to her as a Creole the 'Isle of Springs', and probably with fond memories of the Spring Hill near Black River where she had grown up. Construction of Mary's premises would take several weeks, continuing in fits and starts throughout the summer, yet despite a considerable cost to her of £800, the outward appearance of the grandly named 'British Hotel' would be somewhat haphazard, for it was made from whatever flotsam and jetsam – mainly wood and sheet-iron recovered from Balaklava harbour after the November storm – that could be salvaged and knocked together by two English sailors and some Turkish carpenters. These latter had been provided by Omar Pasha, the Ottoman commander camped nearby.

Later referred to as the 'Half-Way House' or the 'Iron House' by the troops, the British Hotel was essentially a restaurant-cum-general store with a counter and shelves, chairs and tables. It had room for further storage on its upper floor – though everything was regularly assailed by Crimean rats with 'the appetites of London Aldermen' – and a kitchen attached in a lean-to.[5] It did not have its own hospital, as has often been misconstrued, but Mary spent any free time she had visiting and assisting at the Land Transport Corps's hospital just a stone's throw from her door, where she regularly arrived with armfuls of delicacies and copies of *Punch* and the *Illustrated London News*, as well as religious tracts, of which she had a goodly supply. She was a woman of strong religious opinions and abolitionist sentiments and took every opportunity of imparting such opinions to patients and visitors.

Mary did not advertise the fact in her memoirs, but she operated the same basic segregation of the classes as prevailed in Victorian society at large – a separate canteen for the 'soldiery', the rank and file, which was located in another ramshackle building on her site. The main storehouse and restaurant, as famously illustrated by Julian Portch on the day the French chef Alexis Soyer visited, was a place where she prided herself that 'comfort and order' prevailed and from where Mary doled out her mulled claret, hearty stews, 'capital' meat pies and rice puddings.[6] But this was most definitely the preserve of the *officers*. Essentially, it became a kind of clubhouse where they could indulge in private and often riotous parties late into the night – often in Mary's company – or even turn up for cigars at half past one in the morning, as did Captain Scott of the 9th, and be sure of a welcome. Meanwhile, the main canteen was locked up at 8 p.m. sharp to discourage bad habits among the lower ranks and in order for Mary to maintain an outward degree of propriety. By necessity, a double standard was in operation at the British Hotel – the best was saved for the officers who could pay the most or, as it turned out, who ran up the biggest debts, together with a number of incorrigible newspaper correspondents, both of which contributed to Mary's later bankruptcy. But she made money this way with good motives. Those who could afford to pay subsidized the food and drink she carried up to the front lines and gave away gratis to the wounded whenever there was an engagement, as well as funding the medicines she doled out daily from her improvised dispensary.

Close to the British Hotel, Mary had two small wooden houses erected with sleeping accommodation for herself and the mild and unassuming Thomas Day (who remains a cipher throughout her journal, their relationship ambiguous and his loosely defined family 'connection' deliberately disguised). Despite its isolation, the British Hotel must have been a noisy environment at night with a constant barrage of cackles, moos, baahs and whinnying from the menagerie in the nearby yard, stables and pigsty. Here Mary kept sheep, horses, mules, goats, pigs, geese and chickens, which she lost in huge numbers through thieving; even officers arriving at the hotel for a meal often found that their horses had been stolen from the hitching post outside. Mary's own fine black mare Angelina went that way, as did the French chef Alexis Soyer's horse when he visited.

Finally, Mary had a collection of 'outhouses for our servants' as she put it; though in her memoirs she was never specific about precisely who they were and when or how they joined her in the Crimea. She certainly had two black, probably Jamaican, cooks, one of whom, Francis, appears to have 'slept among the flour barrels' where he was often attacked by marauding rats. We do not know the other servants' names, but Mary's opinion of them was low – they were 'good for nothing' and she took great pleasure in bawling them out for their misdemeanours in her rich Creole patois.[7] Edwin Galt, a gentleman tourist, once encountered Mary in full, glorious idiosyncratic throttle: 'Her English is not the purest description, although there is a lurking desire to introduce fine words, and thus the reproofs she is constantly administering to her servants in her Negro-Anglo dialect become amusing and at times positively ludicrous,' he wrote.[8] Army chaplain J. B., who came to know Mary well, agreed that although she was large and unwieldy in size and when roused could seem intimidating and harsh, her 'bark [was] worse than her bite'. He had no doubt that her heart was 'soft' and she 'had a good deal of the milk of human kindness in her bosom'. Also there to assist in the running of the hotel were 'Jew Johnny' and the enigmatic Sally or Sarah, a beautiful young mixed-race girl whom visiting soldiers assumed was Mary's daughter, because, like everybody else in the Crimea, she addressed her as 'Mother'. Whether or not Mary openly admitted that Sarah was her daughter or ever introduced her as 'Sarah Seacole' is not known, but certainly one soldier, William Douglas, who stopped off at the British Hotel late one night was delighted to have a 'long chat with the old dame and her daughter about the West Indies'; and Surgeon William Menzies Calder of the 49th thought Mary's daughter 'a great character'.[9] This certainly was the impression too of Alexis Soyer when he visited Mary Seacole's establishment and struck up quite a friendship with her, as well as an admiration for Sally, whom he named the 'Dark Maid of the Eastern War'. But such was the pressure of Victorian convention and propriety that Mary could never admit, in her post-war memoir written for an eminently shockable, white middle-class audience, to the existence of her own mixed-race, illegitimate daughter, the product of a liaison with a British officer, one 'Colonel Bunbury', as Florence Nightingale alleged.

Mary Seacole had been extremely shrewd in her choice of location for her hotel. As a respectable woman of business she wanted no truck whatsoever with the many rapacious traders in operation in the Crimea. She sought deliberately to distance herself too from the riotous sutlers' village near Kadikoi. It was to Kadikoi that the multinational community of traders – Greeks, Turks, Jews, Tatars, Croats, Armenians, Maltese and Bulgarians – who had been crowding every available pestilential hovel in Balaklava had now been drummed out by a General Order from Lord

Raglan to make way for the construction of a railway from Balaklava harbour to the front lines. The goods such traders had on offer were largely unappetizing: sour beer, crude and fiery raki, mildewed cabbage all the way from Malta, cheeses the size of a 32 lb shot, that 'in the absence of a supply of ammunition . . . might have been thrown against the Russian walls with startling effect', and plug tobacco so hard it might, in an emergency, 'have served to spike down a railway track'.[10]

With its gaudy collection of temporary booths, grimy tents, marquees, wooden cabins and sheet-iron lean-tos, as well as street vendors squatting in the mud with trays of fruit and nuts, Kadikoi had a fairground atmosphere of barter and carousing, with traders ready to do 'anything to catch the soldier's penny'.[11] Prices were extortionate: up to 500 per cent of an item's original value, two guineas being the going price for a small ham and three shillings for a bottle of porter. Thus Kadikoi soon earned a variety of nicknames among the British troops who patronized it, notably 'Vanity Fair' – in an allusion to the original sense in Bunyan's *Pilgrim's Progress* – but it was also referred to as 'Buffalo Town', 'Donnybrook' (among the Irish troops), 'Log Town' and 'Hut Town'.[12] The ready availability there of alcohol – especially gin and the gut-rotting Greek raki – soon turned the place into one vast drinking den that did much to nurture the already endemic drinking problems in the army. Here, too, the British, French, Turkish and Sardinian troops could sprawl on Oriental cushions smoking tall chibouks in the Turkish cafés. Whether other, sexual services were on offer from local women is not known – soldiers' letters home to wives, sisters and mothers remain understandably silent on the subject.

British officers, many of whom were lucky enough to have hampers of goods shipped out specially from Fortnum & Mason in London by doting relatives, no doubt heaved a sigh of relief when the German purveyor Oppenheim's, 'the Rothschild of the provision market', transferred their operation from the now disbanded camp at Varna to Kadikoi.[13] Soon Oppenheim's planked storehouse with its eight large windows rose on a half-acre site, finding itself in competition not long after with Crockford's with its large yellow flag emblazoned 'Crockford & Co., Wine Merchants from St James's Street London', who opened up in a less salubrious location near a swamp full of frogs. Then came Thomson of Edinburgh, Messrs Gardner & Goulbourn, Booker & Barker, Goldstein, Borkheim – the latter's store complete with 'dimity curtains' at its windows.[14]

Eventually, with trade booming, even Fortnum & Mason set up shop in the Crimea. So successful was Oppenheim's that they later were allowed to build a second outlet in a smaller bazaar at the 4th Division camp right up near the observation point at Cathcart's Hill.[15] At Kadikoi, Oppenheim's monopolized trade with the best champagne, hock, claret and bottled beer, as well as every kind of cured and potted meat, pickles, preserves and hams, French chocolate, roasted coffee, tins of Albert biscuits, toiletries, paper, pens and ink, cutlery, and cigars at 30 shillings a 100. It became a venue, much like Mary Seacole's, where officers could gather off duty for a smoke and a chat and the latest copy of *The Times* sent from England. The tone of Kadikoi would be further raised by the arrival of craftsmen: saddlers, shoemakers, bakers, tinsmiths and armourers, with the shops offering 'every species of goods under the sun, from Cheshire cheeses to mittens and from saucepans to the last volume of the "Shilling Library"'. Mary Seacole was not therefore alone in priding herself in offering for sale 'everything from an anchor down to a needle'.[16]

In a post-war review of Mary's *Wonderful Adventures of Mrs Seacole in Many Lands*, the *Athenaeum* made the point that her honest and philanthropic activities in the Crimea had at last given a good name to the profession of sutler, in striking contrast to the immoral and grasping 'Moll Flagon' camp followers of the battlefields of the British campaigns under Marlborough, as depicted in Henry Fielding's *The Adventures of Ferdinand Count Fathom* (1752).[17] In their former guise as *vivandières* the French *cantinières* too had traditionally followed their armies into war, providing food and drink and other supplies and a welcome and reassuring female presence. During the winter of 1854–5 and with the war now static, they had been busy establishing their mobile canteen tents – some opting for bright, colourful Turkish-style ones – to attract customers, where they installed tables and chairs, a bar and a crude kitchen. They had also been much occupied in scavenging and haggling for stores in and around Balaklava and Kamiesh, for although one of their designated tasks was cooking for the NCOs, they also sold drink, tobacco and hot dinners to the

French rank and file. Some even became adroit at horse trading during the winter when horses were at a premium, earning huge profits, mainly from English soldiers, most of whose horses had died.[18]

In the sunshine of the now approaching spring the perky *cantinières* seemed 'full of life and spirit amid all that "slough of despond" before Sebastopol'. Unlike the poor army wives in the British lines, who had to struggle everywhere on foot through the mud, the *cantinières* would ride into Balaklava 'in full Bloomer costume, booted and spurred', 'sitting on their horses in manly fashion, and carrying as much provender as they can manage to stow away', evoking memories of the famous opera singer Jenny Lind's recent sell-out performances in London as *La Figlia dell Regimento*. The correspondent of the *Patriotic Fund Journal* commended their sociability and vivacity: 'Well done! little vivandières! There is nothing like keeping up a good heart and showing a smiling face.'[19] It did much to raise French male morale, as it did to shock and disconcert officers and their wives of the British camp who were outraged at the *cantinières'* forward manner and the fact that they rode masculine fashion, astride the horse. By no means all the *cantinières* were attractive, but the British, so deprived of the sight of a 'petticoat' during the long hard months of the siege, rated them as 'stunning'.[20] The French knew better: there was an old army saying, 'The quality of the wine is in inverse proportion to the beauty of the *cantinière*.' Rumour spread, in the form of a joke told by W. H. Russell, that they offered other, sexual, services too:

> Two sailors walking up to the camp met a French vivandière riding
> down. 'Hullo Jack,' says one, 'is that what they call a She-Dragoon?' –
> 'Oh no,' says the other, 'that's what they call their Hors de Combat.'[21]

The *cantinières* took pleasure in their uniforms and made sure that they were kept regularly supplied with corsets, fine trimmings and beauty products specially imported for their benefit, but as businesswomen they were as wily as any trader at Kadikoi. As 'priestesses of the *petit verre*', their fundamental trade was no different from that of anyone else – Mary Seacole included. They all sold alcohol and alcohol brought big profits. Nor were the *cantinières* slow to discover that there were better financial pickings to be had among the British than the French troops. One pretty *cantinière* confided to a British officer that 'she intended to desert to the English, as the Zouaves, though the grandest and bravest fellows in creation *had no money*'.[22] Soon officers such as George Cavendish Taylor were recording that the canteen tents of the *cantinière* 'offer great attractions to our soldiers, who go to them and get most gloriously drunk'.[23]

Many of the *cantinières* in the Crimea came on campaign without ever being married to their 'husbands'; one American captain who transported French troops to the Crimea observed that the word *femme* was most convenient, as 'its ambiguity often serves a very desirable purpose'.[24] During the war, some *cantinières* were prevailed upon to legitimize their relationships, for, much like the British army wives, some had made their way there illegally to be with their men. One who did so was Henriette Moutier, an illegitimate foundling, who made her way to the Crimea to join her man in the 8th Artillery Regiment, the colonel taking a sympathetic view and issuing her with a permit to operate as a *cantinière*. Another woman, a cook from Toulouse, had stowed away on a ship out of Marseilles, hiding herself in the coal hold and then making her way from Kamiesh to the French lines. She begged her boyfriend's officer to allow her a permit as a *cantinière* and he agreed, knowing that she was a good cook and hoping that 'she would in return repair my socks, through which my toes were beginning to stick'.[25]

By the time Mary Seacole arrived in the Crimea, therefore, competition was getting stiff. She by no means had a monopoly at her outlet on the wharf at Balaklava, where Mr Day spent most of his time supervising things, nor was she the only female trader. A similar French operation to Kadikoi was in full swing at their supply base at Kamiesh, and there was another traders' village at 'Cannonville' located up near the HQ of the French commander-in-chief, General Pélissier, with its rue de France and rue Napoléon, and its own French-style *estaminets*, *boulangeries* and *épiceries*. It also had some excellent restaurants, one with a notable French rival to Mary Seacole, the wonderful Madame Gallien – *La Reine de Cannonville*, a woman of some pretensions to beauty and grace, who 'dressed with the most becoming taste . . . with a small white cap on the crown of her head and a silk embroidered apron and served her patrons in white kid gloves from behind her table'. Her 'style', according to Edwin Galt was most definitely 'Parisian'.[26] Nevertheless, word quickly spread about the freshly cooked wholesome food to be found at Mrs Seacole's, and no doubt too about the glorious idiosyncrasies of the hostess herself, and Mary was soon entertaining not only British officers but also French Zouaves and Chasseurs, as well as the Turkish general, Omar Pasha himself. He had taken a shine to Mary and soon became a regular customer, putting to one side his religious faith to enjoy champagne, sherry and bottled beer with the best of them, to the strains of his own military band ordered down specially to play for him.

How the British troops in the Crimea reacted to the sight of a black woman unexpectedly appearing in their midst is impossible to gauge, but it must have caused something of a sensation; as for the Russians, their eyes were on stalks at the sight of Mary when the hostilities came to an end. Certainly the sight of *any* woman aside from the army wives, nurses and *cantinières* who had some legitimate reason to be there was enough to cause gossip during the winter of 1854–5. In particular, officers' diaries and letters of the war are full of largely sarcastic and uncomplimentary remarks about Fanny Duberly, who was derided as 'Mrs Jubilee' and criticized for her strong-mindedness, with no admission made of her courage and steely determination in seeing the winter out in the Crimea. It was enough that Mrs Duberly paraded herself around the front lines wearing leather-lined riding trousers under her gown, but the sight of Mary Seacole would have been even more extraordinary. It certainly was for 'Assistant Chaplain J.B.' (probably John G. Boudier) who wrote one of the most vivid accounts of her:

> I shall not easily forget the first glimpse I had of her. I was sitting in the hut of an artillery officer, when I perceived a peculiar object in the distance. I took it at first for an ostrich, but on nearer approach I observed the flutter of a veil.
>
> 'Who, in the name of Crimean incredibilities, is that?' I exclaimed.
> 'Oh! That is Mrs. Seacole.'
> 'And who is Mrs Seacole?'
> 'Why, don't you know? She is grand purveyor to the army, doctor of

medicine, cook, confectioner, and nurse – in fact, quite a Caleb Quotem [Jack of all trades] in her way; and, in a word, the soldier's friend.' . . .

'But is she anything like a woman in her conversation and manners? Is she not rather a sort of giraffe?'[27]

Mary might have seemed, at first encounter, a figure of fun for some, but for the good chaplain she possessed, as he later discovered, 'the kindest disposition in the world'. She had the same practical sense as Fanny Duberly, choosing a bloomer-type costume to enable her to ride up near the front lines, and also sported a riding hat and veil. But here conventional sartorial taste stopped, for Mary was a warm-hearted and exhibitionist Creole woman who had grown up loving the vivid colours of the West Indies and favoured dresses in bold primary colours – red, blue, yellow. Her wearing of such colours was undoubtedly an allusion to her Creole roots and her childhood at Black River, when the annual *John-Canoe* (Junkanoo) celebrations would have seen rival factions in the town dress in the Blue of Scotland (of which ancestry Mary was inordinately proud) and the Red of England. Both colours signified for her a fierce loyalty to Jamaica, Britain, Empire and Queen and would have signalled as much to her clientele.

Mary would have needed to have powerful friends in the army to operate as an independent woman in a war zone. In the Royal Navy, too, she counted many old favourites from Jamaica days, among them the queen's nephew Count Gleichen, who in 1871 executed a terracotta bust of her. Something of her reputation had clearly gone before her, facilitating a unique social and racial acceptance of Mary's presence in that strange, hermetically sealed part of old England that the Crimea became, for by the spring of 1855 it had transformed into one great country club to which the war was increasingly an adjunct. One of Mary's most powerful patrons, alongside senior commanders such as Lord Rokeby, was the Inspector-General of Hospitals, Sir John Hall, himself an army-trained surgeon who had served many years in the West Indies with the 33rd and twice survived attacks of yellow fever. Hall it was who, no doubt having witnessed the efficacy of Creole medicine, gave tacit approval to Mary's nursing activities. In a conversation she had with Nightingale after the war, her sister Parthenope noted: 'Dr Hall looked over her [Mary's] medicine chest & gave her his sanction to prescribe to mark the difference with F, i.e. that he extended his protection to Seacole & opposed F to his utmost.'[28] A bitter animosity between Hall and Nightingale had existed from the first and Hall's action further fuelled Nightingale's implacable opposition to Seacole. But it was not simply a matter of racial prejudice; Nightingale's antipathy to Seacole was more complex. Here was one loose cannon – a black woman, nurse, doctor, healer and herbalist – whom the Lady Superintendent knew she would never ever get to toe the line. Mary Seacole spelled trouble in Nightingale's eyes. Seacole presented a direct threat to her own nursing experiment by seeking to disseminate her 'quackery' throughout the army in defiance of Nightingale's own rigid standards of nursing. But there would be issues of good old Victorian propriety at play too, for, to make matters worse, Mary Seacole readily sold alcohol to the troops. In the course of the warm-hearted and good-natured welcome she gave to all and sundry who visited the British Hotel, a fact which even Nightingale attested to, Mary had, however, 'made many drunk'. And to Nightingale, who saw alcoholism among the troops as 'the real pestilence with which . . . we have to struggle in an army idle and sick', that was anathema.[29]

It was not just the good food and drink to be had at the British Hotel that soon had the camp before Sevastopol buzzing; it was also something far more important. Mother Seacole, it appeared, had her own highly specialized cures, for she 'had the secret of a recipe for cholera and dysentery; and liberally dispensed the specific, alike to those who could pay and to those who could not'.[30] By the standards of traditional medical practice of the day, Mary Seacole undoubtedly had as much professional qualification and hands-on experience as any average British doctor. Conventional treatments for enteric disease at the time included the use of fluids such as camomile tea, gruel, barley water, chicken broth; compounds of chalk, powder of rhubarb and, if worst came to worst – opium and chloroform for the agonizing cramps of diarrhoea or dysentery. Quinine added to wine was also found to be effective against cases of chronic fever, but many British doctors, Dr James Barry included, did not approve of chemical astringents, and suggested small doses of sulphuric acid with opium added.[31] All too often though, opiates, of which Mary Seacole disapproved, were heavily relied on as a failsafe.

In contrast to Barry's stern warning against astringents, Mary was very much an advocate of their use, as too was Deputy Surgeon General Bostock, who, having witnessed the terrible malignancy of the cholera at Varna, had despaired at how nothing seemed to alleviate it except slightly acid drinks.[32] In Jamaica Mary had been trained by her mother in the use of an extremely diverse native pharmacopoeia, much of which had been developed to treat the sick African slaves on the plantations and had been gathered together in 1801 in Thomas Dancer's *The Medical Assistant, or Jamaica Practice of Physic*. Such remedies had saved the lives of many British servicemen who had succumbed to fever in the West Indies, including Horatio Nelson, who himself had been nursed back to health when sick with fever at Port Royal in 1780 by a Jamaican doctress, Couba Cornwallis.

Mary had thus become conversant with a range of treatments based on natural barks and fruit rinds, particularly pomegranate, which would be boiled in water with cinnamon bark (one of her most-favoured ingredients), or sometimes ground into a powder, to which could be added port wine or guava jelly to sweeten. A decoction of the leaves, buds and fruit of the guava was also popular, as was the juice of the cashew fruit squeezed into wine and turned into a refreshing 'sangaree' (sangria). But the most common form of treatment for diarrhoea and dysentery and the many 'bilious fevers' that plagued the British army and navy in the West Indies was the shavings of bitter bark from the logwood or mahogany trees that grew in such abundance and were essential to the Jamaican export trade.[33] These chippings would be boiled into an astringent decoction, again flavoured with cinnamon and with guava jelly. In the Crimea, of course, Mary's herbal remedies would be severely limited by the availability of the fruit, barks and spices she needed; but, located as it was on the Black Sea, there would have been a regular supply of pomegranates via Constantinople and Balaklava, for the fruit grows in profusion around the Black Sea coast in Asia Minor, Bulgaria and Georgia.

With this rich tradition behind her, one might even argue that Mary Seacole was far better experienced in nursing the diseases so prevalent in the Crimea – cholera, fever, dysentery, diarrhoea – than any of the British medical men out there. Surgeon William Menzies Calder certainly thought so. Her fame 'as a doctress for Cholera and Diarrhoea are spread all over the camp', he asserted. He had witnessed at first hand how a man from the Land Transport Corps had come 'to ask her advice, and buy some camphor as a preventative against cholera'. Mary, he said, had 'laughed him out of his fears and sent him away a different man though without his camphor and giving him sound practical advice as regards regimen, drinking, etc.'. From all Calder had heard, Mary's powders had 'worked miracles' and 'certainly cannot be *less efficacious* than all our drugs &c for cholera, from all the varieties of which I have as yet seen little benefit here'.[34]

It did not take long for the ordinary soldiers to make the correlation that those who went to Mary Seacole for a cure had a far better chance of recovery than those taking themselves off to the nearest army hospital. She was equally adept at stitching a wound and setting a broken bone; extracting bullets, too, was a skill learned long ago among the gun-slinging prospectors of Panama. Certainly, whenever men of the nearby Land Transport Corps were injured or fell ill, they were brought straight to Mary rather than their own doctors. By July, the *Morning Advertiser* would be telling its readers of Mary Seacole's skills as 'both a Nightingale and a Soyer in her way', for so great was her experience in treating cholera (now again plaguing the British camp) and diarrhoea that 'she is constantly beset with applications, and it must be stated, to her honour, that she makes no charge for her powders'.[35] Such was the demand too for Mary's remedy for jaundice that she 'kept it mixed in a large pan, ready to ladle it out to the scores of applicants who came for it' every morning.[36]

But nothing could beat the good food, the soups and broths and roast chickens, jellies and blancmanges that she dispatched on request or delivered in person to those lying sick in camp and in need of invalid food. However, as time went on, the demands on Mary as doctor, nurse and cook become so huge that she rarely had time to eat or get enough sleep. Her day started at 4 a.m. – cooking, plucking fowl, cleaning and readying the store for the breakfast rush for hot coffee at nine, followed promptly afterwards by her morning surgeries when she spooned her cures for dysentery and diarrhoea into lines of grateful mouths. The work was never-ending, as was the constant pilfering and thievery. And with such a motley crew of unreliable servants as she claimed to have, she was never able to delegate. Then, on 9 April, came the renewal of the artillery bombard-ment of Sevastopol – the start of a long softening-up of the Russian defences as a prelude to a major assault on the city. It was followed by two more bombardments in June, which meant her attentions were increasingly diverted to the front lines and the needs of the wounded.

Meanwhile, the Crimea was becoming host to an influx of new women. But they shared neither Mary's class, colour not sentiments; nor were they army wives, nurses, washerwomen or cooks. This new breed of 'female amateurs' – complete with maids and band boxes, opera glasses and tele-scopes as well as the latest fashionable crinolines – now began to arrive in the company of 'TGs' (Travelling Gents) by private yacht and steamer to visit the sites of the battles of Alma, Balaklava and Inkerman and thrill to the live action of the bombardment of Sevastopol. Taking advantage of the £5 all-in tours to the sights of Constantinople and the Crimea on offer in the British press, the lady war tourist was about to distract, attract, obstruct and infuriate those in the military who were already most decidedly of the opinion that the Crimea was positively 'no place for ladies'.[37]

TWELVE

A Morbid Taste
for Horrors

'Can this be a journal of a campaign? I think I must change its name to a new edition of the "Racing Calendar".'[1] So wrote Fanny Duberly in March 1855, anticipating the start of the racing season, as she looked out on a Crimean plateau where the sky was a cloudless blue, the birds were singing and underfoot was a carpet of glorious spring flowers. Even the war correspondent W. H. Russell could not fail to note that the Crimea was, after such a cruel winter, now magically transformed into a place of great beauty. The bird life was wonderful, with 'brilliant gold-finches, large buntings, golden-crested wrens, larks, linnets, titlarks and three sorts of tomtits, the hedge sparrow, and a pretty species of wagtail'. Nevertheless, how strange it was, Duberly wrote, to hear the birds 'piping and twittering about the bushes in the intervals of the booming of cannon'.[2]

With the whole of the Crimea now a profusion of spring flowers, especially crocuses and snowdrops, soldiers found time to stop and dig up bulbs and roots to send home to their families in England. There was no doubt in their minds that the Crimean snowdrop was the true snowdrop. Taller and robuster than the English variety, it seemed to have a powerful significance for everyone on the peninsula as the agonies of winter receded, for it was the first flower to push its graceful head 'like a resurrection for the dead' through the piles of shot and shell and the last of the winter snow. It was a flower of consolation, a '"memory's flower", for many a dear friend who has gone down into a *cold, cold* grave in the service of his country'. It also somehow brought hopes of an end to the war, 'of brighter skies, of comfort and plenty, and glory in the field'.[3]

Even the most hardened soldiers were taking time in their letters to describe the beauties of the Crimea and its natural life. Those parts of it away from the booming siege guns now made the most perfect of locations for relaxing rides where the rye grass was three or four feet high, and there was 'dwarf oak, burbury, hornbeam, patches of wild bearded wheat, barley & every conceivable wild flower, acres of musk, mignonettes, lavender . . . burrage . . . which is the most perfect turquoise blue, very large harebell, such quantities of mallow, and pink and rose coloured gladiolas, that you never saw a rosery more full of colour'.[4] Hearing such testaments from Lord Rokeby, commander of the 1st Division, Queen Victoria, who had since girlhood made a sentimental collection of pressed flowers from the places and events in her life, sent him instructions to go out and pick a selection of flowers for the royal album. Rokeby politely contained his annoyance at such a time-wasting diversion from his military duties, warning Her Majesty that now high summer was approaching it might be impossible to 'collect any tolerable amount of specimens' because the extreme heat combined with the 'diligent use of their teeth, and trampling of the hoofs of thousand upon thousands of animals of all descriptions, has rendered the whole of the great position occupied by the Allied armies as barren and brown as the desert of Sahara'. Nevertheless, he dutifully went out in search of a nosegay for the queen, which survives, carefully preserved in the royal flower album at Windsor Castle.[5]

After being so long confined to the narrow quarters of the *Shooting Star*, Fanny Duberly was now living in camp, the proud possessor of a wooden prefabricated hut sent out from England. Her Crimean residence was in fact a very cramped affair, with only room for the basics of bed, stove, table and personal possessions, but she brightened up the interior as many did by papering it with engravings from the *Illustrated London News*, painstakingly colouring them in to add cheerfulness. It was however decidedly infra dig to entertain her officer friends sitting perched on her rickety bed, so Fanny organized an additional reception room for entertaining – a Turkish marquee attached to the hut. This became her 'salon' – with a blue lining to keep out the heat, cocoa-mats and rugs on the floor, a table, chairs and one solitary armchair for special guests. She filled it with the flowers now growing in such profusion. Suddenly life seemed so much brighter: she went into Balaklava and bought chickens; she planted a vegetable garden, hired a good Maltese cook and ordered a tailor-made riding habit from a Zouave tailor at the French camp – sky blue with black braid trimming in the style of the uniform worn by the illustrious *Chasseurs d'Afrique*. Later, a black and white cat made her happiness complete.

The spring race meetings held by the British on 5 and 17 March had been the first of a calendar of social events that Fanny was now revelling in. She had thought it quite remarkable that men who had survived the miseries of winter 'drowned in rain and mud, wounded in action, and torn with sickness' should, in the first warm, balmy days of spring, 'start into fresh life like butterflies, and be as eager and fresh for the rare old English sport, as if they were in the ring at Newmarket'.[6] She also was greatly heartened to see that the few horses that had miraculously survived the terrible winter were now recovered and going at the fences 'as if they like the fun'. The French staged their own races three weeks later in the valley of the River Chernaya, attracting a crowd 'as large as that at Epsom or Ascot', as General William Codrington wrote to the queen. It was, for him, a 'wonderful feat' to see such a 'peaceable assembly' of British, French and Sardinian troops, and all 'within talking distance of a small portion of a Russian army, all to see a national English sport on Russian territory'.[7] For the British officer class so far from home, the Crimea took on an air of normality with the resumption of traditional sports of racing, hunting (the quarry being not foxes but the feral dogs that roamed the Crimea), bathing parties on the shingly beach east of Balaklava, fishing in the River Chernaya, cricket matches, and that enduring military standby, camp theatricals. What better recreation could there be than taking lazy picnics at the exquisitely situated Monastery of St George, five miles east of Balaklava, perched on the Crimea's craggy coast with its spectacular views, its atmosphere of utter tranquillity matched by the gentle rippling of the clearest and bluest of seas down below. It must have seemed bizarre to the enemy. 'The Russians must certainly think us an odd race of people,' observed George Cavendish Taylor, 'to carry all our national institutions about and establish them wherever we go – even to a railway and electric telegraph'.[8]

In the meantime, the bombardment of Sevastopol intensified, but with the war essentially static and a supply of horses now readily available, visitors were arriving in the Crimea in ever greater numbers to take a look at the action and join in the bizarre country-club atmosphere of this 'very personal war'. Many officers and tourists knew each other, coming as they did from the same well-to-do social circuits in England and from old military families; Captain Henry Clifford, for example, wrote home enquiringly about one officer's wife who was living in camp: 'Can you tell me who is Mrs Van Straubenzee – wife of Colonel Straubenzee of the 3rd Buffs, now Brigadier General of the Second Brigade, Light Division? She is a Catholic and was at Taunton with Elly. She knows . . . many others of our lot, so that it is quite delightful talking to her about my people.'[9]

Male visitors certainly were generally welcomed as guests of the army, prompting lavish dinner parties and drinking sessions. Fred Dallas was only too happy to welcome friends of his who came to the Crimea as Travelling Gents, to show them the sights and take them to the siege lines at night for a pot shot at a 'Rooshian' or two. 'If a shot will only come at the right time they are quite delighted & we always tell them that it went quite close to them, which completely satisfies them & they wisely go home again. Altogether I cannot fancy a pleasanter trip for a man with many acquaintances in the army than a week or two here . . . They do not find champagne at dinner & a bed in a tent in this weather at all disagreeable.'[10]

But it was a different matter when it came to the ladies; there being so few of them, they were a constant distraction wherever they went. This was all very well at the Crimean race meetings, where their presence in dainty muslins and veils, sitting in carriages, complete with their picnic baskets, parasols and opera glasses was a great novelty to many, such as Lieutenant Francis Gore Currie, who had complained of hardly 'seeing a petticoat' in months except 'Mrs Jubilee'. Had the ladies been 'some strange animals they could not have been more stared at'.[11] But the increasing presence of officers' wives in camp kept their husbands away from their duties and raised a chorus of disapproval among many of their fellow officers.

Mrs Forrest, wife of Lieutenant Colonel William Forrest of the 4th Dragoon Guards, was certainly neither pretty nor endearing, and Colonel

Edward Hodge rued the day she returned to camp. Her husband was not the most 'active' officer at the best of times, and his wife's return meant that 'the regiment may go to the dogs, for all that he will do for it'. Hodge had far more time and respect for the stalwart Mrs Rogers, camp cook and laundress; he ensured she featured in two photographs of the 4th taken by Roger Fenton and vowed that he would apply for a Crimean Medal for her as she 'deserve[d] it ten times more than half the men who will get it'. Hodge was horrified when the 'horrid' Mrs Forrest duly arrived and then, horror of horrors, was installed by her husband in his half of the hut he shared with Hodge. Unable to bear the sight and sound of the couple 'washing, and dressing and talking to each other', Hodge did as much as he could to avoid her, refusing to invite her to dine with them and sending down her daily ration of rum in a jam pot, since he considered her being in the Crimea and trying to muck in with the men was 'not quite what a lady ought to do'. The hapless Mrs Forrest grew thinner and more miserable and hungry by the day, 'screaming for our cook to bring things to her' and 'sponging upon us for her food'. Then she turned the hut into a kitchen; the stench of 'some greasy concoction' prepared in it made Hodge's stomach turn. The final insult to his sense of propriety was that Mrs Forrest, lacking her own female attendant, was obliged to empty her own leather slop bucket every morning. Worse still was the public display of Mrs Forrest's unmentionables: one morning Hodge saw the lieutenant colonel's own batman picking the fleas from a pair of Mrs Forrest's drawers, 'after which he hung them out to air'. It was more than any respectable officer could stand. How Forrest could permit his wife to be the 'common gossip of the camp' Hodge did not know. As for her 'infernal cackle', it was driving him demented and would do so until the Forrests decamped to winter quarters in Pera in December.[12]

Those officers' wives who did not choose to rough it and run the gauntlet of the fleas in camp usually stayed on board ship in Balaklava or Kamiesh harbours, from where, instead, they would 'seduce their husbands to run there after them, as many a weary staff officer has found to his sorrow'.[13] Despite this influx of what one would imagine to have been a welcome addition to her own sex, Fanny Duberly remained curiously resistant to admitting their existence in her journal. In mid-April she remarked in a letter home to her sister Selina that Roger Fenton had come and taken her photograph (sitting on her favourite old horse Bob with Henry proudly holding the reins). She claimed an 'incredible' number of copies had been made and sold of it, for 'every man I meet seems to have one'. Fenton, she said, had not charged her anything for the photo, 'I being the only woman'. Fanny was desperate to cling on to that pretence for a little longer. Quite aside from the lowly army wives in camp, including her own servant Mrs Finnegan, who clearly didn't register on her radar as female, Fanny resolutely refused ever to acknowledge the presence in the Crimea of that other well-known female figure – Mrs Seacole – of whom she must by now have heard tell. The curious failure of both Fanny Duberly and Mary Seacole to acknowledge each other's presence in the Crimea not only confirms the social and racial barriers that prevented fraternization, but also reinforces the determined objective both women had in their post-war memoirs of creating a mythology about themselves as gutsy lone women in a violent man's world. Certainly the British Hotel would have been decidedly off limits for an officer's wife and a lady such as Fanny Duberly; she had found it hard enough disguising her jealousy of Lady Erroll in camp at Varna, had made only a few sour comments about the eccentric Mrs Cresswell there, and would now be just as resistant to lauding the virtues of a beauteous and head-turning rival in the figure of Lady Agnes Paget. Fenton had nominated Lady Agnes the 'belle of the Crimea' and she would soon set all the camps of the Crimea talking.

Meanwhile, Fanny was intent on raising her own public profile, going everywhere and doing everything in her inimitable style, constantly riding up to Cathcart's Hill to watch the bombardment of Sevastopol and then seeing the wounded and mangled bodies being carried off. This, in the opinion of many officers, was distasteful in the extreme, not to say unsexing.[14] Mrs Duberly had no business parading herself, for she was not a nurse with a valid reason to be there; instead she was constantly 'à cheval, a pushing, vulgar woman [who] treats her husband more as a servant than what he is'. There was no doubt in the mind of Captain Robert Hawley that in that particular marriage Mrs Duberly wore the trousers – 'and the boots too'. So confident was she of her own position that Hawley reported how Duberly had inserted an advertisement in the army newspaper, the *Hue and Cry*: 'Lost: a lady's spur without a rowel. Please return it to the Camp, 8th Hussars' – on the assumption that everyone knew where to find her.[15]

The British privately referred to Fanny Duberly as 'the Vulture' due to her predilection, as they perceived it, for riding round the battlefields after a fight 'among scenes of peculiar fascination'. But for Fanny herself, day followed pleasant, hot summer day. She found herself much admired by the French, who unlike the British appeared to like her strong-mindedness and courage and who, in deference to her riding skills and her sporting of a Chasseur-style riding habit, called her the *Amazone* and dedicated a polka of that name to her. Fanny now made regular visits to the French camp, with the ubiquitous Henry in tow, where she sparkled with her natural vivacity and wit and joined in games of écarté. Here she was quite the social butterfly, breakfasting at French headquarters one morning with General Féray, followed by lunch with the commander of the Heavy Brigade of the French Cavalry, General Forton, followed by an energetic gallop across the Crimean valleys to a Russian hunting lodge, the Château Perovsky, before dinner and champagne under an arbour of trees back at General Forton's and then to General Féray's again until past midnight.[16] As Captain Anatole Berthois, the officer who accompanied her, remarked, she was a 'true Clorinde' (in the style of the female Saracen knights sent to fight against the Crusaders). The French had a knack for making the most of a situation, he observed: 'one does all sorts of things in the French cavalry, and none engender melancholy'.

During the miserable weeks of despair after the debacle of the Charge of the Light Brigade, in which he had lost some of the finest soldiers in his regiment, the 4th Light Dragoons, Lord George Paget had grown ever more homesick for the beautiful wife he had married on 27 February 1854 – his much younger cousin Lady Agnes Paget. The lovelorn Paget saw no point in spending the winter in command of 'fifteen horses' and returned to England intending to resign his commission (which he had decided to do before the war).[17] However, for a senior officer to depart the field of war was not a gentlemanly thing to do. Paget had a difficult time back home, being cut at White's, his club in London, and effectively white-feathered for leaving his comrades to the worst of the Crimean winter. He therefore returned to the Crimea in March 1855, much aged and 'with a defeated air',[18] comforted by the fact that Lady Agnes, who had accompanied him as far as Constantinople, was soon to join him for a few weeks. She arrived on 26 April on the Leander in the company of the British ambassador at Constantinople, Lord Stratford de Redcliffe, with his wife and their three daughters the Miss Cannings, and Lady Ann Carew and her daughter Bessie (who were visiting their son and brother, Walter, in the Horse Guards). The uxorious Lord George was so distracted by the presence of Lady Agnes that his ADC, Captain Robert Portal soon was complaining that he 'saw nothing of him'.[19] Lord George, who now appeared to fellow officers to look after his wife more than his brigade, was only too happy to play the part of spectator, accompany his wife out on excursions around camp, listening to military bands and watching cavalry parades and reviews, enjoying private dinner parties with Lord Raglan, his wife always surrounded by an entourage of eager officers. First stop was the view of Sevastopol from the Maison d'Eau – a water tower near the French batteries; then on to the scenes of the Battle of Balaklava, where Paget painfully recounted his own experiences that day when the 4th Light Dragoons had formed the third line of the charge; and then Inkerman, where the ladies excitedly later related that they had actually been *fired at* from the heights opposite by the Russians. Young Bessie Carew confided to her journal that she was having 'capital fun', though she disapproved of her brother Walter's blatant flirtation with 'that minx, Miss Canning'.[20] Later, the Paget party ventured by steamer, courtesy of Admiral Lyons, along the south coast to Yalta, joined by General Estcourt's wife Caroline (who had charmed Roger Fenton in her white bonnet and muslin, such a 'refreshing sight . . . among the warlike dresses round'[21]), together with her sister-in-law Marianne. At Yalta, the party could not resist taking a peek at the seaside villa of Prince Vorontzov at Alupka, with its beautiful terraced gardens. The captain's decision to venture close inshore so they could all raise their telescopes provoked a hail of gunfire from the Russians until the ladies boldly paraded on deck and 'put the Russkies to the blush', upon which they ceased firing.[22] On the steamer's return voyage the same Russians who had fired at them now stood waving and cheering.

During her stay, Lady Paget regularly visited Lord Raglan, who sent up his carriage for her and laid on capital dinners for her benefit, delighted to have the pleasure of a lady's presence. In the company of Raglan she visited the Sardinian camp at Kamara to hear its much admired military band play at the little church there. Here the Sardinian commander General Alfonso La Marmora was so inflamed by Lady Agnes's beauty that he ordered his band down to play for her at Lord Raglan's HQ on regular occasions.

But not all the British officers in the Crimea were so enamoured of Lady Agnes and her sycophantic clique of officers. 'Lady George Paget is here with a great proportion of the Paget beauty,' wrote Captain Henry Percy, 'and from what I hear, the *whole* of the Paget presumption and insolence. But as she and Mrs Duberly are the only ladies here except the *revêche* [grumpy] nurses, she is in full plenitude of power, and rides out with a cortege composed of officers from every regiment (though principally the Dragoons) who can only say "ya-as."'[23] Fanny Duberly found herself excluded from such a 'charmed circle of privilege'; her husband Henry was not highly ranked enough to facilitate an introduction to Lady Paget's very select party, and so she chose to sulkily say little of her in her journal, unable to resist the observation that Lady Agnes was a nervous horse-woman and preferred Lord Raglan's carriage.[24] What is more, she was, in Fanny's opinion, clearly not in love with her bore of a husband.

On 27 May Fanny finally decided to make a pilgrimage to the Valley of the Charge of the Light Brigade. She found it 'gaudy with flowers and warm and golden in the rays of the setting sun'. After stopping to gather some flowers and ponder the tragedy that this now luxuriant valley had been witness to, she returned and later wrote to her sister: 'I send you some flowers from where the flowers of our chivalry were reaped away.'[25] Not long before, the youngest Miss Canning, Mary, aged 17, took a ride out to the field of the Battle of Inkerman. In a letter, she described how the view of the undulating mountains in the background had been 'quite lovely'. There was now little to indicate that a battle had taken place, 'flowers now grow on the spot so lately strewed with corpses, and all that remains to tell the tale are the mounds of earth under which they are buried and the pieces of shell lying hid among the turf and flowers'. For a girl of such a young age, she seemed particularly sensitive to what had gone before: 'It was indeed strange to stand on those heights of Inkerman now looking so calm and peaceful in this first flush of summer, the echoes only now and then awakened by the booming cannon, and then to carry back one's thoughts to the day of battle.'[26]

As time wore on, the presence of 'shiploads of tourists . . . with telescopes of all sizes . . . roaming wildly about the heights' became an increasing annoyance.[27] The lady tourists in particular were disapproved of. Captain Hodge of Paget's own regiment, the 4th Dragoons, had found their attention-grabbing presence in camp and 'out grazing' on their public picnics unladylike and 'very disgusting'. Captain Strange Jocelyn of the Scots Fusilier Guards, who also witnessed much of Lady Paget's visit, whilst undoubtedly enjoying the rare sight of pretty women in the war zone, nevertheless thought it 'rather an odd place for ladies to make a party of pleasure when so many are dying every hour in the trenches'.[28] Up at Cathcart's Hill, where the Rifle Brigade band often played between lulls in the fighting, the 'lady amateurs' were now jostling for the best view of the cannonade – and for the killing – with travelling gents, 'excurtionists' and other package tourists, as though they were out for a day's rabbit shooting. 'It really seems a morbid taste for horrors which has gotten up among them,' remarked Lieutenant Colonel Anthony Sterling in bafflement.[29] On one occasion Captain James Creagh found himself standing next to a 'pretty but simpering and affected young person' in view of the British, French and Russian fortifications just as a massive explosion hurled eight or ten British artillerymen high into the air. Their bodies 'appeared in the distance like birds on the wing', recalled Creagh. On being told they were 'human beings, and not, as they seemed, crows flying', the young woman could only exclaim after a moment's hesitation, 'how funny!'[30]

Soon there would be a renewed vigour in the bombardment of Sevastopol for all these lucky tourists to witness. On 24 May the capture of the crucial Russian supply base at Kerch and the town of Yenikale across the strait by a combined British and French operation had signalled the beginning of the end of the war. Located to the north-east on the Sea of Azov, Kerch commanded a powerful vantage point and, with this strategic supply route from the Russian interior now seized and its powerful batteries destroyed, the defence of the city of Sevastopol was weakened. With morale high in the Crimea – '"We must have a try for Sebastopol now" is the cry from the General to the newly arrived Ensign,' wrote Fanny Duberly – the allied commanders set about planning a major assault on the Malakhov and Redan Towers that guarded the city and its dockyards.[31]

Fanny Duberly was out of bed at 3 a.m. on 8 June to ride out to watch from the Picquet House where a crowd of spectators was gathering. The long wait left her exhausted from heat stroke, but eventually, at 4 p.m., with allied guns pounding all around and in a choking barrage of smoke, fire and gunpowder, the French moved off toward the Mamelon, one of Sevastopol's numerous fortified hill defences, and the British to the quarries that guarded the Malakhov beyond. Roger Barnston noticed the many tourists crowding to catch the view, Lady Agnes Paget and several other ladies among them, and was appalled: 'It's bad enough for ladies to be in camp at all, but when they come to see a couple of thousand men put an end to all at once, one might find a better title than "ladies" for them'.[32]

Up at her own vantage point Fanny Duberly saw how disconcerted Lady Agnes seemed by it all, 'sitting on the rock-work, vainly endeavouring as were many more to trace the operations through the fog'.[33] Soon Fanny's vantage point became extremely dangerous, as she later told her sister:

> The Russians fired right and left. Whizz went a round shot over our heads directly we got up. Whop went another into the ground alongside us. Whizz comes a third over our heads and rolls backwards down the hill. Clatter went a fourth into some loose stones.

She therefore moved to a safer position on Cathcart's Hill, from where she saw the French running up the hill towards the Malakhov in their thousands 'like sheep – all scattered as gun after gun opened upon them. Forward they ran, and then forming charged. One officer raising his sword arm falls dead.'[34] The Mamelon was quickly taken but then the Russians launched a counter-attack, and drove the French back from the Malakhov, despite now suffering ammunition shortages as a result of losing their supply base at Kerch. But the losses were terrible: over 6,000 French and British dead, piled in great heaps all around the base of the Russian batteries. The whole of the march of the attack beyond Cathcart's Hill was strewn with the dead and wounded also.

The next objective, a joint attack of the French on the Malakhov and the British on the Redan – both heavily defended with cannons surrounded by protective embrasures – was to come on 18 June, the anniversary of the British victory over Napoleon at Waterloo. Such a significant day in British military history sent word round the camp like wildfire that probably the most important engagement since the battles the previous year was about to take place.

Spring Hill was buzzing with talk about the engagement to come. Mary Seacole woke up with a restless air of excitement and spent the 17th frantically making piles of sandwiches, slicing cheese and cooked meats, and filling her panniers with these and bottles of wine and spirits, as well as lint and bandages and medicines, which she loaded onto two mules before heading off for Cathcart's Hill three and a half miles away the following morning. Every day she had walked out from the door of the British Hotel to shake hands with men as they passed by on their way to the front lines, many for the last time, knowing that many would not return. 'I used to think,' she wrote, 'that it was like having a large family of children ill with fever and dreading to hear which one had passed away in the night.'[35] Occasionally the death of a favourite had filled her with gloomy retrospection and grief, but she always pulled herself together: 'a day was a long time to give to sorrow in the Crimea'.[36] Fanny Duberly, too, aware of the no doubt momentous day to come, made sure the day before that she went round to see her many officer friends who would be taking part in the attack – in case it would be for the last time. With 600 allied siege guns opening with 12,000 rounds of ammunition during the barrage of the 17th to soften up the Russian defences, the tourists began to assemble. They hauled their picnic baskets up to Cathcart's Hill that midsummer night just in time to see dawn blot out the twinkling stars and then sat all day long in the broiling heat watching the action. So many spectators had seemed intent on being there that Lord George Paget and a detachment of officers of the Light Cavalry were delegated as special constables to 'keep the crowd back from showing themselves'.[37]

Among the army wives watching that day was Margaret Kerwin of the 19th, who was offered the loan of his telescope by W. H. Russell: 'it brought the battle under my eyes – men bayoneting one another and drawing back and meeting one another again. When I saw this, I could stand it no longer, and I gave the gentleman his telescope back again. He told me that I had seen something that very few women in England had seen, and that was a heavy battle fought.'[38] Kerwin at least shrank from the horror, and having seen too much of it already, turned away, but the eager spectators out from England could not get enough. They would, however, be disappointed in what they saw, for the mass of stinking acrid smoke and flashes of fire from the guns on both sides all but obliterated the view. Gradually, the walking wounded began to straggle back with defiant courage through the smoke. Then the news sunk in – the attack had been a disaster.

Up at Cathcart's Hill during the attack, Margaret Kerwin recalled how the Russians had opened fire on the crowd and, as they rushed to disperse, a gun had gone off accidentally in a sergeant's hand and knocked the bonnet off her head and stunned her. She came round to news that the 19th's gallant commander, Colonel Unett, had been mortally wounded in the ditch before the Redan. Margaret went down to see him, 'the shot and shell flying in every direction . . . I took my handkerchief out to wipe his face and he asked after my husband. He did not live many days after that and both myself and my husband went to the funeral. It was a sad day for both of us to lose Colonel "Daddy" Unett as he was called in the Regiment.'[39] Nell Butler, too, had been up near the front lines during the assault on the Redan, working all summer in the 95th's hospital tent; so heavy had been some blasts of the attack that the poles of the tent had lifted out of their holes, bringing the canvas down on the wounded, the doctors and Nell.

After the attack, Mary Seacole hurried down to the temporary field hospital on the Vorontsov Road, under constant fire, ignoring the orders to go back, in order to do what she could in binding the wounds of the less seriously injured and offering them drinks, before returning to Cathcart's Hill to offer help to the wounded there. But it was a hopeless task. The French had lost 3,500 men on the killing ground in front of the Malakhov, which they failed to take; the British had lost about 1,500, cut to ribbons as they attempted to cross the ditches and set up scaling ladders under a murderous hail of grapeshot and bullets at the Redan. It had been nothing less than slaughter. Sevastopol, which the British had optimistically hoped would be theirs by the evening, was still defiantly Russian.

A truce was held the following day for the dead to be taken away, their bodies hideously blackened and bloated after only 24 hours out in the scorching Crimean sun. The bursting flesh, the maggots that now swarmed over the dead that filled the ditches around the Malakhov and Redan Towers, and the stench all made even the most hardened of soldiers vomit. But Mary Seacole was there to see the body of one of her old favourites, Sir John Campbell, commander of the 5th Brigade, brought back. The assault on the Redan had been 'a fearful sight for a woman to witness', but whilst she prayed to God that she might never see its like again, she was certain of one thing: 'in scenes of horror and distress . . . a woman can do so much'.[40]

A weary and deeply distraught Lord Raglan had left the field on the 18th, knowing the responsibility for the disaster was his and that yet more criticisms of his conduct of the campaign would follow. He looked like a haunted man. On 22 June Raglan heard that his great friend and comrade General James Estcourt had sickened with cholera, which had reappeared in the British camp at the beginning of the month. Estcourt, another favourite with Mary Seacole and one of her best customers, had duly done what all soldiers going down with cholera did: taken draughts of rum and water in an attempt to keep warm during the fits of terrible shivering, then sipped lime juice and seltzer water and even champagne (a popular remedy) – but nothing could stop the prolonged and violent vomiting, not even the doses of castor oil and laudanum, and finally opium, administered by his doctors. It happened that his wife Caroline and sister Marianne had been on a visit to the Crimea from Pera and were there to witness Estcourt's last hours:

> The sickness continued very violently & when we found him at
> 10½ [a.m.] his voice was very much altered, weak & hollow . . . We
> laid him down on his bed & presently he got cooler, cooler, cooler, till

the clammy cold of cholera came on, his skin hard, and whilst he fancied himself burning hot, he was cold as ice, he never got warm again. As soon as he was laid down and made as comfortable as we cd make him he kissed us so touchingly holding Caro in his arms, with such a look of quiet, peace and love . . . So we passed the afternoon fanning him, keeping off the flies, bathing him with lavender-water, now giving him drinks . . . soon I felt there was but one end . . . the restlessness returned and never ceased, the rest was a dreadful trial, continually asking to be lifted up, longing for air, and being laid down in a painful state of exhaustion . . . About 11½ [p.m.] he sprang up in bed had a sort of dreadful convulsion his jaw rigid & his eyes – no words can describe this. We thought it was quite the last . . . till so distressing the restlessness at last I prayed that he might be taken – at 5 min to 9 the pulse ceased to beat, the eyes had long been fixed & Caro & I closed them, those beautiful eyes, we closed them & his mouth, that darling mouth – we laid him down to rest in the full assurance that his spirit was gone to God.[41]

Estcourt was buried on the 25th just outside British HQ, rather than up at the cemetery at Cathcart's Hill, at Lord Raglan's particular insistence. But Raglan had been too sick and too grief-stricken to attend the funeral. Three days later the Estcourt women sailed for Trieste, Marianne's last wish being that a slab be placed over her brother's grave in remembrance of him, for they were leaving 'whatever we loved so dearly in this most miserable country'.[42]

Four days later, at 9 p.m. on the 28th, Lord Raglan died also, probably of cholera brought on by the exhaustion and despair of the debacle of the 18th. Lady Paget was among the VIPs solemnly gathered at his deathbed. Later, Mary Seacole too contrived, heaven knows how, to be admitted into the room to pay her last respects and touch a corner of the Union Jack that covered Raglan's coffin. Then she stood and watched it 'wind its way through the long lines of soldiery towards Kamiesch, while, ever and anon, the guns thundered forth in sorrow, not in anger'.[43]

Lady Agnes Paget quit the Crimea for Constantinople soon after Raglan's death, Lord George in tow, the two of them taking up three cabins in the *Imperador*, a crowded hospital ship, despite the objections of the medical staff. At Therapia, installed in the more salubrious comforts of the Hôtel d'Angleterre, the Pagets enjoyed the sights of the Bosporus for two more weeks before the reluctant Lord George was obliged to kiss his wife goodbye and return to camp.

Two and a half years later the beautiful, spoilt Lady Agnes, who had witnessed violent death on the grand scale in the Crimea, succumbed to that most prosaic of deaths suffered by women – in childbirth, at her home in London's fashionable Berkeley Square.

THIRTEEN

Do Hurry Back and Take Sebastopol or It Will Kill Mama

In the kitchens of Balaklava General Hospital Elizabeth Davis, 300 miles away from the ubiquitous and critical presence of Florence Nightingale, was enjoying a free run, requisitioning unchallenged supplies of wine, sherry and brandy, rice and sago and sugar in her drive to produce extravagant treats for her patients. Having seen supplies go to waste and sit rotting at Scutari because of bureaucratic delays, Davis was determined that the same should not happen to the Balaklava Free Gift Store.

On her arrival at the hospital early in the year Davis had been greeted with the same terrible sights she had encountered at Scutari – cases of frostbite so bad that hands and feet came away with the bandages when they were unwrapped; wounds alive with maggots; overcrowding, lack of beds and medical supplies, and a plague of rats which even climbed on the beds at night. But soon the hospital had been knocked into shape thanks to the hard work of the nurses there led by Nightingale's reluctant appointee, Lady Jane Shaw Stewart. Stewart, one of the best connected of the Crimean nurses (daughter of a Scottish baronet and sister of Sir

Michael Shaw Stewart MP), won the highly critical Davis's respect for her unstinting devotion: 'I think she was the only lady who went to the East in all respects really capable of a nurse's duties', she wrote.[1] There was, however, something of the martyr about Stewart, so much so that Eliza Polidori and the other nurses were of the opinion that she was 'a little cracked'.[2] She certainly drove herself to the point of exhaustion, working all day and then sitting up nearly all night with the worst fever cases. Dr George Lawson thought her obsessive behaviour 'perfectly mad': Stewart rested only 'by snatches', seldom stopped to remove her clothes when she did so and 'when she is craved to take a little rest, wraps herself up in a cloak and lies down on the ground'.[3] Stewart, for her part, disliked having administrative responsibility thrust upon her by Nightingale and in May accepted a transfer, at Lord Raglan's request, to the smaller Castle Hospital, a row of prefabricated huts newly erected on the Genoese Heights above Balaklava. Here her nursing qualities were again lauded, but Stewart failed to endear herself to colleagues with her severe, ascetic manner: 'She is no doubt a most excellent creature,' remarked Captain Robert Portal, 'but her appearance in drab, and her gaunt grim figure, made me congratulate myself on being sound and not in need of her kind services.' He found her 'colder than ice'.[4]

In early May 1855 Nightingale herself had finally managed to get away from Scutari to make her long-intended inspection of the Crimean hospitals. The Secretary of War Lord Panmure had now acknowledged her superintendency over all nurses, although this was contingent on the approval of Sir John Hall. Davis, who believed, as others did, that Nightingale's authority extended only over the nurses in Turkey and not the Crimea – which was part of Russia – gave her short shrift when she arrived, grumpily remarking that 'I should have as soon expected to see the Queen here, as you.'[5] It did not take long for Nightingale to conclude that the elderly and somewhat eccentric Miss Margaret Wear, the woman she had appointed to replace Jane Shaw Stewart, was incompetent and ineffectual – and had no more control over Davis's profligacy with the Free Gift Store than Stewart had had. She proceeded to lock horns with Sir John Hall over the proper management of the hospitals in the Crimea and her insistence on the imposition there of her own system, but this did not come into effect until mid-July, nor was she able to recall Miss Wear to Scutari, though eventually Wear transferred voluntarily to the much smaller Monastery convalescent hospital. Davis, still simmering with resentment and now suffering from chronic dystentery and diarrhoea, finally elected to go home on the *Calcutta*; she left with ill grace after a final row with Nightingale over the wages owing to her, despite Nightingale's recommendation that she be given one's years pay at 18 shillings a week as a gratuity when she was invalided home. It was a recommendation Nightingale made also for her best and most loyal nurses, such as Mrs Noble.

No sooner had word spread among the British troops that the sainted Miss Nightingale had come to visit the Crimea than Nightingale fell dangerously ill with fever, probably brought on by her long months of overwork and self-neglect. She was whisked off to the Castle Hospital where she was devotedly nursed through two weeks of life-or-death delirium by her stalwart ally Mrs Roberts, who had accompanied her from Scutari. Everyone held their breath – including Queen Victoria and the British public at home – and prayed for her recovery. For a while it looked as though the British authorities were about to invalid Nightingale home, a fact which caused great anxiety among the rank and file. Undoubtedly she represented the last hope to the wounded and desperately sick in their thousands. The thought of her loss brought tears to their eyes, as one sergeant in the 56th wrote: 'All the soldiers was cryin because Miss Nightingale was goin away for sure all their comfort & succour was in her along with the Almighty. And what should they do for mother when she was gone!'[6]

It was a close-run thing, but Nightingale had recovered enough by the end of May to make the journey back to Scutari, though now painfully thin and with a shaven head. As soon as she recovered she found fresh battles to fight – against army bureaucracy, the same old Commissariat inefficiences and the misconduct of her recalcitrant hospital nurses. Nurses Howes and Hawkins were, she observed, drinking heavily; Nurse Tainton had 'made love' to an orderly who turned out to be a married man and was promptly put on the boat back to England. And then the hard-working and loyal Bracebridges, exhausted from their nine months at Scutari – having stayed much longer than they originally intended – decided to leave for home.

The departure of the Bracebridges was followed by the deaths of one of Nightingale's favourites – Mrs Drake, one of the St John's House nurses – in August and then of Martha Clough. Clough had found the privations of life up at the secluded Highland Hospital a challenge and had sought comfort in the claret bottle – about which word filtered back to Nightingale. It was not quite the usual life of a gentlewoman to live in an army camp as the only woman (bar her female servant), though she did not mind the loneliness and rebuffed the accusations of impropriety, insisting she was treated 'with kindness, consideration, respect and even deference'.[7] She welcomed the occasional visits of Lord Raglan and Lady Stratford de Redcliffe and had no fear of Nightingale's presence in the Crimea, supremely confident that her position was unassailable, for Lord Raglan and all the officers 'had taken up the cudgels in my behalf'. She was, she believed, 'the favourite, and I have been so perfectly quiet – never going out but to my wards, attending to nothing in fact but my sick – that without any self-laudation I hope I may bear a comparison with Miss Nightingale'.[8] Then, in June, Clough had suddenly fallen ill. A month later she still was confined to her bed; in August, just as she was recovering, she suffered a relapse. Jane Shaw Stewart took her to the Castle Hospital to be nursed, after which Martha was taken down to the *Orinoco* at Balaklava for passage home. But on 24 September she died on board ship in the Black Sea; her remains, in a rapid state of decomposition, were laid out by Nightingale and Mrs Roberts, Nightingale deciding it inadvisable to send them back to England. Instead, Clough was buried at Scutari, her grave marked by Nightingale with a small wooden cross. 'Poor Miss Clough,' she remarked, 'I little thought that the first time I should see her face would be in death.'[9] One of Nightingale's last tasks was one which the highly secretive Clough would have hated – to go through her effects and send them back to England. Here, Nightingale found the little leather case containing the portrait of Colonel Lauderdale Maule, Clough's constant companion in her solitude; she ensured it was safely returned to a friend in England. But across the waters of the Black Sea, Colonel Maule's lonely grave at Devna remained unvisited.

...

Inside the city of Sevastopol, as the long hot summer of the siege dragged on, everyone was being worn down by the war. The teams of nurses and doctors had found themselves continually overstretched by outbreaks of typhus, which reduced their own numbers too. The terrible ten-day allied bombardment of March and April had resulted in another 6,000 dead and wounded, and there were a further 5,000 casualties after the unsuccessful French and British attack in June. It was now becoming more difficult each day to repair the breaches in defences made by the constant bombardment. There was never any respite inside the Assembly of Nobles either, where most of the Sisters of Mercy were now working, having retreated from the more dangerously located dressing stations on the south side of the city. Here even the nights brought fresh casualties from sorties across the siege lines. The women stayed at their posts through constant shell and rocket fire that made the operating tables reverberate, as well as risking their lives to help move the wounded to places of greater safety under fire across a temporary pontoon bridge of floating logs over Sevastopol Bay to the north side. Some were wounded and even killed in the process; Sister Budberg was caught in the shoulder by shell fragments whilst moving wounded to safety; another sister was killed by a direct hit on the Asssembly of Nobles; several more died of typhus as the year went on. The letter of one Russian, 'Sister B' – it was in fact Ekaterina Bakunina – describing to her sister the bombardment of Sevastopol, eventually found its way into the British press and gave readers a most graphic account of the horrors being endured there:

> In the evening all was again expectation. Every preparation was made . . .
> The room is nearly dark, and a peculiar stillness reigns around, as in the
> air before a thunderstorm. Fifteen surgeons and more, are seated around
> Pirogoff in the room for operations, or are walking up and down in pairs
> . . . As you stand at the door or look out through the lofty windows at
> both sides of the room, you see a bright, quiet night, for the moon is
> shining, and the stars are twinkling, without a cloud. Between 9 and 10
> o-clock there is a flash like that of lightning at the windows, and
> suddenly it roars till every pane of glass rattles. By degrees, flash follows
> flash, more frequent and rapid; you can no longer distinguish the shots

from each other. The fifth and six bastions are lit up with fire, but the enemy's bombs do not reach the city. We sit and listen, ever in the same sort of twilight, and about an hour passes over. Then comes a litter [carrying wounded], another, and another – it has begun. The candles are lit; folks run hurriedly backwards and forwards, and the large room is soon filled with men. The floor is covered with the wounded – everywhere, where they can sit, they who have crawled in do sit. How they shriek! What a din! Hell is let loose around us. You cannot hear the thunder of the guns for this wailing and groaning.[10]

Given the option to move further inland with the wounded, Ekaterina Bakunina, who had become one of Pirogov's most trusted nurses, opted to stay where most needed – in the city. But after all hell broke loose in Sevastopol the night of 17 June, when the city suffered its worst bombardment yet, there were few buildings left standing in which the wounded could be effectively cared for. With supplies now dwindling dramatically, the Sisters had to be dispersed with their charges to field hospitals on the Inkerman Heights (the Russian HQ), at the River Belbek and at other inland towns such as Simferopol, whose every available public building was taken over to house some 13,000 wounded.

On the British front lines, Elizabeth Evans had no doubt that she lived a life 'as few women in existence can speak about . . . short of food, without a bed, scarcely knowing what decent clothing meant, and witnessing heart-breaking spectacles of suffering in hospital and elsewhere'. But even she, resilient though she was, and having spent what time she could helping in the regimental field hospital, eventually fell sick with fever. She was left to await what seemed her inevitable fate lying on the bare ground, with only a stone for a pillow. Then some soldiers came carrying planks – she thought to make her coffin, but in fact it was to make a bed for her. For days on end she hovered near death: 'I used to scream at a shadow when people passed, fearing that they had come to bury me.' And now she no longer had the protection of her husband, who had been sent to Scutari with a batch of Russian prisoners.[11] Margaret Kerwin also remembered how concerned the men of the 19th had been for her safety during the savage bombardments of that summer. On one particular day, with the shot and shell so fierce, two sergeants had pulled out trusses of hay for the horses' feed and 'trusseled me in between them like a dog to save me'. The risks for women near the front lines remained considerable. On 29 August, Margaret Kerwin had a near miss after an explosion in the Mamelon trench. She had been on her knees ironing at the time when four shells had hit her tent and showered her with earth. Now so inured to the bombardment, she was more concerned about the state of a dozen fine shirts belonging to Mr Beans of the Commissariat that she had been washing, for they were riddled with holes.[12]

On 16 August the desperate situation inside Sevastopol forced the Russians to go on the offensive once more, as they tried to cross the River Chernaya in an attempt to recapture the Fedyukhin Heights. The river was defended at its major crossing point, the Traktir Bridge, by French Zouaves, with back-up from newly arrived Sardinian troops. The Russians prepared well in advance for this attack, ensuring that 35 doctors and six Sisters of Mercy were on duty at a first-aid station on nearby Mackenzie Heights. The sisters were taken out there in the dead of night on rickety carts and were ready and waiting for the wounded at 5 a.m. on the morning of the 16th when the Russians attacked through the mist across the river. Mary Seacole was there and watched as wave after wave of Russians waded the river and were shot down in scores, whilst 'quiet and expectant' squadrons of English and French cavalry waited impatiently to be called to attack. The Russian assault was muddled and poorly organized and they were quickly beaten back by the 'dark-plumed Sardinians and red-pantalooned French' who spread out in pursuit. They formed, Seacole wrote, 'a picture so excitingly beautiful that we forgot the death and suffering they left behind'.[13] The Traktir Bridge was one great mass of corpses, so dense that it was now impassable.

During the Russian retreat, so Assistant Chaplain J.B. wrote, Mary 'was found administering creature comforts to the wounded utterly unmindful of the shot and shell flying about her in all directions'. Mary herself marvelled at how tenacious some of the wounded were, how the body's 'sacred spirit struggles to loose itself from the still strong frame that holds it tightly to the last'. One such sufferer was a Russian, whom Mary tended:

One of them was badly shot in the lower jaw, and was beyond my or any human skill. Incautiously I inserted my finger into his mouth to feel where the ball had lodged, and his teeth closed upon it, in the agonies of death, so tightly that I had to call to those around to release it, which was not done until it had been bitten so deeply that I shall carry the scar with me to my grave. Poor fellow, he meant me no harm, for as the near approach of death softened his features, a smile spread over his rough inexpressive face, and so he died.

There were many she helped that day – Russian and allied wounded, who tried in their different languages to thank Mary for her help. In the end they could only communicate their gratitude 'in that one common language of the whole world – smiles'.[14]

Although Sister Alexandra Krupskaya had had enough experience of the wounded in Sevastopol already to be hardened to most sights, nothing had prepared her for the experience of attending them so close to the scene of battle. There were so many wounded crowded onto the Mackenzie Heights, all simultaneously begging for attention, that the medical team worked for days without stopping. Wherever the hard-pressed sisters turned the wounded blessed them and thanked God for their presence: the doctors might cut off their arms and legs but only the sisters could attend to them like mothers did their own children.[15] Sixteen days later, not having even had time for a change of clothes, the sisters were sent to bathe in the sea before returning to the hospital at Belbek.

After the Chernaya, and sensing the Russians were now weakening, the allies decided to launch another major attack on the seemingly impregnable Malakhov tower and the Great Redan nearby. A sense of portentous events to come filled the camp the evening of the 7th. Lieutenant General Sir William Codrington, commander of the Light Division that was to play a leading role in the attack, addressed the men on parade that afternoon, confident that it would 'nobly do its duty'. That evening, at about 8 p.m., the correspondent of the *Illustrated London News* walked towards the Victorian Redoubt in the British lines to take one last look at the 'terrible batteries of Sebastopol'. It left an indelible memory: hundreds of allied soldiers were sitting out on the hillside in the already crisp

September air doing pretty much the same, their thoughts inevitably turning to home and loved ones and the girls they had left behind all those many months before.

Then somebody in the 2nd Rifle Brigade began to sing. It was 'Annie Laurie', the song most loved in camp:

> He had a tenor voice, tolerably good, and sang with expression, but the chorus was taken up by the audience in a much lower key, and hundreds of voices in the most exact time and harmony sang together –
>
> 'And for bonnie Annie Laurie
> I'd lay me down to die!'
>
> The effect was extraordinary; at least I felt it so. I never heard any chorus in an oratorio rendered with greater solemnity. It was more like a psalm than a ballad, for at such a time, on the eve of a great battle, a soldier thinks only of his love and his God.[16]

Then the bugle sounded and the men dispersed back to quarters, many never to meet again.

Fanny Duberly had heard news of the impending attack that afternoon, when General Markham had ridden past her hut and called out: 'Mrs Duberly, we shall have a fight to-morrow. You must be up on Cathcart's Hill by twelve o'clock.'[17] She would not be the only woman gathering to 'see the fight' that morning. Mary Seacole, who, day in, day out, had taken refreshments up to those watching the bombardment, was up early, loading her panniers with bandages and medicines, anxious 'to repeat the work of the 18th of June last'. Surgeon Thomas Buzzard could not miss her, 'mounted on a horse, and conspicuous by her costume, which was bright blue in colour relieved by yellow'. Later she was seen generously distributing provisions and refreshment to exhausted or wounded soldiers as they struggled back.[18] Numerous lady amateurs were present too, getting within range of the Russian guns and once again causing the cavalry to undertake the 'ungracious work of special constables'. The desire of these tourists to witness the assault was extremely distasteful even to Fanny Duberly, who considered herself a special case.

For three days before the attack, it had sounded as though the end of the world had come; as Mary Seacole recalled, 'every battery opened, and poured a perfect hail of shot and shell upon the beautiful city'.[19] On the morning of the 8th it drowned the whole of the southern side of Sevastopol in a choking pall of smoke that blotted out the sun. The French moved off at midday and speedily 'rolled into the Malakhov like a human flood'. They captured it with ease, having had only 30 yards to cover between them and the Russian trenches and gaining an element of surprise. But the British faced the same problem as on 18 June – an attack uphill across 200 yards of open ground followed by an attempt to raise assault ladders at the base of the Redan for the storming party. Many of the British troops were terrified raw recruits who refused to go forward, confronted as they were by a 'lava flow of lead and cast iron' from the Malakhov. They fell 'like autumn leaves in a storm'.[20] A gallant few managed to scale the Redan, but this was not enough to encourage the vast numbers down below who could or would not penetrate it in pursuit of the Russians. The men seemed 'stunned and paralysed', fearful that the Redan was mined, lacking the savage bravado of the battles of the year before. They now began to panic as their junior officers (many mere boys who had been only a month in the Crimea), unable to induce them to attack further, were felled all around them amid a last and often heroic attempt to get them to follow. A bayonet charge of Russians from within the Redan was the last straw; in the mad stampede to retreat, the ditch around the Redan collapsed. As the British struggled to right themselves they were picked off by Russian guns and grenades.

By sunset, scores of those who had joined in the chorus of 'Annie Laurie' the previous evening were now 'lying stiff and stark in the ditch of the Redan', having 'laid down and died at the command of a sterner mistress than any of womankind'.[21] It was yet another military disaster for the British. There would be no more chances for them to redeem themselves in battle during this war. The capture of the Malakhov was sufficient to precipitate the beginning of the end, for General Mikhail Gorchakov, now highly pessimistic about Russia's position, made the decision to abandon the southern side of the city. The 349-day siege came to an end in a rage of flame as for hour after hour tens of thousands of Russians retreated across the pontoon bridge to the north side. By now, the once grand Assembly of Nobles had been reduced to a ruin by a direct hit and the wounded had been moved to the Nikolaevsk battery, where many of the women and children from the city had been sheltering since the bombardments of May and June.

One of the last to cross the bridge was Ekaterina Bakunina. With up to a thousand wounded a day coming into Sevastopol, she had refused to abandon her post. Naval officer Mansurov witnessed her heroism:

> In the midst of total confusion at the Assembly of Nobles, where the main dressing station was situated, Sister Bakunina of the Community of the Holy Cross declared that she would not leave the building until the last patients had been evacuated, and that she would take her oath on it. Not only did she keep her word, on several occasions she accompanied the wounded to the quayside and helped ensure that they came aboard the launch in safety. This woman demonstrated the kind of self-sacrifice and courage few men possess.[22]

Looking out on the verdant green meadow and pine wood beyond her window as she wrote her memoir of the Crimea in 1898, Ekaterina said she had sometimes stopped to wonder during her 'quiet and secluded life' whether it had all really happened. Had she really witnessed all this horror? So many wounded; so many violent explosions; the pontoon bridge swaying and writhing like a snake as the wind lashed the waves up and over it and men, women, children, horses struggled to make the crossing. Two days after the evacuation, she had written a letter from the north side of Sevastopol, describing the 'deep and universal grief' that had overcome everyone at the abandonment of the city, and the 'horror of desolation – a chaos – more dreadful than hell' that Sevastopol had become on that final day: 'What a sight met my eyes! . . . our troops had set the town on fire . . . the bridge was broken away, the ships of the line and the frigates sunk, the city was in flames, black smoke mounted to the clouds, and explosions of powder made the earth tremble on every side.'[23]

Queen Victoria was with her family at Balmoral when news reached her of the fall of Sevastopol. The young prince, who was so anxious about his mother's obsession with the war and who had so eagerly begged Lord

Cardigan the previous year to 'hurry back and take Sebastopol or it will kill mama', was at last gratified.[24] Immediately, Prince Albert, accompanied by gentlemen of the royal household, gamekeepers, ghillies and workmen from the nearby village, all went up to the top of a nearby hill to light the bonfire they had laid the previous year in premature anticipation of Sevastopol's fall. From the castle the queen could see how it 'blazed forth brilliantly'. There was much dancing and shouting and drinking of healths in good Scotch whisky (the whole proceedings turning into a veritable 'witch's dance', as Albert noted), after which the people 'came down under the windows, the pipes playing, firing off guns, and cheering – first for me, then for Albert, the Emperor of the French, and the "downfall" of Sebastopol'.[25]

In England church bells pealed and the guns boomed out in St James's Park as the public pushed and jostled for copies of the evening papers and the pubs and coffee shops filled with people discussing the momentous news. Jane Welsh Carlyle, travelling into town by coach at the time, recalled 'such a row of bells as we got near London!':

> 'Does thou know why the bells are ringing?' asked a Quaker beside me at a working man opposite. 'Well then, I suppose something is up; they were saying at the station Sevastopole was took and the Russians all run away!' Presently I had the pleasure of reading on a placard
> 'Hurrah! Hurrah! Hurrah!
> Glorious news!
> Sevastapool in possession of the allies!'
> Don't they wish they may keep it![26]

At the Haymarket Theatre that evening the manager came on stage between acts and read out the newspaper dispatches to an excited audience which rose en masse cheering as the orchestra struck up 'God Save the Queen' followed by Handel's 'See the Conquering Hero Comes'. And the next day the whole of the city of London was still 'on the *qui vive*'.[27]

The allies waited for two days after the Russian withdrawal before entering the scorched and ruined shell of the city in force. When they did so, they encountered terrible sights: pile upon pile of black and bloated

Russian dead; worse still, amidst the desolation of the deserted city remained vast numbers of the near-dead, those Russians (and a few French and British prisoners) too severely wounded to be evacuated, who had been abandoned in appalling states of suffering. W. H. Russell described the horrors:

> I beheld such a sight as few men, thank God, have ever witnessed . . . the rotten and festering corpses of the soldiers, who were left to die in their extreme agony, untended, uncared for, packed as close as they could be stowed, some on the floors, others on wretched trestles and bedsteads, or pallets of straw, sopped and saturated with blood, which oozed and trickled through upon the floor, mingling with the droppings of corruption . . . Many, nearly made by the scene around them, or seeking escape from it in their extremest agony, had rolled away under the beds, and glared out on the heart-stricken spectator – oh! With such looks! Many, with legs and arms broken and twisted, the jagged splinters sticking through the raw flesh, implored aid, water, food, or pity . . . Could that human being, or that burnt black mass of flesh have ever held a human soul?[28]

Eustace Murray also witnessed the scene and described the sense of impotence everyone felt: 'I do not believe that history tells of anything more dreadful than the state of the Russian hospitals . . . What can one man with a flask of sherry do among 10,000 wounded men, mostly speaking an unknown language?'[29]

With her usual persuasive manner and good connections, Mary Seacole had managed to get a pass from General Garrett allowing her to ride into Sevastopol the day before the official entry on the 9th – at a time when 'even general officers were refused'. She was determined to be the first woman into the city, entering by mule, loaded with baskets of provisions which gained her 'a hearty welcome from the hungry officers and soldiers'.[30] Scenes of looting greeted her, much of it by the Zouaves. Everything that could be carted away was taken – clothes, samovars, icons, furniture, even livestock. Mary was offered many trophies but chose to keep only a few, her most precious being a painting of the Madonna cut from the altar of a church that she bought from a French soldier.

It wasn't until four days later – the 13th – that Fanny Duberly managed to get permission to ride into Sevastopol, much to the disgust of several officers who saw her, for all the horrors of the siege and piles of unburied corpses made such a spectacle 'surely no place for an English lady'.[31] It was an enervating experience for Fanny: 'eight consecutive hours spent in sightseeing under a blazing sun is no light and ladylike *délassement* at any time'.[32] But she could not fail to admire the magnificent engineering of the Russian batteries on the Redan and Malakhov, nor turn a blind eye to the horrific signs of slaughter – pools of half-dried blood, bloodstained caps, human brains and entrails, broken bayonets, dead horses. Yet on entering the city, it had from a distance seemed 'so calm, and white and fair'. Close to all was desolation, buildings full of shell holes, the cupola of its finest church 'split and splintered to ribands', dead Russians everywhere in appalling states of decomposition, the air thick with an intolerable, putrid smell:

> I think the impression made upon me by the sight of that foul heap of green and black, glazed and shrivelled flesh I never shall be able to throw entirely away. To think that each individual portion of that corruption was once perhaps the life and world of some loving woman's heart – that human living hands had touched, and living lips had pressed with clinging and tenderest affection, forms which in a week could become, oh, so loathsome, so putrescent![33]

Time, and a beautiful Crimean autumn, saw the burial of the dead and the erection of memorials in many graveyards dotted over the Crimean plain. The winter of 1855–6 was a great deal different from the previous one, with most of the army housed in huts by November, their animals sheltered and fed, and supplies of wood and warm clothing in abundance. The absence of vultures was marked; the previous winter there had been hundreds of them. Meanwhile, the influx of war tourists continued. English transports were still offering free passage from Constantinople to Balaklava, bar a small payment for food, 'boots' and 'bedmaker' (passenger steamers charging as much as four or five guineas for the pleasure). But visitors were warned in advance that they would be hard-pressed to find a bed in Balaklava and would have to be prepared to pay for the use of some 'flea-ridden shakedown' from a local tradesman or throw themselves on the hospitality of 'some jolly English skipper' in hopes of a berth in dock.[34] New arrivals included 'amateur females' such as the 'plucky' Virgy Sandars. With 'true woman's persistence' she showed herself prepared to rough it in the face of Admiral Lyons's hostility to women's presence and live on board ship, in her case a 'dirty, dingy' steam transport, the *Holyrood*, with a captain 'addicted to drinking and swearing'.[35]

With so many visitors still pouring in, trade was brisk for all the sutlers, including Mary Seacole. Her restaurant was the venue for many noisy dinner parties given by British officers for their French allies. As Christmas drew near, the Crimea might not have many turkeys but there were plenty of other game birds to be had – including the indigenous bustard. Mary had one for sale weighing 19½ lb. She also came into her own as a prodigious mistress of the plum pudding and mince pie. When he visited one day, the Revd J.B. found her 'deep in the mysteries of baking and boiling', for she had orders for eighty or more plum puddings from her officer clients.[36] Meanwhile, Christmas cakes arrived unscathed from doting families in England. Officers drank champagne out of marmalade pots (there still being a shortage of mugs), but dined on all the best that Oppenheim's, Fortnum's and the sutlers of Kadikoi could offer. Huts were festooned with artificial flowers and decorations made of coloured tissue paper, bows of bright calico and spruce and fir branches; some officers rode out to Miskomiya to gather mistletoe that grew there in abundance on wild pear and apple trees. Mary lent gay-coloured muslin dresses as costumes to the 'lady' actors of the 1st Royals and even struggled with their tight lacing till she made them 'blue in the face'. Lieutenant Lacey of the 63rd was the star of theatricals that lasted well into the new year, playing a most fetching lady in tableaux such as 'The Mustache Movement', 'To Paris and Back for Five Pounds' and 'Betsy Baker'. For a jape he even went to one of the French dances at Kamara dressed as a woman; so convincing was his disguise that 'his hand was squeezed and kisses asked for in the most tender manner'.[37]

The French 'dancing saloon' at Kamara with its 'fashionable' Sunday-evening balls at half a guinea was much talked about. The attendance of ladies at these events was 'most respectfully invited' but none would venture there from the British camp. 'It is an objectionable practice, and I never go even on week-days,' wrote an officer. 'There are no ladies to dance with, only *vivandières*, who are generally the wives of the restaurant-keepers'.[38] Mary Seacole and her daughter Sally certainly did not approve: 'Do you think mother or myself would go to such a place, where the women wear soldiers' clothes?' remarked the modest Sally.[39]

But there was one grand ball for which hopes were raised of some British female attendance: the celebration of the birth of a son and heir to Napoleon III of France on 16 March 1856. For weeks everyone had been talking about it, whilst a special board and canvas ballroom was constructed on the great Balaklava plain, visible for miles around. Eventually, eight English ladies (all of them married bar one) were persuaded to venture out for the occasion. But their sense of propriety was so deeply shocked when a troop of *cantinières* walked in sporting their 'scarlet trousers and shiny hats' that the good ladies made a hasty exit.[40] It was one thing for women of a lower class to infiltrate such an occasion, but to do so in *trousers* was unconscionable. The *cantinières*, in the opinion of a British officer, were 'typical of the lowest and vilest Parisian *bals*'. To add further insult, they were having such a good time that they danced '*cancans d'enfer* with generals and elderly officers, in a manner really revolting to witness'.[41]

With the war effectively over but protracted peace negotiations in Paris dragging on for months, boredom set in and everyone welcomed the return of the racing season and the Great Sebastopol Spring Meeting staged by the allied armies on 24 March 1856. Here 'canteen-cartloads of *cantinières* from Kamiesch and a donkey carriage or two of ladies' turned out to watch the fun whilst Mary Seacole was there with a 'store of thirst-compelling and thirst-assuaging edibles and drinkables'.[42]

When the Treaty of Paris officially ended the war on 30 March 1856, a disgruntled Queen Victoria was loath to accept it, the nation having been denied a final decisive victory over the Russians. 'I own that peace rather sticks in my throat,' she had written, 'and so it does in that of the *whole* Nation.'[43] But at least now she could adoringly watch her returning troops, who were showered with bunches of laurel as they marched through the streets of London 'very sunburnt . . . the picture of *real* fighting men, such fine tall strong men, some strikingly handsome – all with such proud, noble, soldierlike bearing'.[44] The queen's hero-worship and military mania would continue throughout that summer, with military parades and a grand review at Aldershot at which, in a handsome scarlet tunic with gold braid and brass buttons, Victoria rode a horse called Alma. There were public award ceremonies too for the Crimean Medal and the Victoria Cross (a medal newly instituted) at which the queen took centre stage.

The final great public celebration came with the end-of-war illuminations – £20,000 worth of gunpowder and combustibles – let off across London's parks on 29 May, as well as bonfires and events elsewhere throughout the country. Hyde Park that night was one great, dense mass of people. From their balcony at Buckingham Palace the royal family had a magnificent view of the displays not just in Hyde Park but also on Primrose Hill and Victoria Park in East London. On 8 July the queen watched an enormous march past, sadly marred by pouring rain, of the largest fighting force assembled in England since the Battle of Worcester in 1651. She gave a rare public speech in which she expressed her confidence that should her troops be needed again, they would be 'animated by the same devotion, which, in the Crimea rendered you invincible'.[45]

In April 1856 the allies began winding down their presence in the Crimea, the British being the last to leave. In May, Mrs Emilia Hornby, wife of a British official in Constantinople, paid a longed-for visit. Like other lady visitors before her she made the pilgrimage out to the ravine known as the 'Valley of the Shadow of Death', where she gathered up shot and shell fragments as mementoes. They made her think all too painfully of the terrible suffering that the struggle had cost to thousands of human lives. But beyond she could see the mountains and to the west the wonderful blue waters of the Black Sea glittering in the late-afternoon sunshine. Rising up beside it were the white stone ruins of Sevastopol, its bay full of sunken ships. Most of the ruins had been powdered almost to dust, and all around were shattered gardens, broken trees and ploughed up and scorched turf. Everything blackened; 'ruin on the most gigantic scale, everywhere'. The wrecked bastions of the still imposing Mamelon and Redan were now a mass of wild purple irises, all bathed in the glorious light of the setting sun. Despite all the images of war and destruction still lingering, there was something eerily tranquil about the scene:

> Nature seemed to remember that it was spring-time, even in this scene of desolation, for a nightingale was singing in the distance, and a few wild flowers springing up in companionship with some bright tufts of turf beyond the line of earthworks. A starling sat whistling on a piece of broken wall to the left, and frogs were croaking contentedly in a grass-grown pool, probably once belonging to the poor farmhouse of which only those few scorched bricks remained . . . Then in the profound silence, when the grey twilight came falling sadly over all, it seemed to us that the splendour which had entranced us was like the glory our brave men had gained, and the darkness, like the pain and sorrow for their loss. We paced the fearful path up which our soldiers trod, and gathered from around the huge holes made in it by bursting shells, many of the same wild irises . . . their lovely violet colour, mixed with a brilliant yellow, gleaming like jewels among the stones, and looking strangely beautiful amidst those signs of war.[46]

Before departing the Crimea, Alexis Soyer took a last ride round the familiar landmarks of the British camps – all now silent and deserted. Some were derelict, some already destroyed, others taken over by gypsies and Russian soldiers. The vibrant sutlers' camp at Kadikoi was broken up and demolished; the 'Seacole Tavern', as he described it, already no more than a pile of ruins. Soyer remained in the Crimea, like his new-found friend Mary Seacole, to witness the formal handing back of Balaklava to the Russians and the departure from the Ordnance Wharf of the last British regiment – the 56th – on 9 July. It was a fine sunny day and Mary was, as usual, conspicuous in her colourful riding habit with a plaid shawl and natty feather in her hat, to watch 'the last scene of the great drama enacted upon those shores'. Soyer appreciated the poignancy of the moment only too well; he watched in admiration as 'this excellent mother' bade farewell for the last time 'to all her sons, thus ending her benevolent exertions in the Crimea'. He gave Mary a parting salute and then rode off, leaving 'the *mere* [sic] *noire* for the Black Sea'.[47]

Throughout the war Queen Victoria had claimed that her 'whole soul and heart were in the Crimea'.[48] But of course she never went there, even after the war. She did however receive a sentimental gift from the field of battle to serve as a living reminder of the conflict. In November 1855 Colonel H. G. Daniell wrote to the queen's secretary offering the gift of a stray dog from the ruins of Sevastopol, 'knowing Her Majesty's predilection for dogs'. The animal had been found wandering up in the quarries near the city and had been adopted by his men. It was 'young and thoroughly good tempered and could,' asserted Daniell, 'from its great intelligence soon make a capital Retriever'. A few weeks later, Quarry the dog was most gratefully received by the queen into the royal kennels at Windsor, where he lived out a happy and contented life.[49]

Long after the last of the officers' wives – Mrs Birne, Mrs Monro, Mrs Tinley, Mrs Forrest and Mrs Van Straubenzee among them – to whose existence Fanny Duberly had remained determinedly oblivious, had left and the last of the British nurses were on their way home from Scutari, two women remained. Both had claimed the title of 'mother' to the British Army and both had made a unique contribution to the war effort, so different yet in each case so emblematic. Florence Nightingale and Mary Seacole both returned home as national heroines. But as fate would have it, the woman whose name would be immortalized in poetry and prose and song, on statues and public institutions, streets and public houses up and down the land and who would set her stamp on the training of nurses for over a century to come, turned her back on all the fame and acclamation offered her. It was instead the vibrant and life-loving Mary Seacole who took full advantage of the unprecedented accolades uniquely accorded her as a woman of colour in white middle-class Victorian society. Like Florence Nightingale, she had had to fight the enormous gender battle that had made women's work in the Crimea so frowned upon. But she had also crossed racial and social divides too, in the only way she knew how – by letting nothing stop her in her drive to care for her 'sons' of the British Army in her own inimitable, hands-on manner, whilst trusting to the instincts of her own very large and generous heart.

FOURTEEN

The Roll Call

The Crimean War lived on in the public consciousness for many years after it was over – partly buoyed up by the industry of commemoration, partly by the strong sense of social conscience the war had provoked in the sight of its many returning disabled and amputees. Politically, England was forced to come down from the unchallenged pedestal it had occupied in Europe since the Napoleonic Wars and examine and reform its old and corrupt systems. Cardwell's army reforms of the 1870s and Florence Nightingale's detailed, persistent and swingeing recommendations on changes to the Army Medical Services also had helped keep the memory of the war alive. The names of those who had been killed and wounded had long since been published in great lists in the newspapers and carefully memorialized in town halls and churches throughout the land; old soldiers continued to claim their Crimean Medals and pensions for decades after the war; institutions and public houses were named after the major battles and the war's distinguished military leaders. The names of Alma, Sevastopol, Balaklava, Inkerman, Raglan and Cardigan still remain on British streets and pubs today.

When John Henry Foley's bronze Crimean War Memorial was erected in London in 1915 near the junction of Lower Regent Street and Pall Mall, it contained only one reference to a woman – Florence Nightingale. Much against her own wishes, Nightingale had become the repository of the public perception of woman's contribution to the war. Her 'singular endowments' and 'powers of consolation' had been celebrated in journals such as the *Englishwoman's Domestic Magazine*, positioning her at the head of a band of 'pitying women', a 'sisterhood of Mercy' that underlined woman's pacifist, nurturing and ultimately passive roles: 'The word nurse will from henceforth be no longer associated with clinking pattens, damp umbrellas, and unlimited gin, but with the soothing voice, the sleepless care, the heroic zeal of Florence Nightingale'.[1] Memoirs, letters and journals by soldiers and politicians about the war often talked of the female nursing effort as though it had been invested in one woman only; it is certainly clear from the accounts of nurses such as Catherine Hobson that the sick and delirious often thought the nurse who attended them in their hour of need was indeed 'the Lady of the Lamp' herself. Hobson, who in fact bore a resemblance to Nightingale, was one of them. She resented the fact that back in the British press '"Miss Nightingale" was for many a generic name to whom many things were assigned through mere ignorance and mistake', whilst many other fine nurses went uncredited.[2]

But in all the post-war glorification of Florence Nightingale the quiet but devoted French Sisters of Charity were not forgotten by the British press either. They too had produced a heroine: Soeur Prudence, whose selfless dedication was spoken of in the *Illustrated Times* of July 1856. Much like Nightingale, she had 'obtained from the patients a degree of attention which could not have been enforced by the most severe military discipline. A single glance from her was a command, and one that was never disobeyed.' In summarizing the work of the French and British nurses during the war, a Zouave officer observed:

> Were it not for the difference of costume, it would be impossible to tell one from the other. Englishwomen and Frenchwomen, Catholics and Protestants, all have shown themselves equally devoted and equally admirable. Ask the English soldiers who leave the hospitals what they think of the saints who have nursed them . . . and you will see whether those who have just escaped from death do not bless the straw bonnet and green veil of Miss Nightingale as we bless the black dress and white hood of Sister Prudence . . . No one who has been under her care, can deny the highest merits to our Sisters of Charity; but it would be false to suppose that the English ladies have not shown the same devoted spirit.[3]

But what had the war really done for women other than keep them for ever locked into this sanitized role of ministering angel? Certainly nursing as a profession for women moved inexorably ahead with the establishment of Nightingale's training school at St Thomas's Hospital, but not until 1860. Meanwhile, the prevailing mindset about the woman question in Britain did not progress very far at all; if anything, the Crimean War set it back. The poet Elizabeth Barrett Browning had had no doubt that Crimean nursing would not help matters, as she explained in a letter to her friend Anna Jameson:

> I confess myself to be at a loss to see any new position for the sex, or the
> most imperfect solution of the 'woman's question' in this step of hers
> [Nightingale's]. If a movement at all, it is retrograde, a revival of old
> virtues. Since the siege of Troy and earlier, we have had princesses
> binding up wounds with their hands; it's strictly the woman's part and
> men understand it so. Every man is on his knees before ladies carrying
> lint, calling them 'angelic she's' whereas, if they stir an inch as thinkers
> or artists from the beaten land (involving more good to general humanity
> than is involved in lint) the very same men would curse the impudence
> of the very same women and stop there . . . I do not consider the best use
> to which we can put a gifted and accomplished woman is to make her a
> hospital nurse. If it is, why then woe to us all who are not artists![4]

By a strange twist of fate that Browning could not have predicted – dying as she did in 1861 – a 'gifted and accomplished' woman did finally make a significant contribution to the iconography of the war, and thus drew attention to woman's creative potential.

In December 1873 the promising young artist Elizabeth Thompson, who earlier that year had scored a modest success with her painting *Missing*, depicting a scene from the recent 1870–1 Franco-Prussian War, announced that her next project would be a winter scene from the Crimean War. Her father shook his head in disbelief. The Crimea, he said, was 'forgotten'; as for her mother, she 'rather shivered at the idea of snow'.[5] But Elizabeth had been carrying an image in her head of the war and how she wished to portray it for some time and would not be dissuaded. Inspired by the French narrative painters Detaille and Meissonier, she was determined to depict the suffering of the ordinary foot soldier in the Crimea in a way that was as accurate and authentic as she could make it. She sought out Crimean veterans as models and with the help of a Jewish old-clothes dealer found the correct uniforms, helmets, haversacks and other items she needed to start making preparatory sketches.

Completed in late March 1874, *Calling the Roll after an Engagement, Crimea* – or *The Roll Call* as it soon became popularly known – was sent to the Royal Academy by Thompson with a sense of foreboding. She was sure they would disapprove. It was not the usual, conventional and heroic depiction of war – of gallant officers pointing the line of attack to legions of men in line. Instead it presented a raggle-taggle of exhausted Grenadier Guards gathering in the snow, cold and in tatters after an engagement, for their names to be called. Some said it depicted the aftermath of the Battle of Inkerman, but in fact the painting was archetypal of the collective experience of the war, a painting that stripped away the heroics and showed, in all its sombre honesty, that war brought no victories – only an overwhelming sense of futility and exhaustion.

Much to Thompson's surprise, her painting immediately caused 'quite a commotion' when it arrived at the Royal Academy for hanging in that year's exhibition.[6] As the first major painting to depict the Crimean War, it was given a prime position in Room II and word quickly filtered back to Thompson about 'the stir the picture was making behind the scenes prior to its launch'. The sober Selection Committee at the Royal Academy had greeted it with cheers; a private view had already heralded it as the 'coming picture of the year'; the academician Sir John Millais was one of its eminent champions. And it was now 'the talk of the clubs', populated as they were by so many military men. Members of the royal family came and saw *The Roll Call* in a private view on 30 April, the Duke of Cambridge, former C-in-C in the Crimea, expressing his astonishment that any young lady could so 'grasp the speciality of soldiers'.[7] The Prince of Wales immediately announced his wish to buy it. In fact, everybody wanted it, and the offers flooded in.

The Roll Call proved to be the star attraction at the RA exhibition when it opened on 4 May. It received magnificent reviews in the papers. Art critics such as John Ruskin, who till then had been convinced 'no women could paint', changed their minds. Thompson became an overnight sensation, her work compared to that of the finest male academicians. The correspondent of the *Spectator* complained that such was the 'inconvenient' crowd around Miss Thompson's painting that it was impossible to see it.[8] So large was the crowd in fact that the Academy had to put a policeman on duty in front of *The Roll Call* to protect it from damage. Parthenope Nightingale came and asked if it could be removed from the exhibition and taken round to her sister Florence's sickbed in Harley Street so she could see it; the request was declined.

It all got too much for the insatiable curiosity of Queen Victoria, who had no qualms about using her royal prerogative, ordering the painting removed to Buckingham Palace one evening so that she could take a good look at it. Her response was unequivocal: she *must* have it. But the painting was already sold, to Charles Galloway, the Manchester industrialist who had commissioned it. So delighted had he been in fact that he had paid Thompson £126 – £26 more than the asking price. But how could Galloway resist the persistence and determination of his queen? He tried hard to hold on to the painting but eventually capitulated and sold it to Queen Victoria, though not without retaining the copyright on a popular and highly lucrative engraving produced by J. Dickinson & Co.

Meanwhile, *The Roll Call* went on a solo tour to provincial cities. No one could have predicted its impact on the British population.[9] Word was out: 'The Roll Call is Coming' shouted newspaper headlines in Newcastle.[10] Everywhere people queued to see it – 20,000 in Liverpool alone. Over and over again, people would come away profoundly moved and often in tears. The painting had clearly touched the nation's heart. Such was the curiosity about its attractive 27-year-old artist that 250,000 *cartes de visite* of Elizabeth Thompson were sold. People were astonished that a woman who had never seen or experienced war – a war that had ended when she was only 10 – could have produced it. There was no doubt about it: Thompson was a miracle worker, the 'Florence Nightingale of the Brush'.[11]

The Roll Call would remain the most popular painting exhibited at the RA during the nineteenth century. Nor was Thompson a one-hit wonder. In later life, as Lady Butler, she produced a series of stunning battle images of the Crimean, Napoleonic and Boer Wars, to become the most famous woman artist of the day. And though she never ceased to thank God that she had 'never painted for the glory of war, but to portray its pathos and its heroism',[12] nothing ever quite equalled the power and poignancy of *The Roll Call*. Elizabeth Thompson had done for the ordinary British soldier in art what Rudyard Kipling later did for him in literature: she had 'taken the individual, separated him, seen him close, and let the world see him'.[13]

After the Crimean War, 275,000 Crimean Medals were issued in Britain with additional clasps for Alma, Inkerman, Balaklava and Sevastopol for the men of regiments that had fought in those battles. But not a single medal was given, officially, to a woman (although several French *cantinières* were awarded military decorations). Nor were any of the 229 British nurses who served in Turkey and the Crimea, eleven of whom had died out there, honoured, let alone the numerous unofficial nurses – army wives like Nell Butler who had served in the field hospitals. Eventually, a handful of survivors including Sarah Anne Terrot received a retrospective award in 1897 of the Royal Red Cross, a medal that had been instituted in 1883 to commend 'exceptional services in military nursing'.

Mary Seacole, meanwhile, had for many years after the war proudly walked the streets of London wearing Crimean medals given to her by the British, French and Turks – though how and when they were awarded remains a mystery. It is most likely they came via the back door, thanks to the influence of her highly placed military and royal patrons. Fund-raising appeals were made for her in 1857 and 1867, and in the latter, supported by three royal princes, Queen Victoria permitted the publication of 'her approbation' of Mary Seacole's services. But Mary was never officially recognized with a medal, nor granted an introduction to the queen. No more was Fanny Duberly, who petitioned for a campaign medal, very rightly thinking she had more than deserved it, but who was snubbed by the queen when she asked permission to dedicate the published edition of her *Journal* to her. And although Florence Nightingale received a personal gift from the queen of a brooch designed by Prince Albert 'as a mark of esteem and gratitude for her devotion toward the Queen's brave soldiers', she received no official decoration until she accepted the award of the Order of Merit – but this was not until 1908, two years before her death.[14]

NO PLACE FOR LADIES

The heroism of the 120 or so Russian Sisters of Mercy, 17 of whom died in the Crimea, was doubly recognized, however: with the award of the silver medal for the Defence of Sevastopol, as well as a medal 'For Zeal', which was also presented to some of the heroic women of the city who had carried supplies and ammunition to the bastions throughout the worst of the bombardments. Some women were even granted the higher military medal 'For Gallantry'. In Sevastopol a memorial was erected to Dasha Sevastopolskaya and the work of the Sisters of Mercy of the Community of the Cross in St Petersburg was boosted by considerable private donations in recognition of their work.

When the last of the troops were embarked from the Crimea in the summer of 1856, it was found that 50 or 60 women who had joined their men in camp without permission were now stranded, the army with its usual mean-spiritedness making no provision for their passage home. It took the efforts of both Florence Nightingale (now at Balaklava) and the Deputy Quartermaster General to induce the Army's Chief of Staff to make arrangements for the women to be sent back to England on the *Thames* transport ship, picking up en route those women still lingering at Scutari. 'Let not the wife and child of the soldier be forgotten', remarked Charles Bracebridge in noting this fact at the end of his report on the 'Assistance Given to the Wives, Widows, and Children of the British Soldiers at Scutari, 1854–5–6'.

Alicia Blackwood, for one, had had more than 500 women pass through her care at Scutari, many of whom had found only a grave there. One case in particular had always haunted her, a story more poignant than all the many others she had encountered. In November 1855, one of a handful of women who moved mountains to get to the Crimea to be with their husbands was the wife of a sergeant in the Royal Artillery based at Scutari. She had already lost two of her four young sons to fever whilst he was away at the war and was desperate to be reunited with him. Alicia Blackwood, having received confirmation of the woman's good character from her parish priest, had offered to take the woman in, on arrival, and give her work. But at Liverpool, where she went to board ship for the Crimea, another of the woman's two remaining sons fell sick; she nevertheless wrote informing her husband of her date of arrival. Then, tragically, the sergeant was felled by cholera. He died five days later at Scutari, having begged the Blackwoods to take care of his widow, now en route. As fate would have it, on the very day the sergeant died, his sick child died too. The woman arrived on 13 December to hear the terrible news and 'sank down on a seat and seemed as though turned to stone'. For days she did not eat, speak or even weep and was oblivious to her remaining child. It was only after she visited her husband's grave that the tears came, in great waves. Such was the compassion for the woman's situation that a substantial subscription was raised at Scutari to assist her.[15]

In the main, however, the women who served and suffered with their regiments so devotedly in the Crimea received no such special consideration and care. When they died, as many did – at Gallipoli, at Scutari, at Varna and in the Crimea itself – they were forgotten, their names unrecorded and their courage unsung.

Elizabeth Evans of the 4th King's Own Regiment of Foot was one of the few to be given a farewell befitting a Crimean heroine when she died in 1914. Large crowds attended her funeral in Richmond on 4 February. Six sergeants of the King's Own were sent from barracks in Dover to be her pallbearers, and she was buried with full military honours and the playing of 'The Last Post', with the regimental pall covering her coffin. Nell Butler, her right arm withered by frostbite and scurvy in the war, fought a dogged 39-year campaign for a widow's pension after the war. She too was remembered when she died in 1909, with scores of old soldiers at her graveside to see the coffin lowered, bearing the proud inscription on its brass plate: 'Ellen Butler, Crimean Veteran'.[16] Margaret Kerwin of the 19th lived into old age too, having served in India with her husband John during the Rebellion of 1857–8; as had Fanny and Henry Duberly.

Like Elizabeth Evans, Kerwin never had a moment's regret for the often arduous life she had lived. Both agreed that army life had not been without its happy times: 'If I was young to-morrow, I would take the same travels, but I would be a little wiser,' she remarked modestly.[17] Mrs Mary Ann Jones of Welshpool, an army wife and washerwoman with the militia sent out later in the war to Turkey, had no regrets either. She had spent her war washing for 27 men. When asked if she was glad when the war ended, she had replied in all honesty: 'Well no, I can't say altogether that I was, you see we hadn't done so badly. I went from Welshpool with a sovereign in my pocket – and I came back with seven.'[18] As wars go, Mary Ann had had a good one.

In a letter to Florence Nightingale's sister Parthenope in July 1855, the novelist Elizabeth Gaskell remarked that 'babies ad libidum are being christened Florence here [in Manchester]; poor little factory babies, whose grimed, stunted parents brighten up the name, although you'd think their lives and thoughts were bound up in fluffy mills'.[19] These children and the names they were given were the pride not just of the public back home, but of those ordinary soldiers who campaigned out in that remote and forgotten place. During and after the war there was a flood of girls named Alma and Florence; boys were given the dubious honour of having Sebastopol, Inkerman, Crimea or even Redan as a first name. Nolan, Cathcart and Raglan went down well, too. Balaklava appeared as a middle name – even for girls such as Eliza Balaklava Richards and Alma Balaklava Lloyd; as did Scutari – a possible indicator of where James Scutari Taylor was born. John Malakoff Lomax, born in 1862, must no doubt have been named in memory of a father or grandfather's service in the war. *Punch* magazine, in its usual tongue-in-cheek way, observed that girls might be rather more reticent about owning to Crimean Christian names for, 'some thirty years hence, if not sooner, they will be suggestive of a certain date, which, for reasons best known to themselves, and we would gallantly say, almost all ladies thirty years old, and not a few under thirty, do not wish to be known'.[20] But it's doubtful the sickly infants born to army wives at Scutari and even in the Crimea survived the harshness of their environment. Little Himalaya Strange born on the troopship *Himalaya* in January 1855 survived into adulthood; but died a poor domestic servant, of phthisis, at the age of 22. As for the numberless others – one cannot help wondering how many short lives began and ended somewhere in a dirty ditch near the front lines or a rat-infested cellar in Scutari.

At the British cemetery at Scutari, near Constantinople, only a few of the women – both nurses and army wives – who served and died in the Crimea, as well as some of their small children, are commemorated. Two gentlemen tourists visiting in the summer of 1855 noted the plain cross on white marble of 'Sophia Barnes, Nurse', who had died on 4 April that year. They knew nothing more of the short sad life that had ended here, so far from home, but felt that the simple memorial was enough 'to inspire respect and love' and tell a story:

> She had left her country and home, and all that those two words
> comprehend. She had gone to alleviate sorrow, to nurse the sick and
> the wounded. With a woman's courage, she had braved infection and
> disease, dangers little inferior to those of a battle-field, and wanting its
> excitement. Fatigue, foul air, sights that must have made every nerve
> quiver, turned her not aside. She strove to the last; and in the exercise
> of her angelic mission, fell into the grave she had smoothed the approach
> to for others. God reward thee, Nurse, and those like thee![21]

None of the graves, of some 129 cemeteries the British left behind them dotted over the Crimean plain, have survived the accumulated depredations of neglect, vandalism, weather, revolution, Communist indifference and the fierce fighting that took place in the Crimea during the Second World War. Even the carefully tended British officers' graveyard at Cathcart's Hill, which became the repository of many grand headstones and memorials to the fallen, was eroded and its gravestones destroyed one by one. A new British Memorial was erected by the Russians at Cathcart's Hill in 1993 but, proving to be jerry-built, soon began to fall down. But now there is at least a new memorial to the British dead outside Sevastopol and another in Bulgaria to commemorate the many thousands who died in the cholera epidemics.[22]

No one knows now where the handful of women's graves, recorded on the Crimean peninsula in 1857 by Captain John Colborne and Frederic Brine, are to be found. Graves such as that of Mary Ann, wife of Sergeant Matthew Phenix of the 1st Royals, who died in camp in November 1855. Hers was one of 13 lonely graves that the regiment left behind in their little cemetery. Time, too, has removed all trace of the wooden marker on the grave that once overlooked the River Chernaya, near the field of Inkerman:

TO THE
Memory
OF
MArgretT
STArrETT
LATE WIFE
Of James STArrETT, Pr. 95th Regt who LANDED on the Crimea
On The 14th Sept 1854. This woman TRAVLED with the RegT
Through the Campeign UNTILL Such Times as IT was
PLEASED GOD TO CALL her To himself out of this WORLD
To the next Being in ThE 23rd Year of HER Age[23]

The grave also bore the simple wooden marker at its foot: 'Woman, English', carved so carefully by her semi-literate husband all those years before. But of Margaret Starrett, what she endured on campaign with the army, how she lived and the manner of her death, we know nothing more.

NOTES

For abbreviations of manuscript collections and journals, see Bibliography.

Prologue

1 Benson and Esher (eds), *Letters of Queen Victoria*, vol. III, p. 14.
2 Ibid., p. 170.
3 Information kindly supplied by Nick Mays, Deputy Archivist, News International Ltd.

Chapter 1: The Girl I Left Behind Me

1 Brereton, *The British Soldier*, p. 159.
2 Ibid., p. 156.
3 Arthur Bryant (ed.), *In Search of Peace: Speeches (1937–1938) by the Right Honourable Neville Chamberlain*, London: Hutchinson, 1939, p. 393.
4 Wiseman, 'The Future Historian's View of the Present War', p. 4.
5 Monica Charlot, *Victoria the Young Queen*, Oxford: Blackwell, 1991, p. 350.
6 *ILN*, 25 February 1854, p. 157.
7 Longford, *Victoria R.I.*, 2001 edn, p. 241.
8 *Times*, 15 February 1854.
9 Benson and Esher (eds), *Letters of Queen Victoria*, vol. III, p. 14.
10 *ILN*, 4 March 1854, p. 186.
11 Fletcher and Ishchenko, *The Crimean War*, p. 95.
12 Benson and Esher (eds), *Letters of Queen Victoria*, vol. III, p. 14.
13 Lyrics from http://www.contemplator.com/england/girl.html, on which site the melody can also be played.
14 *Bell's Weekly Messenger*, 4 March 1854; in Chesney, *Crimean War Reader*, p. 29.
15 *Cassell's Illustrated Family Paper*, 15 April 1854, p. 131.
16 Anon [Miss Bird], *Four Days at Portsmouth*, p. 16.
17 Ibid., p. 4.
18 Ibid., p. 12.
19 Ibid., p. 14.
20 Ibid., p. 21.
21 RA/QVJ, 11 March 1854.
22 Barnett, *Britain and Her Army*, p. 271.
23 *ILN*, 18 March, p. 242.
24 Longford, *Victoria R. I.*, p. 244.
25 Seacole, *Wonderful Adventures*, p. 69.
26 Barnett, *Britain and Her Army*, p. 273.
27 *Household Words*, 1 April 1854, p. 161.

Chapter 2: Nothing But My Needle to Depend On

1 *Household Words*, 1 April 1854, p. 164.
2 *ILN*, 1 April 1854, p. 303.
3 *ILN*, 29 April 1854, p. 383.
4 *Times*, 4 March 1854, p. 9.
5 *Times*, 22 February 1854, p. 8.
6 *Times*, 6 March 1854, p. 9.
7 *Times*, 25 February 1854, p. 12.
8 Hobson, *Catharine Leslie Hobson*, p. 16.
9 Evans, 'A Soldier's Wife in the Crimea', p. 265.
10 Patterson, *Camp and Quarters*, p. 114.
11 See articles on 'Solders' Wives' in *United Service Journal*, April and May 1854.
12 Young, anonymously, in *Household Words*, 21 April 1855, p. 279.
13 Young, *Aldershot and All About It*, p. 32.
14 Wyatt, *History of the 1st Battalion Coldstream Guards*, p. 144.
15 Trustram, *Women of the Regiment*, p. 153.
16 *ILN*, 29 April 1854, p. 383.
17 Ibid.
18 Hansard CXXXVI, 26 February 1855, col. 193; Trustram, *Women of the Regiment*, p. 56.
19 *Times*, 27 February 1854, p. 9. Major Colin Robins relates how little had changed in army attitudes to financial provisions for wives even in June 1961, when President Kassem of Iraq announced his intention of annexing Kuwait. Troops of Major Robins's regiment, the Royal Artillery, were hastily sent to the Middle East without any arrangements made for their wives left at home, few of whom had bank accounts, to receive a proportion of their pay. In the end the colonel's wife came to their rescue and lent them money from her own account until several weeks later the army issued the wives with allowance books.
20 *Times*, 26 July 1855, p. 10.
21 *Portsmouth Times and Naval Gazette*, 4 March 1854.
22 *Times*, 22 November 1854, p. 5.
23 Ibid., p. 6.
24 Ibid.
25 See Hagist, 'The Women of the British Army in America'.
26 *Household Words*, 21 April 1855, p. 279.
27 *Cassell's Illustrated Family Paper*, 23 June 1855, p. 196.
28 Evans, 'A Soldier's Wife in the Crimea', p. 265.

Chapter 3: Tramp, Tramp, Tramp for Woman as Well as Man

1 *The Great Gun Song Book*, c.1855, n.p.
2 Compton, *Colonel's Lady and Camp Follower*, p. 29.
3 Duberly, *Journal Kept During the Russian War*, p. 1.
4 Anglesey, *Little Hodge*, p. 9.
5 Duberly, *Journal Kept During the Russian War*, p. 9.

6 Young, *Our Camp in Turkey*, p. 8.
7 *Times*, 25 April 1854, p. 9.
8 Bentley, *Russell's Despatches from the Crimea*, p. 33.
9 Young, *Our Camp in Turkey*, p. 158.
10 Ibid., p. 32.
11 Wyatt, *History of the 1st Battalion Coldstream Guards*, p. 144.
12 *Times*, 8 May 1854, p. 7.
13 Evans, 'A Soldier's Wife in the Crimea', p. 266.
14 Ibid., p. 267.
15 'A Crimean Heroine', *The Thistle*, p. 101.
16 Ibid., p. 102.
17 Young, *Our Camp in Turkey*, p. 120.
18 Ibid., p. 121.
19 Russell, 'The Allied Forces at Gallipoli', *ILN*, 27 May 1854, p. 494.
20 Young, *Our Camp in Turkey*, p. 98.
21 Ibid., p. 115.
22 Ibid., p. 130.
23 Ibid., p. 106.
24 Evans, 'A Soldier's Wife in the Crimea', pp. 266–7.
25 Ibid., p. 266.
26 Young, *Our Camp in Turkey*, p. 33.
27 Ibid., p. 53.
28 Duberly, *Journal Kept During the Russian War*, p. 15.
29 Farwell, *Queen Victoria's Little Wars*, p. 81.
30 *Times*, 16 May 1854, p. 10.
31 Stephenson, *At Home and on the Battlefield*, p. 73.
32 Young, *Our Camp in Turkey*, p. 59.
33 Ibid. p. 56.
34 Compton, *Colonel's Lady and Camp Follower*, p. 43.
35 Higginson, *Seventy-One Years of a Guardsman's Life*, p. 121.
36 Young, *Our Camp in Turkey*, pp. 60–1.
37 Ibid., p. 68.

Chapter 4: The Disease That Walketh by Noonday Was Among Us

1 Anon, *The War, or Voices from the Ranks*, p. 15.
2 Ibid.
3 Ibid.
4 Richardson (ed.), *Nurse Sarah Anne*, p. 138.
5 Airlie, *With the Guards We Shall Go*, p. 32.
6 Glazbrook, letter 12 August 1854, NAM 8401-100. For Glazbrook's tragic death, see chapter 7.
7 Tisdall, *Mrs Duberly's Campaigns*, p. 125.
8 Duberly, *Journal Kept During the Russian War*, pp. 19–20.
9 Ibid., p. 10.
10 Steevens, *The Crimean Campaign with The Connaught Rangers*, p. 66.

11 Emerson, *Sebastopol: The Story of its Fall*, p. 42.
12 *Times*, 18 July 1854, p. 9.
13 Anon, *The War, or Voices from the Ranks*, p. 16.
14 'The French *Vivandières* in Turkey', *United Service Journal*, 1854, part 2, p. 296.
15 For a fascinating account, see Cardoza, 'Duty to the Nation'.
16 Young, *Our Camp in Turkey*, p. 155.
17 Alexander, *Passages in the Life of a Soldier*, p. 90.
18 Young, *Our Camp in Turkey*, p. 156.
19 Kerwin, 'In the Crimea with the 19th Regiment', p. 94.
20 Young, *Our Camp in Turkey*, p. 253.
21 Evans, 'A Soldier's Wife in the Crimea', pp. 266–7.
22 Kerwin, 'In the Crimea with the 19th Regiment', p. 95.
23 Ibid.
24 Young, *Our Camp in Turkey*, p. 230.
25 Lorne, Marquis of, *V.R.I., Her Life and Empire*, London: Eyre & Spottiswoode, 1901, p. 248.
26 H. B., Letters from the Crimea during the Years 1854 and 1855, pp. 27–8.
27 Russell, 'The British Expedition', *Times*, 5 October 1854, p. 7.
28 Hibbert, *The Destruction of Lord Raglan*, p. 32.
29 Duberly, *Journal Kept During the Russian War*, p. 46.
30 Anglesey, *Little Hodge*, p. 26.
31 Russell, 'The British Expedition', *Times*, 5 October 1854, p. 7.
32 Evans, 'A Soldier's Wife in the Crimea', p. 267.
33 Ibid., p. 266.
34 Duberly, *Journal Kept During the Russian War*, p. 54.
35 Letter to her sister Selina, 23 July 1855, in Tisdall, *Mrs Duberly's Campaigns*, p. 49.
36 Ibid.
37 Ibid.
38 Duberly, *Journal Kept During the Russian War*, p. 91.
39 Bentley, *Russell's Despatches from the Crimea*, p. 56.
40 Fisher-Rowe, *Extracts from the Letters of E. R. Fisher-Rowe*, p. 15.
41 Kerwin, 'In the Crimea with the 19th Regiment', p. 95.

Chapter 5: The Queen of England Would Give Her Eyes to See It

1 Tyrrell, *History of the Present War with Russia*, vol. II, p. 218.
2 Bayes, 'Nell Butler was the front line "Florence Nightingale"', p. 20.
3 'The British Expedition', *Times*, 2 October 1854, p. 6.
4 Evans, 'A Soldier's Wife in the Crimea', p. 268.
5 Alexander Kinglake, *The Invasion of the Crimea: Its Origin and Progress to the Death of Lord Raglan*, vol. II, Edinburgh, 1863–87, p. 208.
6 Evans, 'A Soldier's Wife in the Crimea', p. 268.
7 Chapman, *Echoes from the Crimea*, p. 82.
8 Evans, 'A Soldier's Wife in the Crimea', p. 268.
9 Cowper, *The King's Own*, vol. II, p. 96.
10 Compton, *Colonel's Lady and Camp Follower*, p. 77.

11 Evans, 'A Soldier's Wife in the Crimea', p. 268.

12 Anon, *The War, or Voices from the Ranks*, p. 49.

13 Evans, 'A Soldier's Wife in the Crimea', p. 268.

14 Bayes, 'Nell Butler was the front line "Florence Nightingale"', p. 20.

15 The few sources there are on Dasha Sevastopolskaya are patchy and somewhat con-
tradictory. The most recent and reliable is that published in Simferopol in 2005, in
Sestry Miloserdiya v Krymskoi Voine 1853–1856 godov, pp. 157–9.

16 Duberly, *Journal Kept During the Russian War*, p. 83.

17 Bell, *Soldier's Glory*, p. 225.

18 *PFJ*, 10 February 1855, p. 157.

19 Duberly, *Journal Kept During the Russian* War, p. 108.

20 Ibid.

21 Bell, *Soldier's Glory*, p. 229.

22 Emerson, *Sebastopol: The Story of its Fall*, p. 70.

23 Letter to King Leopold, 13 October 1854, in Benson and Esher (eds), *Letters of Queen
Victoria*, vol. III, p. 50; Longford, *Victoria R.I.*, p. 243.

24 Benson and Esher (eds), op. cit.

25 Longford, *Victoria R.I.*, p. 243.

26 Benita Stoney and Heinrich C. Weltzien, *My Mistress the Queen: The Letters of Frieda
Arnold, Dresser to Queen Victoria 1854–9*, London: Weidenfeld and Nicolson, 1994, p.
154.

27 Hector Bolitho et al. (ed.), *Further Letters of Queen Victoria*, London: Thornton
Butterworth, 1938, p. 51.

28 Munro, *Reminiscences of Military Service*, pp. 41–2.

29 Ibid.

30 Duberly, *Journal Kept During the Russian War*, p. 116.

31 'The War in the Crimea', *Times*, 14 November 1854, p. 7.

32 Duberly, *Journal Kept During the Russian War*, p. 118.

33 Kerr, *The Crimean War*, p. 83.

34 Massie, *A Most Desperate Undertaking*, p. 108.

35 Royle, *Crimea*, p. 244.

36 RA/VIC/F1/34 letter, 2 November, letter to her sister Selina.

37 Hamley, E. Bruce, *The Story of the Campaign of Sebastopol*, Edinburgh: W. Blackwood,
1855, pp. 106–7.

38 Chapman, *Echoes from the Crimea*, p. 156.

39 *Times*, 4 December 1854, p. 7.

40 Wylly, *History of the 1st and 2nd Battalions, the Sherwood Foresters*, p. 472.

41 Letter to King Leopold, 14 November 1854, in Benson and Esher (eds), *Letters of
Queen Victoria*, vol. III, p. 52.

42 Letter to Marianne Gaskell, ?13 October 1854, in Chapple and Pollard (ed.), *The
Letters of Mrs Gaskell*, p. 311.

43 Benson and Esher (eds), *Letters of Queen Victoria*, vol. III, p. 52.

44 Royle, *Crimea*, p. 292; Newcastle to Raglan, 27 November 1854. WO6/70/2208.

Chapter 6: Why Have We No Sisters of Mercy?

1 Gail Malmgreen, 'Anne Knight and the Radical Subculture', *Quaker History*, LXXI, 1982, pp. 100–23.
2 *Herald of Peace*, October 1854, p. 113.
3 *Punch*, vol. 27, 1854, p. 96.
4 *Herald of Peace*, October 1854, p. 113.
5 Editorial, *Times*, 28 August 1854, p. 6.
6 See for example 'The Love of Woman', *EDM*, vol. III (1854–5), p. 47.
7 *Times*, 12 October 1854, p. 7.
8 See Eric Gruber von Arni, *Justice to the Maimed Soldiers: Nursing, Medical Care and Welfare for Sick and Wounded Soldiers and their Families during the English Civil Wars and Interregnum, 1642–1660*, Aldershot: Ashgate, 2002. The Army Medical Services Museum at Aldershot, Hampshire holds interesting displays on military nurses in the seventeenth and eighteenth centuries.
9 'Hospital Assistants in the East', *Times*, 14 October 1854, p. 7.
10 'To the Editor of *The Times*', *Times*, 16 October 1854, p. 9.
11 Hobson, *Catharine Leslie Hobson*, p. 49.
12 'The Soldiers' Wives in the East', *Times*, 24 October 1854, p. 9.
13 Summers, *Angels and Citizens*, p. 39.
14 'France: From Our Own Correspondent', *Times*, 30 November 1854, p. 7.
15 Pincoffs, *Experiences of a Civilian in Eastern Military Hospitals*, p. 182.
16 'Nurses for the Wounded', *Times*, 24 October 1854, p. 9.
17 Antony R. Mills, *The Halls of Ravenswood*, London: Muller, 1967, p. 116; Burton and Wilkins, *The Romance of Isabel Lady Burton*, p. 76.
18 Rossetti, *Dante Gabriel Rossetti*, p. 32.
19 Rickards, *Felicia Skene of Oxford*, p. 110.
20 Acland, *Memoir on the Cholera at Oxford*, p. 133.
21 PRO WO 25/264, application of Miss Belgrave.
22 Ibid., application of Elizabeth Purcell.
23 Seacole, *Wonderful Adventures*, pp. 73–4.
24 Goldie, *I Have Done My Duty*, p. 93.
25 Luddy (ed.), *The Crimean Journals of the Sisters of Mercy*, p. 11.
26 Ibid., p. 36.
27 'Nurses of Quality for the Crimea', *Punch*, vol. 27, 1854, p. 193.
28 'Nurses for the East', *Times*, 13 November 1854, p. 10.
29 'The Hospital Nurse – An Episode of the War', *Fraser's Magazine*, p. 97.
30 Quoted in Shepherd, *The Crimean Doctors*, vol. 1, p. 262.
31 Letter to Sidney Herbert, in Osborne, *Scutari and Its Hospitals*, pp. 177–8.
32 Richardson (ed.), *Nurse Sarah Anne*, p. 75.
33 Ibid., p. 80.

Chapter 7: Every Accumulation of Misery

1 Hamlin, *Among the Turks*, p. 230.
2 Wiseman, 'The Future Historian's View of the Present War', p. 20.

3 See Nightingale, *Subsidiary Notes as to the Introduction of Female Nursing*, pp. 20–1.
4 Nightingale, letter, 21 December 1854, to Sidney Herbert, in Goldie, *I Have Done My Duty*, p. 52.
5 Lytton Strachey, 'Florence Nightingale', in *Eminent Victorians*, Harmondsworth: Penguin, 1971, p. 119.
6 Taylor, *Eastern Hospitals and English Nurses*, p. 55.
7 Goodman, *Experiences of an English Sister of Mercy*, p. 105; Taylor, *Eastern Hospitals and English Nurses*, p. 70.
8 Huntsman et al., 'Light Before Dawn', p. 9; Taylor, *Eastern Hospitals and English Nurses*, p. 54.
9 Ken Horton papers, TS of Bracebridge memo, Scutari, 15 November 1855.
10 Richardson (ed.), *Nurse Sarah Anne*, p. 87.
11 Anon, *The War, or Voices from the Ranks*, p. 137.
12 Goodman, *Experiences of an English Sister of Mercy*, p. 60.
13 Letter, 15 February 1855, in Shepherd, *The Crimean Doctors*, vol. 1, p. 281.
14 Bakunina, 'Vospominaniya Sestry Miloserdiya', in Kolesnikova (ed.), *Sestry Miloserdiya*, p. 194.
15 A full account of the grand duchess's work can be found in Dina Yafasova, 'Sisters of Mercy: Women in Nursing in Old Russia', 2002, available in Russian online at http://www.sygeplejersken.dk/nh/manuel/soderjanie.htm. A typescript translation by Hugh Matthews is held at the FNM. See also Kolesnikova (ed.), *Sestry Miloserdiya*, which covers the grand duchess's life and work in detail.
16 Pirogov wrote extensively on his surgical methods and principles, including his work at Sevastopol. See especially his *Sevastopol'skie pis'ma i vospominaniya*, Moscow: Akademiya Nauk, 1950.
17 Pirogov, in Yafasova, 'Sisters of Mercy', part 6, p. 5.
18 Ibid.
19 Ibid., part 6, p. 10.
20 Howson, *Deaconesses*, pp. 250–1.
21 Letter to Karl K. Seidlitz, in Sorokina, 'Russian Nursing in the Crimean War', pp. 59–60.
22 Luddy (ed.), *The Crimean Journals of the Sisters of Mercy*, p. 125.
23 Stanmore, *Sidney Herbert*, vol. I, p. 370.
24 Luddy (ed.), *The Crimean Journals of the Sisters of Mercy*, pp. 128–9.
25 Ibid., p. xxiii.
26 Copy letter in RA/VIC/F1/88.
27 Goldie, *I Have Done My Duty*, p. 43.
28 'Rules and Regulations for the Nurses Attached to the Military Hospitals in the East', 1854, FNM.
29 Summers, 'The Mysterious Demise of Sarah Gamp', p. 381; Summers, 'Pride and Prejudice', p. 44.
30 See Mary Stanley, *Hospitals and Sisterhoods*, London: John Murray, 1854, pp. 54–5.
31 Goldie, *I Have Done My Duty*, p. 56.
32 Ibid., p. 56.
33 Ibid., p. 55.
34 Richardson, *Nurse Sarah Anne*, p. 89; Goodman, *Experiences of an English Sister of*

Mercy, pp. 105, 144.

35 Richardson, *Nurse Sarah Anne*, pp. 83–4.

36 Compton, *Colonel's Lady and Camp Follower*, p. 127; MS letter, extract, n.d., in RA/VIC/F1/79.

Chapter 8: This Little Heroic Wreck of an Army

1 Duberly, *Journal Kept During the Russian War*, p. 131; Tisdall, *Mrs Duberly's Campaigns*, pp. 113–16.
2 Evans, 'A Soldier's Wife in the Crimea', p. 270.
3 Duberly, *Journal Kept During the Russian War*, p. 170.
4 Kerwin, 'In the Crimea with the 19th Regiment', p. 95.
5 Bayes, 'Nell Butler was the front line "Florence Nightingale"', p. 20.
6 Ibid.
7 Neil Bannatyne, *History of the 30th Regiment, Now the First Battalion, East Lancashire Regiment, 1689–1881*, Liverpool: Littlebury Brothers, p. 422.
8 Evans, 'A Soldier's Wife in the Crimea', p. 270.
9 Ibid.
10 Duberly, *Journal Kept During the Russian War*, p. 133.
11 Anglesey, *Little Hodge*, p. 84.
12 Goldie, *I Have Done My Duty*, p. 109.
13 Blackwood, *A Narrative of Personal Experiences*, p. 57.
14 Bell, *Soldier's Glory*, p. 256.
15 Duberly, *Journal Kept During the Russian War*, p. 135.
16 Ibid., p. 140.
17 Ibid., pp. 144–5.
18 Creagh, *Sparks from Camp Fires*, p. 106.
19 Bell, *Soldier's Glory*, p. 263.
20 Anglesey, *Little Hodge*, p. 71.
21 Warner (ed.), *The Fields of War*, p. 110.
22 *Times*, 23 December 1854, p. 9.
23 Frederick Mulhauser (ed.), *The Correspondence of Arthur Hugh Clough*, vol. II, Oxford: Clarendon Press, 1957, p. 497.
24 See *PFJ*, 16 December 1854, p. 14; 23 December 1854, p. 32; 27 January 1855, pp. 116, 122; and Taylor, *Eastern Hospitals and English Nurses*, p. 61.
25 Chapple and Pollard (ed.), *The Letters of Mrs Gaskell*, p. 324.
26 *PFJ*, 27 January 1855, p. 122.
27 Woods, *The Past Campaign*, p. 262.
28 Quoting Shakespeare, *Troilus and Cressida*, III:3; *Times*, 2 March 1855, p. 8.
29 Polidori, letter, 8 June 1855, in Rossetti Archive UBC, fo. 2418.
30 Kenyon (ed.), *Letters of Elizabeth Barrett Browning*, vol. 2, pp. 179–80.
31 Stokes, *Echoes of the War*, p. 76.
32 *ILN*, 30 December 1854, p. 702; *PFJ*, 6 January 1855, p. 68.
33 Taylor, *Eastern Hospitals and English Nurses*, p. 203.
34 Surtees, *Charlotte Canning*, p. 191.
35 St Aubyn, *Queen Victoria: A Portrait*, p. 295.

36 Clifford, *Henry Clifford VC*, p. 124.
37 Fisher-Rowe, letter, 2 December 1854, in *Extracts from the Letters of E. R. Fisher-Rowe*, p. 26.
38 Woods, *The Past Campaign*, pp. 245–6.
39 *ILN*, 23 December 1854, p. 645.
40 Goodman, *Experiences of an English Sister of Mercy*, pp. 120–1.
41 Goldie, *I Have Done My Duty*, pp. 55–60.
42 Duberly, *Journal Kept During the Russian War*, p. 155.
43 Bentley, *Russell's Despatches from the Crimea*, p. 156.
44 Sterling, *The Highland Brigade in the Crimea*, Letter XLVI, p. 94.
45 W. F. Monypenny and G. E. Buckle, *The Life of Benjamin Disraeli, Earl of Beaconsfield*, vol. III, *1846–1855*, London: John Murray, pp. 551–2.
46 Russell, *The Great War with Russia* , London: Routledge, 1895, p. 235.
47 Askwith, *Crimean Courtship*, p. 63.
48 Ibid., pp. 84–5.
49 Ibid., pp. 77, 82, 86.

Chapter 9: Would a Guinea Be Too Much?

1 Shepherd, *The Crimean Doctors*, vol. II, p. 508; Calthorpe, *Letters from Headquarters*, vol. II, pp. 62, 67–8.
2 *Lancet*, 1854, vol. 2, p. 136.
3 *BMJ*, 1899, vol. 2, p. 206.
4 *Lancet*, 1855, vol. 1, p. 141; 1854, vol. 2, p. 136; Edgerton, *Death or Glory*, p. 145; *Times*, 23 August 1855, p. 7; *Royal Army Chaplains' Department Journal*, January 1932, vol. IV(no. 33), p. 144.
5 *Colburn's United Service Magazine*, 1856, vol. I, p. 284.
6 Ibid., p. 12.
7 *Portsmouth Times and Naval Gazette*, 13 January 1855, p. 8. See also 'The First Anniversary Meeting of the Central Association', p. 13.
8 'The First Anniversary Meeting of the Central Association', pp. 14–15.
9 RA/VIC/F1/106.
10 'The First Anniversary Meeting of the Central Association', p. 21.
11 Ibid., p. 17.
12 Nancy Mitford, *The Stanleys of Alderley: Their Letters between the Years 1851–1858*, London: Hamish Hamilton, 1968, pp. 92–3.
13 Burton and Wilkins, *The Romance of Isabel Lady Burton*, pp. 76–9; Mary S. Lovell, *A Rage to Live: the Biography of Richard and Isabel Burton*, London: Abacus, 1999, pp. 188–9.
14 *ILN*, 6 January 1855, p. 6.
15 *PF J*, 16 December 1854, p. 10; *ILN*, 6 January 1855, p. 6; *Morning Chronicle*, 5 January 1855.
16 Bostock, *Letters from India and the Crimea*, pp. 225, 247.
17 Bonham-Carter (ed.), *Surgeon in the Crimea*, p. 164.
18 Smith, *A Victorian RSM*, pp. 179–80.
19 RA/VIC/F2/118.

20 RA/VIC/F3/54.
21 See RA/VIC/F1/66.
22 RA/QVJ, 20 February 1855.
23 RA/QVJ, 22 February 1855; Cecil Woodham-Smith, *Queen Victoria: Her Life and Times*, London: Hamish Hamilton, 1972, pp. 353–4.
24 RA/QVJ, 3 March 1855.
25 RA/VIC/F2/52.
26 See RA/VIC/F3/115.
27 'Stories of the Wounded', *Illustrated Times*, 30 June 1855, p. 50.
28 George Russell Dartnell, 'Notes of Queen Victoria's Visit to Fort Pitt', TS, MC 714, Gillingham Public Library.
29 RA/VIC/F2/135.
30 See *ILN*, 28 October 1854, p. 408; 17 March 1855, p. 17.
31 *Lady's Newspaper*, 31 March 1855, p. 193.
32 Portal, *Letters from the Crimea*, p. 140.
33 *ILN*, 31 March 1855, p. 295.
34 *Art Journal*, 1 May 1855, p. 140; Jeremy Maas, *Gambart: Prince of the Victorian Art World*, London: Barrie & Jenkins, 1975, pp. 70–1; Nicol, *Ismeer, or Smyrna and Its British Hospital*, p. 236.

Chapter 10: Miss Nightingale Queens It with Absolute Power

1 Holmes, *Scanty Particulars*, p. 244.
2 For detailed arguments on this see Rachel Holmes, *Scanty Particulars*.
3 RA/VIC/F2/81.
4 Luddy, *The Crimean Journals of the Sisters of Mercy*, p. 141.
5 Williams (ed.), *An Autobiography of Elizabeth Davis*, p. 154.
6 Goldie, *I Have Done My Duty*, p. 92.
7 Stanmore, *Sidney Herbert*, vol. I, p. 373.
8 Huntsman et al., 'Light Before Dawn', p. 16.
9 Goldie, *I Have Done My Duty*, p. 92.
10 Williams (ed.), *An Autobiography of Elizabeth Davis*, pp. 154, 165.
11 Roxburgh, 'Miss Nightingale and Miss Clough', p. 76.
12 Ibid., pp. 77–8.
13 'Nurses Sent to the Military Hospitals in the East', original ledger, FNM.
14 Goldie, *I Have Done My Duty*, p. 112.
15 Hobson, *Catharine Leslie Hobson*, p. 32.
16 Goldie, *I Have Done My Duty*, p. 42.
17 Blackwood, *A Narrative of Personal Experiences*, p. 232.
18 Goldie, *I Have Done My Duty*, p. 113.
19 Taylor, *Eastern Hospitals and English Nurses*, pp. 140–1.
20 Hobson, *Catharine Leslie Hobson*, p. 46.
21 *Cassell's Illustrated Family Paper*, 13 January 1855, p. 13.
22 Pincoffs, *Experiences of a Civilian in Eastern Military Hospitals*, p. 80.
23 *Cassell's Illustrated Family Paper*, 13 January 1855, p. 13; Murray, *Pictures from the Battlefields*, pp. 58–9.

24 Slade, *Turkey and the Crimean War*, pp. 371–4.
25 Clifford, *Henry Clifford VC*, p. 168.
26 Eva Tappan, *In the Days of Queen Victoria*, London: Hutchinson, 1903, p. 198.
27 Editorial, *Pen and Pencil*, 24 March 1855, p. 98.
28 Skene, *With Lord Stratford in the Crimean War*, p. 119.
29 See Marsh, *Memorials of Captain Hedley Vicars*, chapters IX and X.
30 Blackwood, *A Narrative of Personal Experiences*, p. 255.
31 Anderson, 'The Growth of Christian Militarism', pp. 48–9.
32 *Panama Star and Herald*, 12 December 1854, p. 2. Sadly the paper has nothing to say of Mary Seacole's time in Panama, or the boarding houses cum restaurants she established in the Isthmus, during 1850–3.
33 Tisdall, *Mrs Duberly's Campaigns*, p. 126.
34 Seacole, *Wonderful Adventures*, p. 71.
35 Ibid., p. 74.
36 Ibid., p. 110.

Chapter 11: The Iron House on the Col

1 Seacole, *Wonderful Adventures*, p. 78.
2 Ibid., p. 82.
3 Ibid., p. 86.
4 Ibid., pp. 88, 90.
5 Ibid., p. 102.
6 Ibid., p. 101.
7 Ibid., p. 123.
8 Galt, *The Camp and the Cutter*, pp. 75–6.
9 Douglas, *Soldiering in Sunshine and Storm*, p. 198; Calder, journal for 24 August 1855, RAMC Collection 701, Box 137, Wellcome Institute.
10 Macormick, *Two Months in and about the Camp before Sebastopol*, p. 35.
11 Bell, *Soldier's Glory*, p. 283.
12 Brian Cooke, 'Vanity Fair', *WC*, 16 (1), 1999, p. 16.
13 Tyrrell, *History of the Present War with Russia*, vol. 3, p. 70.
14 'Sutlers in the Camp', *Fraser's Magazine*, December 1855, vol. LII,, p. 693.
15 Ibid.
16 Ibid.; Seacole, *Wonderful Adventures*, p. 102.
17 *Athenaeum*, No. 1552, 25 July 1857, p. 938.
18 Cardoza, 'Duty to the Nation', pp. 197–201.
19 *PFJ*, 20 January 1855, p. 103.
20 'The Canteneer', *Cassell's Illustrated Family Paper*, 23 June 1855, p. 200; Hibbert, *The Destruction of Lord Raglan*, p. 28.
21 Cardoza, 'Duty to the Nation', p. 189; Tisdall, *Mrs Duberly's Campaigns*, p. 125.
22 *Art Journal*, 1 October 1855, p. 285; Robins (ed.), *The Murder of a Regiment*, p. 18.
23 Taylor, *Journal of Adventures with the British Army*, p. 301.
24 John Codman, *An American Transport in the Crimean War*, NY: Bonnell-Silver, 1896, p. 140.
25 See Cardoza, 'Duty to the Nation', pp. 183–5. This anecdote would appear to be

about the same woman as described anonymously in Creed, 'A Trumpeter's Wife'.
26 Galt, *The Camp and the Cutter*, p. 149.
27 'A Military Chaplain', 'Reminiscences of the War in the East', pp. 96–8.
28 Claydon House Trust Collection, MS Nightingale 110; see also Bostridge, 'Florence's Secret War'.
29 Claydon House Trust Collection, MS 9004/60; letter to Queen Victoria, 1 December 1855, RA/QV/F4/15.
30 Kelly, *From the Fleet in the Fifties*, p. 162.
31 See *United Service Journal*, part 3, 1856, p. 20.
32 Bostock, *Letters from India and the Crimea*, pp. 218–19.
33 See Thomas Dancer, *The Medical Assistant, or Jamaica Practice of Physic*, Kingston, Jamaica, 1801; and *Jamaican Historical Review*, XVII, 1991, issue devoted to 'Health, Disease and Medicine in Jamaica'.
34 Calder, journal for 24 August 1855, RAMC Collection 701, Box 137, Wellcome Institute.
35 Russell, letter to John Delane, editor of *The Times*, 21 May 1855, in which he observes that 'the *Morning Advertiser* is represented, I understand, by a Mr Keane, who chiefly passes his time in preparing cooling drinks at Mrs Seacole's'.
36 Seacole, *Wonderful Adventures*, p. 113.
37 Sterling, *The Highland Brigade in the Crimea*, Letter XCV, p. 178.

Chapter 12: A Morbid Taste for Horrors

1 Duberly, *Journal Kept During the Russian War*, p. 177.
2 Bentley, *Russell's Despatches from the Crimea*, pp. 175–6.
3 *ILN*, 5 April 1855, p. 359.
4 Lord Rokeby, copy letter to the queen's secretary Col. Phipps, 25 May 1855, RA/VIC/F2/82.
5 Rokeby to Phipps, 20 June 1855, RA/VIC/F2/130.
6 Duberly, *Journal Kept During the Russian War*, pp. 171–3.
7 Copy letter Codrington to his wife, 25 March 1855, RA/VIC/F4/60.
8 Taylor, *Journal of Adventures with the British Army*, vol. 2, p. 283.
9 Farwell, *Queen Victoria's Little Wars*, p. 79; Clifford, *Henry Clifford VC*, p. 273.
10 Mawson (ed.), *Eyewitness in the Crimea*, p. 112.
11 Currie, *Letters from the Crimea*, letter 25, n.p.; Steevens, *The Crimean Campaign with the Connaught Rangers*, p. 314.
12 See Anglesey, *Little Hodge*: for Mrs Rogers, p. 110; Mrs Forrest, pp. 106, 110–18, 132–3, 138, 143.
13 Sterling, *The Highland Brigade in the Crimea*, p. 178.
14 Alexander, *Passages in the Life of a Soldier*, vol. 2, p. 157.
15 Ward (ed.), *The Hawley Letters*, p. 51.
16 See letter of 16 June 1855, in 'Lettres de Crimée du Capitaine de Berthois', *Carnet de la Sabretache*, no. 414, June 1956, p. 113; Duberly's own account is in *Journal Kept During the Russian War*, p. 218.
17 Carew, *Combat and Carnival*, p. 190.
18 Anglesey, *Little Hodge*, p. 102.

19 Portal, *Letters from the Crimea*, p. 169.
20 Carew, *Combat and Carnival*, p. 193.
21 Fenton, letter number 19, 4 June 1855.
22 Compton, *Colonel's Lady and Camp Follower*, p. 160.
23 Percy, *A Bearskin's Crimea*, p. 156.
24 Compton, *Colonel's Lady and Camp Follower*, pp. 175, 177.
25 Tisdall, *Mrs Duberly's Campaigns*, p. 144.
26 Letter of Miss M. Canning to Lady Canning, 7 May 1855, RA/VIC/F2/89.
27 Ewart, *Letters from the Crimea*, p. 89.
28 Anglesey, *Little Hodge*, p. 104; Airlie, *With the Guards We Shall Go*, p. 261.
29 Sterling, *The Highland Brigade in the Crimea*, p. 158.
30 Creagh, *Sparks from Camp Fires*, p. 144.
31 Duberly, *Journal Kept During the Russian War*, p. 216.
32 Barnston, *Letters from the Crimea and India*, p. 91.
33 Duberly, *Journal Kept During the Russian War*, p. 209.
34 Tisdall, *Mrs Duberly's Campaigns*, pp. 146–7.
35 Seacole, *Wonderful Adventures*, p. 132.
36 Ibid., p. 133.
37 Portal, *Letters from the Crimea*, p. 197.
38 Kerwin, 'In the Crimea with the 19th Regiment', p. 96.
39 Ibid.
40 Seacole, *Wonderful Adventures*, p. 138.
41 Diary of Marianne Estcourt, Gloucestershire Record Office, D1571/F558.
42 Ibid.
43 Seacole, *Wonderful Adventures*, p. 139.

Chapter 13: Do Hurry Back and Take Sebastopol or It Will Kill Mama

1   Williams (ed.), *An Autobiography of Elizabeth Davis*, p. 174.
2   Polidori, letter from Barrack Hospital Scutari, 29 April 1855, in Rossetti Archive UBC, fo. 2372.
3   Bonham-Carter (ed.), *Surgeon in the Crimea*, p. 164.
4   Portal, *Letters from the Crimea*, p. 143.
5   Williams (ed.), *An Autobiography of Elizabeth Davis*, p. 184.
6   Quoted in Bostridge, 'Florence's Secret War', p. 6.
7   Roxburgh, 'Miss Nightingale and Miss Clough', p. 80.
8   Ibid., pp. 81–2.
9   Ibid., p. 85.
10 'Letter by a Russian Sister of Mercy', *Times*, 5 January 1856, p. 8.
11 Evans, 'A Soldier's Wife in the Crimea', p. 272.
12 Kerwin, 'In the Crimea with the 19th Regiment', p. 96.
13 Seacole, *Wonderful Adventures*, pp. 141–2.
14 Ibid., pp. 142–3.
15 Kolesnikova (ed.), *Sestry Miloserdiya*, p. 287.
16 'The Favourite Song at the Camp', *ILN*, 27 October 1855, p. 498.
17 Duberly, *Journal Kept During the Russian War*, p. 272.

18 Buzzard, *With the Turkish Army in the Crimea*, p. 179.
19 Seacole, *Wonderful Adventures*, p. 146.
20 Fletcher and Ishchenko, *The Crimean War*, p. 480.
21 'The Favourite Song at the Camp', *ILN*, 27 October 1855, p. 498.
22 Bakunina, 'Vospominaniya Sestry Miloserdiya', in Kolesnikova (ed.), *Sestry Miloserdiya*, p. 238. It is interesting to note that this letter by the same author of that in n. 10 was not published by the major British papers, considered as it was too compassionate a view of the suffering of the enemy in Sevastopol. It was however printed in the pacifist journal *Herald of Peace*, on 1 February 1856, pp. 21–3.
23 Yafasova, 'Sisters of Mercy', part 6, p. 24.
24 Sarah A. Tooley, *The Personal Life of Queen Victoria*, London: Hodder & Stoughton, 1896, p. 184.
25 Longford, *Victoria R.I.*, p. 254; Benson and Esher (eds), *Letters of Queen Victoria*, vol. III, p. 142.
26 Charles Richard Sanders (ed.), *Collected Letters of Thomas and Jane Welsh Carlyle*, volume 30, *July–December 1855*, Durham, NC: Duke University Press, 2002, p. 64.
27 *Picture Times*, 15 September 1855, pp. 9–10.
28 'The Interior of Sebastopol', *Times*, 27 September 1855, p. 7.
29 Eustace Grenville Murray, *The Roving Englishman in Turkey*, p. 326.
30 Tyrrell, *History of the Present War with Russia*, vol. 4, p. 346.
31 Currie, *Letters from the Crimea*, Letter 32, n.p.
32 Duberly, *Journal Kept During the Russian War*, p. 280.
33 Ibid., p.p. 285–6.
34 'Hints to Amateur Travellers', *ILN*, 13 October 1855, p. 434.
35 R. C. H. Taylor M/S letter 23 October 1855, courtesy Elizabeth Balcombe.
36 'Military Chaplain', 'Reminiscences of the War in the East', p. 103.
37 See Vieth, *Recollections of the Crimean Campaign*, pp. 78–80.
38 'An Edinburgh Boy', *A Story of Active Service in Foreign Lands*, pp. 212–13.
39 Soyer, *A Culinary Campaign*, p. 268.
40 Baylen and Conway, *Soldier-Surgeon*, pp. 128–9, 136.
41 Creagh, *Sparks from Camp Fires*, pp. 203–4.
42 *Times*, 9 April 1856, p. 10.
43 RA/QVJ, 11 March 1856.
44 Ibid.
45 RA/QVJ, 8 July 1856; see also Creagh, *Sparks from Camp Fires*, p. 216.
46 Hornby, *Constantinople during the Crimean War*, pp. 313–15.
47 Soyer, *A Culinary Campaign*, p. 297.
48 Benson and Esher (eds), *Letters of Queen Victoria*, vol. III, p. 52.
49 RA/VIC/F3/121.

Chapter 14: The Roll Call

1 See 'Notes on Nurses', *Englishwoman's Domestic Magazine*, vol. IV, p. 335. See also vol. III, p. 243; vol. IV, pp. 249–51.
2 Hobson, *Catherine Leslie Hobson*, p. 48.
3 *Illustrated Times*, 5 July 1856, p. 10.

4 Kenyon (ed.), *Letters of Elizabeth Barrett Browning*, vol. 2, p. 189.
5 Butler, *An Autobiography*, p. 101.
6 Ibid., p. 104.
7 Obituary – Lady Elizabeth Butler, *Times*, 3 October 1933.
8 Quoted in 'Elizabeth Thompson (Lady Butler)',
   http://www.spartacus.schoolnet.co.uk/Jbutler.htm
9 See Matthew Lalumia, *Realism and Politics in Victorian Art of the Crimean War*, pp. 136–145.
10 Usherwood and Spencer-Smith, *Lady Butler*, p. 29.
11 Ibid.
12 Supposedly from Butler, *An Autobiography*, but not found there despite being widely quoted.
13 Wilfred Meynell, *Life and Work of Lady Butler*, London: Art Journal Office, 1898, p. 31.
14 Woodham-Smith, *Florence Nightingale*, p. 193.
15 See Blackwood, *A Narrative of Personal Experiences*, pp. 212–16.
16 Bayes, 'Nell Butler was the front line "Florence Nightingale"', p. 21.
17 Kerwin, 'In the Crimea with the 19th Regiment', p. 96.
18 Ken Horton, 'The Sad Women of the Crimean War', TS, in Ken Horton papers.
19 Chapple and Pollard (ed.), *The Letters of Mrs Gaskell*, p. 359.
20 *Punch*, 30 August 1856, p. 82.
21 'Two Brothers', *Our Tent in the Crimea*, pp. 38–9.
22 Information from Major Colin Robins of the Crimean War Research Society on the current state of Crimean War graves.
23 Colborne and Brine, *The Last of the Brave*, p. 30.

BIBLIOGRAPHY

Abbreviations used in notes and bibliography for frequently cited sources are given in brackets.

Manuscripts

William Menzies Calder: MS journal 1855–6, RAMC 701/Box 137, Wellcome Institute for the History of Medicine

George Russell Dartnell: 'Notes of Queen Victoria's Visit to Fort Pitt and Chatham', TS, MC 714, Medway Archives and Local Studies Centre

Marianne Estcourt: MS diary 1853–5 and sketchbooks, Gloucestershire Archives, D 1571/F557–60

Captain Charles Stuart Glazbook: MS letters 1854–5, ARC No. 8401–100, National Army Museum [NAM]

Sir John Hall: TS Diaries 1854–6, RAMC 524/15/5-6, Wellcome Institute for the History of Medicine

Ken Horton: TS and MS notes on nurses and army wives, in possession of the author

Florence Nightingale Archive: MS N.1000, 9004/60, Claydon House Trust

Eliza Polidori: letters from Turkey 1854–5, Rossetti-Dennis Collection, University of British Columbia Library, Rare Books and Special Collections

General Sir Richard C. H. Taylor: TS letters 1855 – courtesy Elizabeth Balcombe

Queen Victoria: Crimean Papers F1–F4; Queen Victoria's Journal 1854–6 [QVJ]; Royal Archives, Windsor, by permission of Queen Elizabeth II [RA]

Nurses' Testimonials: War Office 25/264, National Archives, Kew [WO]

Register of Nurses Sent to the Hospitals in the East, MS ledger, Florence Nightingale Museum [FNM]

Journals

Blackwood's Magazine
British Medical Journal [BMJ]
Cassell's Illustrated Family Paper
Englishwoman's Domestic Magazine [EDM]
Fraser's Magazine
Household Words
Illustrated London News [ILN]
Illustrated Times
Lancet
Patriotic Fund Journal [PFJ]
Pen and Pencil
Picture Times
Punch

The Times
United Service Journal (also known as *Colburn's United Service Magazine and Naval and Military Journal*)
War Correspondent [WC] [Journal of the Crimean War Research Society]

Books and Journal Articles

Acland, Sir Henry, *Memoir on the Cholera at Oxford in the Year 1854*, London: J. Churchill, 1856

Airlie, Mabel, Countess of, *With the Guards We Shall Go: A Guardsman's Letters in the Crimea, 1854–55*, London: Hodder & Stoughton, 1933

Alexander, Sir James, *Passages in the Life of a Soldier*, 2 vols, London: Hurst & Blackett, 1857

'An Amateur', *A Trip to the Trenches in February and March 1855*, London: Saunders & Otley, 1860

Anderson, Olive, *A Liberal State at War: English Politics and Economics during the Crimean War*, Hants: Gregg Revivals, 1994

——, 'The Growth of Christian Militarism in Mid-Victorian Britain', *English Historical Review*, 86 (338), Jan. 1971, pp. 46–72

Anglesey, Marquess of, *Little Hodge: Being Extracts from the Letters and Diaries of Col. Edward Cooper Hodge Written during the Crimean War*, London: Leo Cooper, 1971

Anon, *Inside Sebastopol, and Experiences in Camp . . . Autumn and Winter of 1855*, London: Chapman and Hall, 1856

Anon [Miss Bird], 'Four Days at Portsmouth on the Eve of War, March 1854', London: Benton Seeley, 1855

Anon, 'Recognising the Work of Miss Florence Nightingale: Women who Braved the Horrors of the Crimean Campaign', *Sphere*, 29 February 1908, p. 180

Anon, *The War, or Voices from the Ranks*, London: G. Routledge, 1855

Askwith, Betty, *Crimean Courtship*, London: Michael Russell, 1985

'Assistance Given to the Wives, Widows, and Children of the British Soldiers at Scutari, 1854–5–6', in *Statements Exhibiting the Voluntary Contributions Received by Miss Nightingale, for the Use of the British War Hospitals in the East*, London: Harrison & Sons, 1857

Astley, Sir John Dugdale, *Fifty Years of My Life*, London: Macmillan & Co., 1876

Bamfield, Veronica, *On the Strength: The Story of the British Army Wife*, London: Charles Knight & Co., 1974

Barnett, Corelli, *Britain and Her Army: A Military, Political and Social History of the British Army 1509–1970*, London: Cassell, 2000

Barnston, Maj. William and Maj. Roger, *Letters from the Crimea and India*, Whitchurch, Shrops: Herald Printers, 1998

Bayes, James, 'Nell Butler was the front line "Florence Nightingale"', *Portsmouth Evening News*, 3 May 1963, pp. 20–1

Baylen, Joseph O. and Alan Conway (ed.), *Soldier-surgeon: The Crimean War Letters of Dr Douglas A. Reid 1855–1856*, Knoxville: University of Tennessee Press, 1968

Beckett, Ian F. W., *The Victorians at War*, London: Hambledon & London, 2003

Bell, Sir George, *Soldier's Glory: Being 'Rough Notes of an Old Soldier'*, London: G. Bell & Sons, 1956

Benson, Arthur, and Viscount Esher (ed.), *The Letters of Queen Victoria 1837–1861*, 3 vols, London: John Murray, 1911

Benson, Evelyn R., 'On the Other Side of the Battle: Russian Nurses in the Crimean War', *Journal of Nursing Scholarship* 24 (1), Spring 1992, pp. 65–8

Bentley, Nicholas, *Russell's Despatches from the Crimea, 1854–1856*, London: Deutsch, 1966

Billington, Mary Frances, 'Surviving Crimean Nurses', *Quiver*, July, 1908, pp. 739–44

Bingham, Stella, *Ministering Angels*, London: Osprey, 1979

Blackwood, Lady Alicia, *A Narrative of Personal Experiences and Impressions During a Residence on the Bosphorus during the Crimean War*, London: Hatchard, 1881

Bladensburg, Lt. Col. Ross of, *History of the Coldstream Guards from 1815 to 1895*, London: A. D. Innes & Co., 1896

Blomfield-Smith, Denis, *Heritage of Help: the Story of the Royal Patriotic Fund*, London: Robert Hale, 1992

Bonham-Carter, Victor (ed.), *Surgeon in the Crimea: the Experiences of George Lawson Recorded in Letters to His Family*, London: Constable, 1968

Bostock, Deputy Surgeon-General John Ashton, *Letters from India and the Crimea*, London: George Bell, 1896

Bostridge, Mark, 'Florence's Secret War', *Times* Review, 30 October 2004, p. 6

Bratton, J. S., 'Theatre of War: The Crimea on the London Stage 1854–5', in James Bradby et al. (ed.), *Performance and Politics in Popular Drama . . . 1800–1876*, Cambridge: Cambridge University Press, 1980

Brereton, J. M., *The British Soldier: A Social History from 1661 to the Present Day*, London: Bodley Head, 1986

Buchanan, George, MD, *Camp Life as Seen by a Civilian*, Glasgow: James Maclehose, 1871

Bunkers, Suzanne L., and Cynthia A. Huff, *Inscribing the Daily: Critical Essays on Women's Diaries*, Amherst, Mass.: University of Massachusetts Press, 1996

Burgoyne, Roderick, *Historical Records of the 93rd Sutherland Highlanders*, London: R. Bentley & Son, 1883

Burton, Isabel, and W. H. Wilkins, *The Romance of Isabel Lady Burton*, London: Hutchinson, 1897

Butler, Lady Elizabeth, *An Autobiography*, London: Constable, 1923

Buzzard, Thomas, *With the Turkish Army in the Crimea and Asia Minor*, London: John Murray, 1915

Calthorpe, Somerset, *Letters from Headquarters, Or the Realities of War, by an Officer on the Staff*, London: Murray, 1856

Cardoza, Thomas J., *Duty to the Nation, Devotion to the Regiment: Cantinières of the French Army 1793–1906'*: thesis, University of California, Santa Barbara, 1998

Carew, Peter, *Combat and Carnival*, London: Constable, 1954

Cartan, William, *Declaration of War: The Regulations Affecting Non-commissioned Officers' and Soldiers' Wives, Considered with Reference to the Army Ordered to Turkey*, London: Thomas Hatchard, 1854

Central Association, 'The First Anniversary Meeting of the Central Association in Aid of Soldiers' Wives and Families', London, 1855

——, 'Third Report of the Central Association in Aid of the Wives and Families of

Soldiers Ordered on Active Service, 7 March 1856', London, 1856

Chandler, David (ed.), Oxford Illustrated History of the British Army, Oxford: Oxford University Press, 1994

Chapman, Roger, Echoes from the Crimea, Richmond: Green Howards Museum, 2004

Chapple, J. A. V., and Arthur Pollard (ed.), The Letters of Mrs Gaskell, Manchester: Manchester University Press, 1966

Chesney, Kellow, Crimean War Reader, London: Severn House, 1960

Chodasiewicz [Hodasevich], Captain Robert, A Voice from within the Walls of Sebastopol, London: John Murray, 1856

Clifford, Henry, Henry Clifford VC: His Letters and Sketches from the Crimea, London: Michael Joseph, 1956

Colborne, Capt. John, and Frederic Brine, The Last of the Brave or Resting Places of Our Fallen Heroes in the Crimea and at Scutari, London: Ackerman & Co., 1857

Colebrook, Sir Thomas Colebrooke, Journal of Two Visits to the Crimea in the Autumns of 1854 and 1855, London: Boone, 1856

Compton, Piers, Colonel's Lady and Camp Follower, London: Robert Hale,1970

Cooper, John, Fort Pitt, Maidstone: Kent County Council, 1976

Cowper, Col. L. I., The King's Own, The Story of a Royal Regiment, vol. II, 1814–1914, Oxford: Oxford University Press, 1939

Creagh, Capt. James, Sparks from Camp Fires: An Autobiography, London: Chapman & Hall, 1901

Creed, C. A., 'A Trumpeter's Wife in the Crimea', Cornhill Magazine, December 1900, pp. 808–11

'A Crimean Heroine' [Mrs Frances Driscoll], The Thistle, August 1899, pp. 101–2

Currie, F. G., Letters from the Crimea, London: Henry Payne, 1899

Curtiss, John Shelton, 'Russian Sisters of Mercy in the Crimea, 1854–1855', Slavic Review 25 (1), 1966, pp. 84–100

Daniell, David, Cap of Honour: the Story of the Gloucestershire Regiment (28th/61st Foot) 1694–1950, London: Harrap, 1951

'Death of Mrs. Evans. A King's Own Crimean Veteran', Lion and the Rose, April 1914, pp. 437–8

Dereli, Cynthia, 'Gender Issues and the Crimean War: Creating Roles for Women?', in Parker, Christopher, Gender Roles and Sexuality in Victorian Literature, Hants: Scolar Press, 1995

Dimond, Frances, and Roger Taylor, Crown and Camera: The Royal Family and Photography 1842–1910, Harmondsworth: Penguin, 1987

Douglas, William, Soldiering in Sunshine and Storm, Edinburgh: Adam and Charles Black, 1865

Duberly, Mrs Henry, Journal Kept During the Russian War, London: Longmans, Brown, Green & Roberts, 1855

Edgerton, Robert B., Death or Glory: The Legacy of the Crimean War, Boulder, Colo.: Westview Press, 2000

'An Edinburgh Boy', Story of Active Service in Foreign Lands. Extracts from Letters Sent Home from the Crimea 1854–1856, Edinburgh, William Blackwood, 1886

Emerson, George R., Sebastopol: The Story of its Fall, London: G. Routledge, 1855

Evans, Elizabeth, 'A Soldier's Wife in the Crimea' as told to Walter Woods, Royal

Magazine, July 1908, pp. 265–72

Evelyn, George P., A Diary of the Crimea, London: Duckworth, 1954

Ewart, Charles Brisbane, Letters from the Crimea 1854–1856, London, 1905

Ewart, Lt. Gen. John Alexander, The Story of a Soldier's Life; or Peace, War, and the Mutiny, 2 vols, London: Sampson Low, Marston, Searle & Rivington, 1881

Farquharson, K. S., Reminiscences of Crimean Campaigning, Edinburgh: privately printed, 1883

Farwell, Brian, Queen Victoria's Little Wars, Ware, Herts: Wordsworth Editions, 1999

Faughan, Thomas Faughan, Stirring Incidents in the Life of a British Soldier, Toronto: Hunter, Rose, 1879

Fenwick, Kenneth (ed.), Voice from the Ranks: A Personal Narrative of the Crimean Campaign, London: Folio Society, 1954

Fisher-Rowe, Edward Rowe, Extracts from the Letters of E. R. Fisher-Rowe during the Crimean War, 1854–1855, Godalming: privately printed, 1907

Fletcher, Ian, and Natalia Ishchenko, The Crimean War: A Clash of Empires, Staplehurst, Kent: Spellmount, 2004

Fluhr, Nicole, "'Their Calling Me 'Mother' Was Not, I Think, Altogether Unmeaning": Mary Seacole's Maternal Personae', Victorian Literature and Culture, 34, 2006, pp. 95–113

Fortescue, Sir J. W., Following the Drum, Edinburgh: W. Blackwood & Sons, 1931

Gadsby, John, A Trip to Sebastopol, London: Gadsby, 1858

Galt, Edwin, The Camp and the Cutter, London: Thomas Hodgson, 1856

General Orders Issued to the Army of the East from April 30 1854 to December 31 1855, London: J. W. Parker & Son, 1856

'The Girl I Left Behind Me', Household Words, 1 April 1854, pp. 161–4

Goldie, Sue, I Have Done My Duty: Florence Nightingale in the Crimean War, 1854–56, Manchester: Manchester University Press, 1987

Goodman, Margaret, Experiences of an English Sister of Mercy, London: Smith, Elder, 1862

Great Gun Song Book: Songs of Our Highland Heroes, Crimean Conquerors, Balaklava Braves, Inkermann Invulnerables, and India Invincibles, London: Pattie, c.1855–60

Grey, Elizabeth, The Noise of Drums and Trumpets: W. H. Russell Reports from the Crimea, London: Longman, 1971

Guedalla, Philip, The Two Marshals: Bazaine and Pétain, London: Hodder & Stoughton, 1943

Hamlin, Cyrus, Among the Turks, London: Sampson Low, 1878

H. B. [Harry Blishen], Letters from the Crimea during the Years 1854 and 1855, London: Emily Faithfull, 1863

Hibbert, Christopher, The Destruction of Lord Raglan, London: Wordsworth Editions, rev. edn 1999

——, Queen Victoria in Her Letters and Journals, London: Viking, 1985

Higginson, Gen. Sir George, Seventy-One Years of a Guardsman's Life, London: Smith, Eldere & Co., 1916

Hobson, W. F., Catharine Leslie Hobson, Lady Nurse, Crimean War, and Her Life, London: Parker & Co., 1888

Holmes, Rachel, Scanty Particulars: The Strange Life and Astonishing Secret of Victorian Adventurer and Pioneering Surgeon James Barry, London: Viking, 2002

Hornby, Emilia, *Constantinople during the Crimean War*, London: Richard Bentley, 1863

Horton, Ken, 'Nurses of the Crimean War', *The Nightingale*, Spring/Summer 2002, pp. 8–9

'The Hospital Nurse – An Episode of the War', *Fraser's Magazine*, Jan.1855, pp. 96–105

Howson, Revd J. S., *Deaconesses; or The Official Help of Women in Parochial Work and in Charitable Institutions*, London: Longman, Green, Longman & Roberts, 1862

Huntsman, Richard, Mary Bruin and Deborah Holttum, 'Light Before Dawn: Naval Nursing and Medical Care during the Crimean War', *Journal of the Royal Naval Medical Service*, 88 (1), 2002, pp. 5–27

Jackson, Major E. S., *The Inniskilling Dragoons*, London: Arthur L. Humphreys, 1909

Keller, Ulrich, *The Ultimate Spectacle: A Visual History of the Crimean War*, Australia: Gordon and Breach, 2001

Kelly, Christine (ed.), *Mrs Duberly's War: Journal and Letters from the Crimea, 1854–6*, Oxford: Oxford University Press, 2007

Kelly, Gen. Sir Richard Denis, *An Officer's Letters to His Wife during the Crimean War*, London: Elliot Stock, 1902

Kelly, Mrs Tom, *From the Fleet in the Fifties*, London: Hurst & Blackett, 1902

Kenyon, Frederic G. (ed.), *Letters of Elizabeth Barrett Browning*, 2 vols, London: Smith, Elder & Co., 1897

Kerr, Paul, *The Crimean War*, London: Channel 4 Books, 2000

Kerwin, Margaret, 'In the Crimea with the 19th Regiment', *Green Howards Gazette*, April 1898, pp. 94–6

Kolesnikova, N. N. (ed.), *Sestry Miloserdiya v Krymskoi voine 1853–1856 godov*, Simferopol: Biznes-Inform, 2005

Lalumia, Matthew P., *Realism and Politics in Victorian Art of the Crimean War*, Essex: Bowker Pub. Co., 1984

Longford, Elizabeth, *Victoria R.I.*, London: Weidenfeld & Nicolson, 1998

Luddy, Maria (ed.), *The Crimean Journals of the Sisters of Mercy 1854–1856*, Dublin: Four Courts Press, 2005

Lunnon, Helen, and Sophie Warner, 'Unsung Heroines', information booklet for exhibition on Crimean War nurses, March–August 2002, FNM

MacMullen, John, *Camp and Barrack Room, or the British Army as it is*, London: Chapman & Hall, 1846

Macormick, R. C., *Two Months in and about the Camp before Sebastopol*, London: William Wesley, 1855

Markovits, Stefanie, 'North and South, East and West: Elizabeth Gaskell, the Crimean War, and the Condition of England', *Nineteenth-Century Literature*, 59 (4), March 2005, pp. 463–93

Marsh, Catherine, *Memorials of Captain Hedley Vicars*, London: James Nisbet, 1859

Massie, Alastair, *A Most Desperate Undertaking: The British Army in the Crimea, 1854–56*, London: National Army Museum, 2003

Mawson, Michael Hargreave (ed.), *Eyewitness in the Crimea: The Crimean War Letters of Lt. Col. George Frederick Dallas*, London: Greenhill Books, 2001

Mayhew, Henry, 'Soldiers' Women', in *London Labour and the London Poor: Those that Will Not Work*, London: Griffin, Bohn & Co., 1862

'A Military Chaplain', 'Reminiscences of the War in the East', *United Services Magazine* Part 1 1857, January, pp. 96–103

Munro, Surgeon Gen. William, *Reminiscences of Military Service with the 93rd Sutherland Highlanders*, London: Hurst & Blackett, 1883

Murphy, David, *Ireland and the Crimean War*, Dublin: Four Courts Press, 2002

Murray, Eustace, *Pictures from the Battlefields, by the 'Roving Englishman'*, London: G. Routledge, 1856

Nicol, Martha, *Ismeer, or Smyrna and Its British Hospital in 1855*, London: James Maden, 1856

Nightingale, Florence, *Subsidiary Notes as to the Introduction of Female Nursing into Military Hospitals*, London: Harrison & Sons, 1858

——,'Soldiers' Wives', in *Notes on Matters Affecting the Health and Efficiency and Hospital Administration of the British Army*, London: Harrison and Sons, 1858

'Notes on Nurses', *Englishwoman's Domestic Magazine*, vol. IV 1855, pp. 333–5

O'Malley, I. B., *Florence Nightingale, 1820–1856: A Study of her Life Down to the Crimean War*, London: Thornton Butterworth, 1931

Osborne, Sidney Godolphin, *Scutari and Its Hospitals*, London: Dickinson Brothers, 1855

'O.W.', 'Sutlers in the Camp', *Fraser's Magazine*, December 1855, pp. 685–95

Pack, Col. Reynell, *Sebastopol Trenches and Five Months in Them*, London: Kirby & Endean, 1878

Paget, Lord George, *The Light Cavalry Brigade in the Crimea*, London: John Murray, 1881

Palmer, Irene Sabelberg, 'Florence Nightingale and the First Organized Delivery of Nursing Services', unpublished paper, FNM, 1983

Patterson, Major J., *Camp and Quarters: Scenes and Impressions of Military Life*, 2 vols, London: Saunders & Otley, 1840

Percy, Algernon, *A Bearskin's Crimea: Colonel Henry Percy VC and His Brother Officers*, London: Leo Cooper, 2005

Pincoffs, Peter, MD, *Experiences of a Civilian in Eastern Military Hospitals*, London: Williams & Norgate, 1857

Poovey, Mary, 'The Social Construction of Florence Nightingale', in Poovey, *Uneven Developments: The Ideological Work of Gender in Mid-Victorian England*, London: Virago, 1989

Portal, Captain Robert, *Letters from the Crimea 1854–5*, Winchester: Warren & Son, 1900

Powell, Geoffrey, *The Green Howards: The 19th Regiment of Foot*, London: Secker & Warburg, 1983

Ranken, Major G., *Six Months at Sebastopol*, London: Charles Westerton, 1857

Rappaport, Helen, *Queen Victoria: A Biographical Companion*, Santa Barbara and Oxford: ABC-CLIO, 2003

Reid, Douglas A., *Memories of the Crimean War*, London: St Catherine Press, 1911

Richardson, Robert (ed.), *Nurse Sarah Anne, with Florence Nightingale at Scutari*, London: John Murray, 1977

Rickards, Edith, *Felicia Skene of Oxford, a Memoir*, London: John Murray, 1902

Robins, Major Colin (ed.), *The Murder of a Regiment: A Crimean War Officer's Journal*, Bowdon: Withycut House, 1994

Robinson, Jane, *Mary Seacole: The Charismatic Black Nurse Who Became a Heroine of the Crimea*, London: Constable, 2005

Robinson, Rod, 'The Travelling Heiress: Ellen Palmer's Crimean Excursion', *War Correspondent* 20 (3), October 2002, pp. 14–16, and 20 (4), January 2003, p. 11

Rossetti, Dante Gabriel, *Dante Gabriel Rossetti: His Family Letters with a Memoir by William Michael Rossetti*, vol. I, London: Ellis & Elvey, 1895

Roving Englishman, *Pictures from the Battlefields*, London: G. Routledge, 1855

Roxburgh, Sir Ronald, 'Miss Nightingale and Miss Clough: Letters from the Crimea', *Victorian Studies* 13 (1), Sept. 1969, pp. 71–89

Royle, Trevor, *Crimea: The Great Crimean War 1854–1856*, London: Little, Brown & Co., 1999

'Rules and Regulations for the Nurses Attached to the Military Hospitals in the East', in Lunnon and Warner, 2002

'Russian Sisters of Mercy', *Herald of Peace*, 1 February 1856, pp. 21–3

St Aubyn, Giles, *Queen Victoria: A Portrait*, London: Sinclair Stevenson, 1991

Seacole, Mary, *Wonderful Adventures of Mrs Seacole in Many Lands*, Harmondsworth: Penguin, 2005

Shepherd, John, *The Crimean Doctors*, 2 vols, Liverpool: Liverpool University Press, 1991

Skene, J. H., *With Lord Stratford in the Crimean War*, London: Richard Bentley & Son, 1883

Slade, Sir Adolphus, *Turkey and the Crimean War: A Narrative of Events*, London: Smith, Elder, 1867

Small, Hugh, *Florence Nightingale, Avenging Angel*, London: Constable, 1998

Smith, George Loy, *A Victorian RSM*, Tunbridge Wells: Costello, 1987

Society for Promoting Christian Knowledge, *Scenes in the Camp and Field: being Sketches of the War in the Crimea*, London: SPCK, 1857

'The Soldier's Wife', *Household Words*, 21 April 1855, pp. 278–80

Sorokina, T. S., 'Russian Nursing in the Crimean War', *Journal of the Royal College of Physicians of London*, 29 (1), Jan./Feb. 1995, pp. 57–63

Soyer, Alexis, *A Culinary Campaign*, Lewes, E. Sussex: Southover Press, 1995

Stanmore, Lord, *Sidney Herbert: A Memoir*, 2 vols, London: John Murray, 1906

Steevens, Nathaniel, *The Crimean Campaign with the Connaught Rangers 1854–1856*, London: Griffith & Farran, 1878

Stephenson, Sir Frederick, *At Home and on the Battlefield: Letters from the Crimea*, London: John Murray, 1915

Sterling, Lt. Col. Anthony, *The Highland Brigade in the Crimea . . . Letters Written during the Years 1854, 1855, and 1856*, Minneapolis, MN: Absinthe Press, 1995 (originally 1895, private circulation)

Stokes, Henry Sewell, *Echoes of the War*, London: Longman, Brown, Green & Longman, 1855

Story of the War: by Collated Passages from The Times *and* Morning Herald *Correspondents and the Evidence before the Sebastopol Committee*, London: David Bryce, 1857

Summers, Anne, 'Pride and Prejudice: Ladies and Nurses in the Crimean War', *History Workshop*, 16 (Autumn 1983), pp. 32–56

——, *Angels and Citizens: British Women as Military Nurses, 1854–1914*, London: Routledge & Kegan Paul, 1988

——, 'The Mysterious Demise of Sarah Gamp: The Domiciliary Nurse and her Detractors, c. 1830–1860', *Victorian Studies*, 32 (3), Spring 1989, pp. 365–86

Surtees, Virginia, *Charlotte Canning*, London: John Murray, 1975

Taylor, Frances, *Eastern Hospitals and English Nurses*, London: Hurst & Blacket, 3rd edn 1857

Taylor, George Cavendish, *Journal of Adventures with the British Army, from the Commencement of the War to the taking of Sebastopol*, 2 vols, London: Hurst & Blackett, 1856

Tisdall, E. E. P., *Mrs Duberly's Campaigns*, London: Jarrolds, 1963

Toft, Simon, 'The Heroine in an Unmarked Grave', *Portsmouth News*, 29 June 2001, pp. 8–9

Trustram, Myna, *Women of the Regiment: Marriage and the Victorian Army*, Cambridge: Cambridge University Press, 1984

'Two Brothers' [G. H. and A. Money], *Our Tent in the Crimea; and wanderings in Sevastopol*, London: Richard Bentley, 1856

Tyrrell, Henry, *History of the Present War with Russia*, 6 vols, London: Printing and Publishing Co., 1854–6

Usherwood, Paul, and Jenny Spencer-Smith, *Lady Butler: Battle Artist 1846–1933*, Gloucester: Alan Sutton, 1987

Venning, Annabel, *Following the Drum*, London: Headline, 2005

Vieth, Frederick H. D., *Recollections of the Crimean Campaign*, Montreal: John Lovell & Son, 1907

Ward, S. G. P. (ed.), *The Hawley Letters*, Society for Army Historical Research, Special publication no. 10, London: Gale & Polden, 1970

Warner, Philip (ed.),*The Fields of War: A Young Cavalryman's Crimea Campaign*, London: John Murray, 1977

Williams, Jane (ed.), *An Autobiography of Elizabeth Davis – Betsy Cadwaladyr: A Balaklava Nurse*, Cardiff: Honno, 1987

Williams, Col. Noel T. St John, *Judy O'Grady and the Colonel's Lady: The Army Wife and Camp Follower since 1660*, London: Brasseys, 1988

Winstock, Lewis, *Songs and Music of the Redcoats, 1642–1902*, London: Leo Cooper, 1970

Wiseman, Cardinal, 'The Future Historian's View of the Present War', London: G. Routledge, 1855

'Woman's Part in War', *Englishwoman's Domestic Magazine*, vol. IV, 1855, pp. 249–51

Woodham-Smith, Cecil, *Florence Nightingale*, London: Constable and Co., 1950

Woods, Nicholas, *The Past Campaign: A Sketch of the War in the East*, 2 vols, London: Longman, Brown, Green & Longman, 1855

Wrench, E. M, 'The Lessons of the Crimean War', *BMJ*, 22 July 1899, pp. 205–8

Wright, Ebba J. D., *Sunbeams in My Path or Reminiscences of Christian Work in Various Lands*, London: James Nisbet, 1900

Wyatt, John, *History of the 1st Battalion Coldstream Guards during the Eastern Campaign*, London: Straker's, 1858

Wylly, Col. H. C., *History of the 1st and 2nd Battalions, the Sherwood Foresters*, 2 vols, Frome: Butler & Tanner, 1929

Young [Postans], Mrs Marianne, *Our Camp in Turkey, and the Way to it*, London: Richard Bentley, 1854

——, 'Women at Aldershot', *Household Words*, 19 April 1856, pp. 318–20

——, *Aldershot and All About It, with Gossip, Literary, Military and Pictorial*, London: G. Routledge, 1857

World Wide Web Sources and Articles

Barham, John, 'Soledad Bazaine', http://www.suite101.com/article.cfm/crimean_war/115598

Fenton, Roger, TS letters for 1855, http://www.rogerfenton.org.uk

Hagist, Don N., 'The Women of the British Army in America', http://www.revwar75.com/library/hagist/britwomen.htm

Henderson, Robert, 'A Soldier's Family in the British Army during the War of 1812', http://www.warof1812.ca/family.htm

Yafasova, Dina, 'Istoki sestrinskogo dela v Rossii . . .' [Sources on Nursing in Russia up to the Mid-Nineteenth Century, and its Development during the Crimean War of 1853–6]. In Russian at: http://www.sygeplejersken.dk/nh/manuel/soderjanie.htm (TS copy of translation, as 'Sisters of Mercy: Women Nursing in Old Russia', in FNM)

INDEX

Cambridge University, 139
Camp and Quarters (Major John Patterson), 19
Campbell, Sir Colin, 82, 83, 106, 169
Canada, 3, 7, 18, 26
Canning, Lady Charlotte, 142, 168
'Canrobert's Hill', 82
cantinières, 57–8, 150, 187–9
Caradoc, 70, 147
Cardigan, Lord, 70, 78, 84–6
Cardwell, Edward, 230
Carlyle, Jane Welsh, 222
Castle Hospital, 212–14
Cathcart's Hill, 186, 204–7, 209, 239
Catholic Church, 95, 99
Causeway Heights, 82–5
Central Association (in Aid of the Wives and
    Families of Soldiers Ordered to the East),
    26, 27, 89, 135, 152–4
Chalmers, Dr, 98
Chamberlain, Neville, 4
Champ de Mars, 46
Charge of the Light Brigade, 85–7, 203
Charge of the Light Brigade (Tony Richardson),
    86
Charing Cross Hospital, 141
Chasseurs d'Afrique, 197
Château Perovsky, 201
Chatham, 12, 152, 160, 161
'Cheer Boys, Cheer', 8, 72
Chenery, Thomas, 94–7, 111
Chernaya, River, 82, 197, 218, 239
Chersonese plateau, 79
cholera, 44–5, 59–62, 67, 69–70, 99, 209
Christmas, 141–6
Clarence Barracks, 152
Clifford, Captain Henry, 142, 198
Clough, Arthur Hugh, 138, 169, 171
Clough, Martha, 169, 214
Codrington, General William, 149, 197, 218
Col, The, 181
Colborne, Captain John, 239
Coldstream Guards, 6, 9, 75, 159
Commissary Department, 130, 158, 162
Commission of Enquiry into the State of the
    Army, 176
Community of the Cross, Sisters of Mercy of
    the, 116–17, 119
Compassionate Widows, 116
Constantinople, 45–7, 49–50
    army wives at, 18
    British bureaucracy, 110
    French hospitals at, 95, 115, 172
    journey to, 33, 45–7, 49–50

Mary Seacole at, 179–80
    telegraph service from, 90
Convent of the Sisters of Mercy, 99
Cornwallis, Couba, 192
Cossacks, 71, 73
Creagh, Captain James, 204
Creoles, 190, 191
Cresswell, Adelaide, 33, 66–7, 80
Crimean Fund, 103, 139, 158
Crimean Medal, 227, 230, 235
Crimean War Memorial, 230
Crockford's, 185
Cuffe, Father Michael, 124
Cuirassier Brigade, 45

Daily News, 52, 56
Dancer, Thomas, 192
Daniell, Colonel H. G., 229
Danube, River, 63
Dardanelles, 13
Davis, Elizabeth (Betsy Cadwaladyr), 167,
    168–9, 211–13
Day, Thomas, 179, 180, 183, 188
de Redcliffe, Lady Stratford, 202, 214
Delane, John, 96, 138
Derriman, Samuel, 147
Detaille, Edouard, 232
Devna, 51, 55, 59, 214
Devonport, 95, 102, 107, 114, 153
Dickens, Charles, 15, 134, 139, 143, 159
Disraeli, Benjamin, 146
Driscoll, Frances, 37, 39–40
Duberly, Fanny, 85–7, 87–90, 199–201
    background and character, 32
    Charge of the Light Brigade visit, 203
    Christmas Day, 145
    clothing, 53–4, 58
    concern for horses, 34, 136
    criticism of, 189
    dining with officers, 70, 78
    eloquent comments, 137
    fame of, 177
    Lady Erroll and, 59, 66, 80, 200
    Mary Seacole and, 200
    new quarters for, 196
    no medal for, 235
    outdoor life and, 80
    servants, 47, 66–7
    Sevastopol, 205–6, 219, 224
    spring in the Crimea, 195
    supply ships sink, 132
    supports war, 63
Duberly, Captain Henry, 32, 78, 90, 237